A

Noose

of

Light

A
Noose
of
Light

Alan Tunbridge

Memories 1940 – 2015

SECOND EDITION

To Beverley, Gabriel, Nathaniel and Dawn

Awake! For morning in the bowl of night
Has flung the stone that puts the stars to flight
And see! The hunter of the east has caught
The Sultan's turret in a noose of light!

Omar Khayyam

Contents

Beatniks

Does the past still exist? What happened to yesterday – all those millions of moments that made up yesterday? More immediately, what happened to the moment in which I typed that sentence, the first one of this book? They say that because of the limited speed of light, someone standing a very long way away and looking through a very powerful telescope could see me type that sentence now, after the moment had entered the past for me – me who is here and now – or was, anyway.

And what if I had not typed that sentence but typed another one, or maybe even deleted this page and gone surfing on FaceBook instead? But that didn't happen: all those alternative possibilities exist only in the world of 'if', and the world of 'if' doesn't exist, and has never existed, and will never exist. I don't care what the quantum mechanics say about multiple timelines and universes, all that stuff is as fanciful as the pagan gods. Maybe the quantum mechanics made it all up because they caught a glimpse of how things really are, and they didn't like it? The way things are, what happens is the only thing that ever happens, and we never get to know what would have happened if what happened hadn't happened. Life is a one-way street, with no you turns allowed, so watch out.

That very far away guy with the very powerful telescope might be pointing it at our little planet right now, watching me hitching down the road to Cornwall in 1959. But there would be nothing he could do to change the events: they are all set in stone, or rather light, which is like being set in diamond – and this setting process is what we call the present moment, the now. Like old Omar said, 'The moving finger writes, and having writ moves on', but maybe he should have picked a less poetic and more robust metaphor: maybe he should have said that the present moment is a universe-sized printing press, stamping out diamond-hard reality nano-second by nanosecond.

The Rubaiyat of Omar Khayyam was one of two books I carried in my duffle bag when I hitched from London down to Newquay, Cornwall, in May 1959. The other one was Dylan Thomas's Collected Poems. The bag also contained a few changes of underwear, a large notebook, and a plastic toiletries satchel. I also carried a packet of Players Weights cigarettes, a box of matches, about five pounds sterling, and a string-bound, small, rolled blanket, with which I planned to protect myself against the unkind elements. I was eighteen, a virgin, and would be nineteen in seven month's time.

My hitching companion was Kevin Mahoney. We had caught the tube as far West as possible and begun hitching down the A30 road at 9am. By 8pm it was dark, and we had only got as far as Basingstoke, scarcely 30 miles from central London. It was no good hitching at night, so we had decided to stop under a large green illuminated road sign, on the scrubby grass strewn

10

with plastic bottles and empty fag packets. Curled up on the icy ground in the baleful amber light, with the big trucks thundering by, I discovered that my blanket was woefully inadequate. I felt very vulnerable and far from home. I stared into the dark and suspected I had made a bad mistake.

A month ago, I had been a junior artist and messenger boy at an advertising agency in Soho, London. In my lunch hour, I had been sitting in a nearby café called 'The House of Sam Widges', listening to Wizz Jones tinkle on his acoustic guitar. He wasn't performing; he was just playing for himself and anyone else who wanted to listen. No one objected. Indeed, some of us complaisantly rejoiced at participating in a scene so authentically bohemian – with the minstrel and the cappuccinos and the spaghetti Bolognese. What Wizz was playing was magical and rare: it was an American folk flat-picking style, which he had taught himself from Ramblin' Jack Elliott and Woody Guthrie records – and he was just about the only person in London who knew how to do it. Lonnie Donegan's skiffle group had gained some fans of their heavy strumming banjo style, but Wizz was the exemplar of the delicate, melodic guitar sound newly being applied to revive American and English folk music. This was four years before Eric Clapton's first amateur pub performances, and the Beatles were still an unknown teenage Liverpool group called 'Rory Storm and the Hurricanes'. Some of the customers in Sam Widges were conventionally dressed, and others, like me, were not. We, the weird ones, were called beatniks because the newspapers called us that, and because everyone had seen movies starring Bob Hope and Bing Crosby in which young, black-clad Parisian existentialists, called beatniks, were ridiculed. But most of us had no notion of existentialism, and our music was mainly traditional jazz and folk and blues, not modern jazz. With Elvis recording 'Heartbreak Hotel' three years ago in 1956, rock was just beginning to impact England, but we beatniks tended to look down on its early exponents such as Cliff Richards and Tommy Steele as vulgar populists. Nor did we adopt uniforms, as did the 'Teddy Boys', with their crepe soled shoes and drape jackets and 'duck's arse' hairdos – although certain fashions did emerge as characteristic of us: long hair, long sweaters and skin tight trousers just about covers it. Wizz Jones had a fetish about leather patches: they were on his guitar, on his corduroy clothes, even on the nose bridge of his glasses. My work colleague Sammy looked quite different. He bought most of his clothes from an antique fashion boutique in the Tottenham Court Road. He wore a genuine nineteenth century coachman's coat with a full frock skirt, self-tailored skin-tight black and green striped banker's trousers, a white celluloid stiff collar with bow tie, and shiny black high boots. Others favoured the Russian peasant look, with extra large belted shirts. It didn't matter what you wore, if it was bizarre you were called a beatnik, and bizarre meant any teenager who did not dress like a middle-aged person. Today, it is difficult to imagine that someone wearing tight trousers, a long black sweater and longish hair would excite general interest and occasional hostility in the streets and shops, but it was so, then. Indeed, the Soho environment was

12

one of the tourist attractions of London, and we were quite used to trippers from abroad, or from Manchester or Leeds, peering in through the windows at us, as if at the zoo.

The sources of the brand 'Beatnik' are said to be Jack Kerouac's 1957 book 'On the Road' and his earlier writings. To my knowledge, few among us had read the book or researched the literature of the 'Beat Generation', but somehow Kerouac's theme of social alienation and the quest for fulfilment filtered down to us – as did the mood of J.D. Salinger's equally famous 'Catcher in the Rye', although no one I knew had read it. No one ever described Holden Caulfield as a beatnik, either – but having now read the book, I can say he was as much a beatnik as we were. Somehow, via the movies of James Dean, and the legends of the remaining old London bohemians from the Augustus John era, and the stories of the Paris Dadaists and Surrealists, everyone was familiar with the great myth of rejecting convention and safety, and launching out on the road to risk all in the quest for we did not know what. Much later on, I heard a ten-year old girl say, fiercely, "I don't know what I want, but I really want it!" That was a way of saying it.

In Sam Widges that afternoon, I overheard Wizz Jones say that he was going down to Cornwall again. He and a few others had travelled down the previous year of 1958 to spend the holiday season doing hotel work. I sat there and felt a warm flush glow in my abdomen and spread up into my head. I immediately knew that this news of the Cornish trip was my call to adventure. I had just read Joseph Campbell's 'Hero with a Thousand

Faces', a compilation of all the world's hero myths, tracing common features of each. All the myths began, said Campbell, with a call to adventure, which if accepted started the hero off on a difficult and dangerous journey, during which he discovered his destiny, or slayed the dragon, or freed the princess, or saved the world or whatever. So strong was the revelation, the conviction that I had been called to the hero quest, that I rose to my feet in Sam Widges and went to the bar, where a fierce Scottish man called Big Frank presided, and I asked Frank if I could try on Dylan Thomas's corduroy jacket which hung on its peg by the coffee machine. I knew what it was because Frank had told me months ago that Dylan himself had given it to him – but I had pretended then that I did not care, though I always gave it a good long look every time I entered the café. Frank passed the jacket over the bar and I put it on and he laughed at the moonstruck expression on my face. But he did not know that this was an omen, that this was a little domestic ceremony, that this was the donning of the sacred mantle to seal my commitment to the quest.

So there I was in the freezing morning on the A30, having survived the terrible night, still huddled on the cold ground, watching Kevin caper about in the grey pre-dawn light, swearing and flapping his arms against his body. I was seriously thinking about crossing the road and hitching back to London. A person could die out here! I had also left behind my girlfriend Janet, a grammar school student of 16 years who was my first love. It had not seemed perverse to leave her, but a proper part of the myth in which the hero was obliged to travel far away and to write beautiful poetry about his estranged and distant love. I had been a little disappointed, though, when she received the announcement of my imminent departure with enthusiasm, not tears. She had said it was just like Mr Darcy in Pride and Prejudice, and that I would return weighty and tempered by grim experience. It did not occur to me that this indicated she thought I needed a bit of weight and experience. No, it just meant that she was with me in the myth, in the quest.

I used to wait for her on Saturday afternoons in Sam Widges, and when she arrived in her bell-shaped cotton skirt and belted blouse, my heart would swell up with awe and disbelief that this vision of loveliness had come to see me. It was embarrassing sitting there with her, holding hands under the table, acutely conscious that my heart had invisibly expanded to fill the whole café with a golden warmth. How could they not notice that I was shining like the sun? We used to share a portion of Frank's powerful Bolognese, and she would eat her half with a teaspoon. When evening came, we walked through Soho to Shaftsbury Avenue, and down into the large cellar which was Cy Laurie's Jazz Club, where we would dance the stomp to such classics as 'Old Rugged Cross', 'Whistling Rufus', and 'Onions'. At intervals, we would climb the steps to the courtyard above, and I would get drinks from the adjacent pub: a bottle of beer for me, and a gin and orange for her. Before closing time, Janet would confer with a group of her Grammar School girlfriends – who had been watching us like meerkats – and return with an alibi allowing her to spend the night with me. Then we would walk, hand in hand, through the Saturday night crowd, across Piccadilly Circus, down Haymarket, to Horse Guards and Whitehall, thence to Westminster Bridge, where we could start to hitch. I was used to it, having hitched home many times after nights out in Soho, but it was all new to Janet, and she glowed and sparkled with the excitement of it. It was always easy to get a ride over the Thames and down the Old Kent Road – and onward along the A2, through New Cross, Deptford, Blackheath – and over Shooters Hill to my parents house in Welling. Beautiful Janet would chatter to the entranced drivers, who often would go out of their way to take us where we wanted. It never took us more than an hour to arrive, and to stealthily let ourselves into the living room. I would make some tea, and put Frank Sinatra's 'Songs for Swinging Lovers' to softly play on the Dansette. Then we would turn off the lights and lie down on the sofa, and snog. In those days, this meant that I had access to the upper half of her body, but not to the lower half, which was defended by a large pair of navy-blue schoolgirl knickers. The other rule was that I was authorised to touch anything above her waist, but she was not authorised to touch any part of me. Honestly, you'd think I was radioactive or something. Later on, in Cornwall, I read T.S. Eliot's 'Lovesong of J Alfred Prufrock', and the line "like a patient etherized upon a table" made me think of Janet – but that unloving thought came after the great betrayal of the three roses, which I'll tell you about later on. On Sunday morning, we were up, demurely drinking tea, when my mother came down to ask Janet what she would like for breakfast. My mother was always good that way, I think she was glad I was normal. After such pleasantries, I would walk Janet to the local railway station, and wave her farewell, while trying not to show how much genital discomfort I was experiencing. I've never consulted any medical advice about this, but imagine that some sort of testicular/prostatic congestion was involved, due to the prolonged but anticlimactic snogging. Some may imagine that I resented Janet's puritanical limitations on my sexual desires, but they'd be quite wrong: I was like an adventurous boy who, having been invited on an Everest climb, was ecstatic just to reach base camp.

My hitching companion on the A30, Kevin Mahoney, was a young man I had met in Cy Laurie's jazz club. After I had committed to the quest, experienced hitchers in Soho coffee bars had advised me that the road was tough on two-man teams, and that it was much better to hitch with a girl. But neither Kevin nor I could find a girl who wanted to go to Newquay, and neither of us was brave enough to go solo. So there we were, at dawn, frozen stiff and starving. We shambled off, heading west, with Kevin still swearing and flapping while I glumly considered abandoning the quest. I would certainly have done so if a lorry had not stopped to offer us a ride all the way to Amesbury. If this had not happened, my life would have taken a different course, and I would have become someone else, someone for whom the moving finger would have written a different story. Fate's messenger, in this case, was a rough diamond truck driver stinking of body odour: a veritable Caliban.

At Amesbury, we sustained ourselves with a meat pie and chips, and endured another long roadside wait before a fat lady in a Morris Minor gave us a ride to Yeovil. It had taken us all day since the crisis under the street sign to arrive in Yeovil at about 10pm. We were so exhausted that we decided, against all ethics of the Hitching Lore, to take a room at an hotel for the night. This decision was made with the implicit agreement that it would not be mentioned to anyone on arrival in Newquay; our fellow beatniks would, we knew, have regarded it as akin to arriving in a limousine. We walked along the deserted dark high street of Yeovil to a public house advertising accommodation. We entered 'Reception' and rang the bell provided on the uninhabited reception desk. A young lady appeared, took one look at us, and screamed in exactly the same tones as heroines screamed when en-countering extra-terrestrial monsters in popular movies of those times. She even raised her clenched fist to cover her mouth, and extended her other hand towards the horrible things, just like they did. Kevin and I stood aghast as thunderous steps were heard descending unseen stairs, heralding the arrival of a burly, red-faced landlord equipped with a mighty walking stick. He brandished this weapon above his head, and said that he did not want the likes of us there and that we should bugger off. We had not uttered a word. While his putative daughter cowered behind the counter, he continued to utter very loud threats as we backed, apologetically gesticulating, out the door. This reaction was entirely unwarranted: Kevin and I were, I suppose, a little dishevelled after our exposure to the road, but there was nothing in our

18

A Noose of Light

presentation to account for such alarm. But this was nothing compared to the reception we received from the Yeovil community as we resumed our trek up the high street. Whole families peered from windows, and even assembled on their doorsteps to witness our banishment; to witness our *expulsion* as we walked up the lamp-lit high street. I do not know how they were alerted to our presence in their town – perhaps they had simply heard the landlord's bellows – but I will never forget the faces of the children gazing blankly at us as their parents clutched them protectively. Outside the town, we found a copse of friendly trees in which to sleep, stunned into mutual silence by our acclaim as public renegades; our acclaim as *outcasts*. We had not imagined that our style could provoke such fear, and our separation from orthodoxy was enhanced thereby. I cannot speak for Kevin, but I rejoiced in it. This was the kind of dark glory that aligned me with the great rejected revolutionaries of the past, and allowed my adolescent ambitions to march shoulder to shoulder with Galileo, Voltaire and Baudelaire.

In the morning, another fat lady picked us up. We asked her *specifically* to drop us off at the nearest place where we could get food, so it was not her fault. She delivered us to a little restaurant just off the road, but it was so early in the day that the sign on the door said 'Closed'. We knocked, and it was opened by a man in a baby blue shirt with a matching brocade necktie who hesitated before admitting us, but did. We were quite literally starving, but politely ordered the 'chef's breakfast', which arrived as microscopic triangles of toast overlaid with one poached egg and a sprinkle of greenstuff, accompanied by weak tea in teeny little flower-patterned Limoges cups. This vanished down our maws like autumn leaves into a volcano. After that, we were kept hanging around, starving by the road for so long that we debated knocking on the nearest door and asking for help: we rehearsed saying, "Hello, have you any food for us, we can pay," but neither of us had the nerve. Eventually, another ride brought us to Exeter, where, at about 11pm, we collapsed onto a grassy bank by the road, only to be awakened at 3am by police, who told us to move on. We asked them to direct us to a source of food, and they pointed the way to a nearby transport café. We walked there as dawn's left hand was in the sky, and stuffed ourselves. Everything was delivered in huge portions, as if serving giants. Even the tea was delivered in pint mugs. Gazing out through the windows at the trucks arriving and departing in the early sunlight, I realised that the social systems of my working classes were strong, and that the norms which I had taken for granted had been won by resentful peasants such as I: restless natives who had stood their ground against the toffs. Invigorated by sustenance, I jotted this observation down in my notebook, and rising from the table, saw Kevin and myself reflected in a mirror behind the serving counter. It was gratifying to see that our three days exposure to the road had transformed us from pallid, effete Londoners into sunburnt and grimy explorers – fit for any mythical adventure.

Kevin and I then had another confidential consultation. We decided to take the 'Cornish Riviera

Express' train from Exeter to Newquay, and to arrive in town without mentioning this fact. If anyone were to ask about the trip, we were to comment that it was rough, and to leave it at that. And that's how we arrived in Newquay. It should be mentioned here that this was the town that the noted BBC Journalist Alan Whicker chose to visit in the following year of 1960 to run a TV expose on the community's persecution of itinerant beatniks. I was there in the year that both preceded and promoted such media attention. But my story, this story, has not been hitherto reported. No one mentioned in Whicker's 1960 TV documentary that the 1959 beatnik community had been involved in a murder investigation. This was because the dead man was not a beatnik but an Oxford undergraduate, and because the circumstances surrounding his death would have been simply too weird for the media of that time to report. For me, an intimate participant, this event became a seminal life experience.

The sun was shining at midday as Kevin and I walked from the station into the town centre and saw a gathering of about 20 beats seated in a ring on the sunlit village green – with the sparkling ocean and rugged cliffs as background. Some I knew from Cy Laurie's and Soho coffee bars, but most I did not. Wizz Jones was playing his guitar as usual, and several dancers were demonstrating the 'stomp' to an audience of holidaying families. We joined the circle and reported the edited version of our journey. The record was held by a boy who bragged that they had made it in under 24 hours, and who proudly described how his girl companion had thumbed at the roadside while he hid in the bushes. When vehicles stopped, he had leaped out from the bushes and into the car or lorry beside her. She had introduced him as her brother, who had just been for a wee-wee. Several drivers had ejected them and driven off, but most had not.

Overnight lodgings and job prospects appeared easily. A boy called Mick said he had an appointment for tomorrow with the manager of the Byron Court Hotel, who had put the word out for casual staff, so we arranged to tag along. Two girls had already begun waitressing at another hotel, and offered us an overnight stay on the floor of their double staff room – but warned that it had to be done covertly otherwise they would be sacked. So that night, Kevin and I sneaked over a back fence and through their window to enjoy whispered conversation with the giggling girls. When the lights went out, Kevin's Irish charm and good looks soon promoted him from floor to bed. The other girl, not wishing to be outdone, extended a slender moonlit hand down to where I lay. The suppressed noises from the other bed indicated that Kevin was more than competent in this situation, whereas I was still virgin and inept and disappointing. She didn't wear any knickers, let alone navy-blue ones, so I didn't know what to do or what not to do.

Next morning, Wizz Jones, Kevin, Mick and I lined up for inspection in the sunlit back yard of the Byron Court Hotel. The saturnine manager, accompanied by an assistant holding a clip board, looked us up and down as if reviewing troops. He indicated Wizz's guitar case and asked for a tune. Stalwart Wizz declined,

A Noose of Light

complaining of an injured left hand. The manager passed on to Kevin, who astonishingly spouted an impressive pedigree as a commis chef at several London restaurants. Mick reported helping his father on his Petticoat Lane barrow. The manager's dark eye then fixed on the folder I habitually held, and asked what was in it. I gave it to him, and he read some pages of my poetry. "Rather formal", he said, handing it back. And that was it: Kevin was appointed as commis chef in the kitchen, and Wizz, Mick and I as plate room staff. The manager walked off and conversed with his assistant, who came back to conduct us to our lodgings. Inexplicably, my companions were delivered to a dormitory room, a Gulag of tiered bunk beds, while I was ushered into a private single staff room overlooking the adjacent golf course. To me, this was a message from the gods that my quest was favoured. I stood alone in the middle of the room, and shuffled around in a full circle like a lighthouse light, beaming my solemn joy at all four white walls, and out the window to the emerald green grass stretching away to the tree-fringed horizon. I placed my few items of alternate clothing in the wardrobe and drawers provided, and arranged my folder and pens symmetrically on the desk (a desk!), then I sat down to write a high-flown poem to my girlfriend Janet.

Our work was governed by the mealtimes of the hotel. We plate room staff were required to wash up the china and cutlery used by up to 200 guests every breakfast time, lunchtime and dinnertime. In between these tasks we were free to surf at the famous Fistral Bay, and to frequent the town cafes or pubs. Quickly understanding this, we devised a system to allow us the maximum free time possible. We identified that the most time-consuming task was transporting the china across the 4-metre gap between the giant plate washer and the stacking shelves. The solution was to throw it across. One of us would stand by the shelves and another would lift each dried plate from the washer and hurl it across to the catcher like a porcelain frisbee, thus emptying the machine and making it ready for the next load. We quickly became so adept at this as to resemble circus performers, and the senior kitchen staff came in to watch. They alerted the manager, and he stood in the doorway watching us as we performed, said nothing, and departed. During the six months of such activity not one plate was shattered.

But as excellence in any trade attracts jealousy, so it was that the Chef's assistant, a man called Heinz, took against us. I think he came from a German town where gypsies were despised, and he thought we were gypsies. His sneering demeanour so annoyed us that I devised a plan to get back at him. One night, when we knew he was on duty alone in the kitchen, I appeared dressed in black and face-powdered pale with flour, bearing a large steel bowl. I hesitantly asked Heinz for some blood. He did not understand, and I explained sincerely that I would like some of the blood, which dripped from the suspended carcasses in the freezer. Doubtfully, Heinz took the bowl from my hand, went into the freezer room, and returned with about two pints of chilled blood in the steel bowl. I sniffed it appreciatively, bowed and thanked him and walked out of the kitchen into the staff room where my eavesdropping friends were near suffocating themselves. The very next day, I was moved from my olympian private room into the Gulag dormitory. A friendly waitress told us that Heinz had reported my Dracula act, and that management feared I might disturb guests on the golf course. I sincerely disagreed with what the finger had written here: Heinz had well deserved his satirical attack, and my theatrical performance was deserving of an award rather than a punishment. Nevertheless I stayed faithful to the heroic principle, and thought it would somehow work out.

Two other incidents are worth reporting as examples of the beatnik lifestyle in that year. In our breaks from work we used to go snorkeling and surfing off the coast around Newquay. While doing so one day, I confessed to a companion – a guy called 'Black Roger', who had gained notoriety and admiration by picking up a dead fish on the beach and eating it raw in front of several holiday families – that I feared looking down through the water at the long green seaweeds waving to and fro beneath me. He said that he had felt *exactly* the same until he had allowed himself to drift down right into the underwater weeds, letting them wrap themselves around him. After that his weed fear had vanished. So I went back into the water and swam out to where I could look down and see the dreaded weeds, and I swam down into them and allowed them to wrap me in their clammy clutches. Returning triumphant to the beach, I reported my experience to Roger. He asked me if I had really done it. I said yes. He said that he would never do that for a thousand pounds.

The second is when were seated late at night around the staff room table where Wizz was teaching me how to play guitar. Kevin walked in, dripping wet, carrying a heavy sack, which he emptied onto the table before us. Thousands of green-tinged pennies and threepenny bits and sixpences and shillings spilled out over the table and onto the floor. Kevin had robbed the town's wishing well. I told Kevin that he had *stolen all the people's wishes,* and that no good would come of it. He remembered that when the scary stuff started happening.

After a few months of life in Newquay, I became anxious that I had not received a single letter from girl-friend Janet, after I had mailed her at least one letter every week. I was not used to *expecting* correspondence, and was quite fully engaged in writing and playing guitar and hanging out with friends at the beach, but the imbalance of her zero letters to my eight or ten gradually became too great to ignore. I began to think that something had happened to her. In those days phones were not so broadly employed as they are today, and it simply did not occur to me that I might find her number and call her. So I presented my fictitious excuses to the hotel manager and gained a week's leave. I used the town's Interflora shop to send a poetic two red roses to her address as heralds of my coming, and then, at dawn next morning, caught a bus to the A30 to begin hitching – stoically prepared for a rough trip. To my astonishment, the first car that came along was going all the way to London. Its driver was a young man who wanted to know all about me, and we conversed pleasantly for a long time before I started to notice certain abnormalities – little anomalies of behaviour, which accumulated into an alarming conclusion. He did not seem familiar with the car's controls, and often revved the engine and grated gears painfully. He rummaged in the glove box and produced a pair of sunglasses, which he put on. They were lady's sunglasses. His driving style was to put his foot down on the accelerator and hold it there – while overtaking around blind corners. It was only a little car, and he more or less had his foot to the floor all the way for 300 miles. I coldly weighed the odds, concluded that he had probably stolen the car, and/or was an escaped lunatic. I decided to talk to him in a manner promoting calmness and safety, and thus improve my chances of arriving in London intact. So I told him all about Omar Khayyam and Sam Widges, and Janet, and Cy Laurie's, and Dylan Thomas all the way to London. I think this did slow him down a bit. He dropped me right outside Janet's postal address in Kilburn at 3pm, and gave me a present of an ivory penknife with a little mother-of-pearl ship inset in the handle. It wasn't his, but I thought I deserved it.

I had never visited Janet's home before, so I just knocked on the door. A woman I assumed to be Janet's mother opened it, and I explained who I was. The woman said that Janet was out. I asked when she would be back, and the woman said she would be back in the evening. I asked if she would be arriving at the train station and she said yes. I walked about a mile to a cafe opposite Kilburn tube station, and sat there snacking and drinking tea, watching passengers come out until

6.30pm. Then I returned to the house and knocked on the door. The same woman answered and broke down in tears and led me through to a bedroom where Janet was laying, pale in a white nightdress, with an enormous red pimple in the very middle of her forehead. She was in tears, also. I looked around the room and immediately noticed *three* red roses in a vase with an Interflora label attached. I had specifically ordered *two* red roses. The shop girl had said that Interflora's minimum order was six, and I had said clearly that I would *pay* for six but they were to send *only two*. But the fools had sent a meaningless three! At that moment I was separated from all the world. I regarded these weeping women and the stupid Interflora girl as a job lot, a job lot of mere puppets. Janet choked back her tears to utter the words, "Why aren't you angry?" I could not be angry. They both knew they had treated me unforgivably, and were crying only for themselves: *they had betrayed Mr Darcy!* And they could never henceforth read romantic fiction in the same way again – a fitting punishment. On the way to the door, the mother sobbed that Janet was studying at school and could not be romantically involved. I said nothing, it was but the twittering of a shade. I left, caught the tube to London's Western outskirts, and started hitching back to Cornwall, comforting myself with the conviction that this was exactly the sort of thing heroes and poets had to endure. I felt darker, and that was good.

The seasonal workers in Newquay that year included a number of Oxford undergraduates, one of whom was a slim and handsome young man called Tom, who worked as a porter at the prestigious Headland Hotel. He befriended us in pubs and cafes, and I guess we adopted him as an honorary beatnik – but one who was upper class, better educated, older and happened to prefer classical music.

One morning Tom's body was found dead on the beach at the foot of a tall cliff. Nobody had come forward to explain how he had come to be there. Some among the beatnik community were interviewed by the police, without result. On the night in question Tom had been seen drinking in a pub near the cliff edge, but no one could account for his movements thereafter.

On the night after receiving news of Tom's death, Wizz, Kevin, David, Arnold, Mick and myself were talking about the tragedy, wondering how Tom had fallen over the edge. We were all seated round the staff room at about 10pm, when we noticed that Mick had grown pale and silent. There occurred an inexplicable alteration of the atmosphere, like a drop in temperature. Whatever it was, it made us all look at Mick at the same time. His head had stooped into his hands on the table. Someone asked if he was okay, but he did not reply. He stood up and was still, staring at nothing, and we all watched him. Without a word he turned and walked out, and by unspoken agreement we all stood up and followed. Mick walked out of the hotel grounds and along the silent street leading to the beach, then he collapsed onto the road under a street lamp, clutching his head and screaming in pain. We ran up as several lights went on in the dark houses, and faces appeared at windows. Mick writhed on the ground shouting again and again that he had a key in his head and it was hurting him. We picked him up, carried him back to the staff room and sat him back down in his chair, where he rocked back and forth, still holding his head and talking about a key. Not knowing what to do, I asked him what the key was like. Mick opened his eyes and calmed down. He said it was an old fashioned key attached to a big brass tag with a saw-toothed edge, and that there was a number on the tag, and that it was the tag that was hurting him. He grew calmer, and we led him to his bunk and he went to sleep. Back in the staff room we discussed what had happened, and decided to keep an eye on Mick tomorrow. Kevin, however, took me aside to whisper that Mick had fallen to the ground outside a Catholic church, and had stopped screaming when carried outside the area of consecrated ground.

Next morning, as normal, we did the breakfast shift, but covertly watched Mick. He did his work but was silent and withdrawn. I asked him how he felt, and he looked at me in puzzlement. We realised he did not remember the drama of last night, and none of us wanted to mention it. We went to the beach and he sat apart, sometimes looking across at us, as if puzzling about something.

That night in the staff room, exactly the same thing happened again. We were all waiting for it. Mick's head stooped into his hands, he stood up and began to walk out the door. We stopped him and led him to the dormitory and sat him on his bunk. I asked him if it was the key again. He looked at us blankly and then started

A Noose of Light

to speak to us in Tom's voice. Mick was a cockney kid whose father was a trader in Petticoat Lane, and here he was addressing us in the accent and syntax of an Oxford undergraduate. Worse than that, it was Tom's voice. We all recognised it. He said this:

"I am walking towards the railing along the cliff edge. I fall over the railing and turn over in the air twice. My head hits a stone. Under the stone is the key."

We were terrified. Two of us immediately left the room, but I could see them standing outside, listening. I stuttered, "Is that you, Tom?"

Mick looked at me calmly, and in Tom's voice said, "I am able to communicate with you because a man is coming to this place who must be prevented from fulfilling his plans. He is a magician and he always dresses in white. A great destruction may happen if he is not stopped. You are the only people to whom this can be communicated."

Then Mick lay down on the bunk and went to sleep.

While the normally cheerful Mick remained quiet and withdrawn over the following days, strange and frightening events began to occur in the beatnik community. Within days, everyone had heard the story of Mick's behaviour and Tom's message, and people began to visit us at the Byron Court to report. The two waitress girls Kevin and I had stayed with on arrival came to tell us that they had finished their lunch-time shift and gone to their room to get changed for an afternoon at the beach. Three hours later, the restaurant manager banged on their door, and they found themselves sitting on their beds with no recollection of the three hours that had passed. They were so disturbed by this and by other reports that they quit their jobs and returned to London.

Sandy was a drummer who worked with a local dance band. He said that he had been walking down the high street one afternoon when an unknown man had greeted him like a friend. Sandy met lots of people in his job, and he had assumed the man to be an audience member at one of his gigs. The man had insisted that Sandy meet his friends, and had led him to a nearby bookshop. The shop was empty, and the man disappeared into the back section saying that he would bring his friends out. Sandy stood around for a few minutes, and then an elderly couple appeared from the back section and apologised that he had been kept waiting. Sandy explained about the man, but the couple had no knowledge of him. I asked Sandy to describe the man, and Sandy said that he had been short, balding and dressed all in white.

Kevin came into the staff room on the night following the 'message', and dropped a key on the table. It was an old fashioned key with a heavy brass tag, which had a saw-toothed edge. On one side of the tag was an engraved number, and on the other the logo of the Headland Hotel where Tom had worked. Kevin explained that he had found it under a rock at the base of the cliff where Tom had been found. We decided to go to the Headland Hotel and find out which door the key opened. We did not show the key to Mick because we feared provoking another visitation from Tom. Next morning, after the breakfast service, Kevin, Wizz and

A Noose of Light

myself walked out to the Headland Hotel and asked the doorman to show us which room it opened. He thought it an odd request, but led us into the staff entrance and down to the basement and along a dark corridor to a door which bore the same number as the key, and he opened the door. It was a broom closet, and it contained only brooms and cleaning equipment.

These and other less-dramatic events, together with the police investigation into the death, generated such an atmosphere of tension in the beat community that some returned to London. Somehow it was decided that as many as possible of the remainder should assemble at night, with Mick, on the beach at the spot where Tom had been found. We did this, and we stood in a silent group on that spot for a long while, waiting for something to happen. Some girls became frightened and left, and nothing else occurred. But the next day, about a week after Tom had been found dead, something did happen.

Wizz Jones returned from a trip to the town centre and reported seeing a white jeep driven slowly down the high street by a man dressed all in white. Also in the jeep was a woman in white. The white jeep was towing a white caravan, and stuck on the side of the caravan was a large poster advertising 'Peter Casson's Hypnotism Show', with dates and times when the show would be presented at the Newquay Town Hall Theatre. Some loud speakers in the jeep had been broadcasting military marching music, and the man and woman had been waving and smiling.

The entire beat community purchased tickets, and on the opening night occupied the whole back row of seats. I sat down between Kevin and Mick, and Kevin nudged me and pointed downward with his eyes to where his hand held his jacket slightly open. Sewn into the lining inside was a leather sheath holding a chef's knife with a five-inch blade.

We all watched, stony faced among the giggling audience, as the magician summoned sunburnt cheerful holidaymakers up on stage, and made them believe things were true that were not true, and made them act in ridiculous ways to make the audience laugh at them. Here was the answer to our confusion and doubt. The magician who must be stopped had appeared as foretold. I turned to Mick, and said, "Is he the man?" But Mick just looked worried and upset.

A conference was held in a pub after the show. Yes, we had all seen him hypnotise the holidaymakers, a veritable Svengali. Yes, he must be the man dressed in white foretold by Mick in the dead Tom's voice. Yes, many weird and scary events had occurred before he arrived. But how are we going to "stop" him? We knew where his caravan was parked. We could sneak up there to the council campsite tonight, and lure him outside and......? When it came down to it, none of us was up for it. Even Kevin declined to volunteer. But something had to be done! It was eventually decided that a *confrontation* was necessary, a confrontation between Mick and the magician: Mick, the spiritual medium of the recently disembodied Tom must come face to face with the man accused, and.....*expose* him. Then, if any unimaginable thing happened, Kevin would rush forward and finish him – somehow assisted by everyone else. But

A Noose of Light

what about the woman? What about Mrs Casson? It was agreed that Mrs Casson was too much to deal with. Mick/Tom had not mentioned any woman in white, so she would just have to take her chances. Next morning, after the breakfast shift, the Byron Court contingent kept a rendezvous at the Newquay council caravan site with beatniks from other hotels. It should be noted that no one chickened-out, they all took the responsibility very seriously. Thus it was that about 15 grim-faced young people sat, at 10.30am, in a semi-circle on the grass facing Peter Casson's caravan door. I led Mick up to it and knocked. Mrs Casson opened it, and I started to explain why we were there. She interrupted me to say, in a practised official voice, that private consultations were only available by appointment – but then she saw the silent assembly behind me, and decided to summon her husband. Peter Casson appeared and impassively heard me stutter through the whole story. He did not seem very interested, and perhaps was irritated that his breakfast had been disturbed. When I finished, he said that it was all a fairly typical example of mass hysteria in an isolated community. He said that Mick had been attached to Tom in a deeper way than he understood, and that Tom's death had shocked Mick into a temporary state akin to psychosis, in which he briefly took on Tom's persona as a sort of compensation for his death. The close knit and exclusive beat community had been a highly suggestive breeding ground for delusory beliefs to spread like a biological contagion. He asked Mick a few questions, and then said that he saw no reason to advise treatment but, if Mick would prefer, he could refer him for a stay in a nearby sanatorium with which he was associated. Mick declined this offer, and we all went home.

Every time I have told this story over the fifty years since it happened, listeners have asked about certain 'holes in the script', which are seemingly not explained by Peter Casson's cool, detached analysis. I have come up with the following answers:

How did Mick speak in Tom's voice? People experiencing psychotic breaks often exhibit behaviours and abilities that are unavailable to them in their normal state of mind. Before Tom's death, Mick used to entertain us with imitations of Hotel staff with Cornish accents, and TV and radio commercials – particularly one about Kraft Crackerbarrel Cheese – which were very funny. The psychological impact of the death seems to have amplified Mick's talent for mimicry to truly extraordinary levels.

How did Mick know about the key? I was not aware that Mick had many meetings with Tom on the beach or in pubs and cafes, but he must have done so to develop such a deep attachment. At those meetings Mick must often have seen Tom carrying such keys, which were common to the Headland Hotel where he worked. My cod psychology opines that the key image symbolised the mental pain or shock Mick felt about Tom's death.

How did Kevin find the key? He simply went down to the beach and found it where it had fallen from Tom's pocket.

A Noose of Light

What about all the other reports of weird happenings? It doesn't take much to trigger paranoia and delusions in a tight knit and socially estranged adolescent community. Google 'mass hysteria' for many similar examples.

How did Mick know that 'the magician' would be wearing white? Peter Casson, an established London psychologist, took his caravan on tour around the English south and west seaside towns every holiday season. It's possible that Mick saw one of Casson's hypnotism shows when he was holidaying with his family in earlier years.

How did Tom die? The coroner's verdict was accidental death. No one knows how it happened.

What happened to Mick afterward? I never saw him again after that season ended. I assume he resumed his normal life. Of course, those who find this ending anticlimactic can always imagine that Tom's message through Mick set us, the beatniks, to confront 'the magician' – thus alerting him to the fact that his activities were being monitored from the 'spirit world', and consequently dissuading him from going ahead with his plan. What plan? We'll never know.

As for us, the rest of the season was anticlimactic, and possibly as a result of this, we devised a 'happening' to liven things up. Such happenings were to become popular in the fast-approaching new decade of the sixties. I don't think it was coincidental that ours had a psychological theme. One afternoon, in Newquay's high street at the busiest time of day, Wizz Jones was seen sitting on the kerb, fishing down a drain in the road directly outside Woolworths supermarket. He had a proper rod and basket, and repeatedly reeled up his baited hook, theatrically shaking his head and stamping his foot in disapproval when it caught no fish. The passing throng of holidaymakers twigged that some entertainment was afoot, and a small crowd gathered in the sunlight on the other side of the road. Sure enough, a white van screeched to a halt beside Wizz, and three white-coated young men jumped out, one of which was clearly wearing a blonde wig, lipstick and a padded bra. Wizz dropped the rod, flung his hands to heaven and cried, "The men in white coats! The men in white coats!" Then he ran into Woolworths and was pursued around the store by the three 'nurses'. Everything would have gone as planned, and Wizz would have been bundled into the van and driven off, to the amused mystification of the crowd, had not an unforseen circumstance occurred. The 'nurse' in the blonde wig was Kevin, and he galloped out of the store much too fast to avoid colliding with a child in a wheelchair, catapulting the little boy *and his plaster cast-encased leg*, up and then down, sickeningly, on to the road. Worse, much worse as fate would have it, a photographer from the local newspaper had been alerted by reports of a beatnik fishing down a drain in the high street, and had miraculously arrived on the scene *precisely* when Kevin collided with the wheelchair. It was probably his lifetime finest achievement: the black and white shot showed the boy actually suspended in the air above the tumbled wheelchair, his plastered leg aloft, and Kevin with his tits and lipstick legging it out of frame. This picture appeared on the front page of the next day's newspaper accompanied by an article deploring this further atrocity by the 'beatnik invaders'. From the beginning, we had not been a welcome addition to the residents of Newquay. Indeed, our popularity throughout the holiday season could be measured by the number of cafes and pubs from which we had been banned: quite literally, we started at the cafes at one end of town, and were sequentially banned until we reached the other end. Our presence in venues, they said, dissuaded normal people from entering. It was this history, I think, and the terrible photo of Kevin's wheelchair accident, which attracted Alan Whicker and the BBC to make the documentary in the following year. How much meatier, I wonder, would have been the media lure if the moving finger had allowed Kevin and his knife to have had their way with the magician?

But what the finger wrote was me, travelling back to London in October 1959 on the pillion seat of a Vespa scooter – with my future wife driving. Ann was a beautiful and wilful girl of Scottish ancestry who had arrived mid-season and mid the Mick/Tom event, and taken a fancy to me. We lost our virginity together on my dormitory bunk: a very painful process which no one had told either of us about. Briefly, my foreskin was too tight, and her hymen too tough. She must have been as disappointed by the whole thing as I was, but nevertheless she suggested that we should get married when we went back to London. When I hesitated to rejoice at this generous offer, she said that she was going to walk down to the beach and surrender herself to the sea. So naturally I acquiesced.

The Victorian Nightdress

When I came back to London from my Newquay experience, I was no longer a virgin in any sense. My marriage to Ann lasted 4 years, during which time my taste for sex increased while hers declined. In the fourth year, at the age of 24, she took to wearing a long-sleeved, frilly linen Victorian nightdress as a barrier against sexual advances. Like some inverse example of a Pavlovian dog, I became exquisitely sensitive to the appearance of this garment at bedtime. On one such appearance, I ripped the hated thing to shreds, then I flung some stuff into a small suitcase and rode off into the night on my scooter – leaving behind the nice East Finchley flat, the chessboard orange-and-black fitted carpeting, the 1950s Scandinavian furniture, the Bush radiogram, the Westinghouse fridge and the frigid wife.

After 4 years of building up our little household, my Heinkel scooter was the only possession I cared about. It was factory finished in a pale gray, but had been superbly decorated all over with a black rococo drawing of angels, nudes, cherubs and centaurs cavorting among Grecian temples. It looked like an 18th century engraving on wheels, and always attracted attention wherever it was parked. The artist responsible was my workmate and occasional music partner Mike McGann, who also played banjo in a traditional jazz band. We met as the two in-house graphic designers of a large London-based photographic enterprise called Woburn Studios, where we were mainly responsible for designing the page layouts for a number of mail order catalogues. The unique studios, owned and run by the photo entrepreneur Peter Peck, were enormous – big enough to shoot a dozen models, precisely posed in a stage set, be it a farmyard, a sultan's palace or a spaceship. When not busy in our tiny studio, Mike and I played our guitars, or played pranks on the models. A favourite trick featured a giant spider, about a metre wide and terrifyingly detailed, which Mike made from black 'colorama' background paper, and suspended from the ceiling over the door. Whenever an innocent new girl appeared on set, the photographer's assistants would lure her into our studio to "see the artists' work". She would step through the door to see our horrified faces staring fixedly up at the ceiling. Naturally, she would look up, too. We were forced to stop this jolly jape when the cosmetics department complained that we were ruining the girls' makeup.

Researching to jog my memory, I found no trace of Woburn Studios or Peter Peck other than links to a Peter Rand – one of Peter Peck's assistants – who later distinguished himself by taking the first photo of a black woman ever to appear in Vogue magazine. I cannot even call Mike McGann to reminisce, because he, too, is now safely dead. I would like to remind him of the spider, and of the millionaire Lancashire catalogue owner who refused to have the colour yellow used in his page layouts, crying, "I 'ate yelloooow!" Perhaps someone on a far away planet is watching him say it now.

After we were married in 1960, before the ice set in, Ann and I kept in touch with Wizz Jones and a few of the other Newquay beatniks, and it was during a chat with Wizz that the idea of starting a folk club was mooted. Wizz said he would play, and get us some other performers, too. Ann and I looked around for a venue, and decided on a large 'function room' above the saloon bar of the King's Head pub at the north end of Putney Bridge. Within a month, our display advertisement announcing the opening of The Mojo Folk and Blues Club appeared in the New Musical Express. We had managed everything very carefully, booked several 'known' performers such as Alex Campbell, and the Strawberry Hill Boys – as well as lined up Mike and Wizz – but we were still stunned when almost 200 people turned up and bought their tickets at the door. It was a degree of responsibility for which we were not prepared. Nevertheless, Wizz, a hardened busker, took control and the evening went off very well. The Mojo ran for a further three Saturday nights, by which time Ann and I had learned that 'unprofitable' was an understatement when referring to folk club takings. By the time we had paid the landlord and the performers, there was hardly anything left for the managers. On the forth night, Ann and I arrived to be told that the pub landlord had let the room to a large wedding party – because he thought the wedding guests would drink more beer than the music enthusiasts. The booked musicians arrived, and made no fuss about the sudden cancellation, nor did they demand payment.

They were used to it: it was the stuff they wrote and sang their songs about. When the world proved to be the treacherous and heartless place they sung about, it was almost cause for celebration! I understood this better when, later on, I read about the 12th century Albigensian Crusade, when the Pope launched France's greedy northern barons, with their murderous rabble armies, down upon the Cathar heretics in Provence. Compared to the money-grubbing 'indulgences' scam the Vatican's Cardinals were running on European peasants, the Cathar heresy looked more like true Christianity, with its devout, penniless priests, and charitable society. Oddly, however, the Cathars believed that God had left the scene after creating the world, and had put the Devil in charge – which is why the world was the rather nasty place it was. As a religion, this seemingly unsavoury idea works rather well in practice. When your prize cow falls off a cliff, or when a September storm flattens your crop, or when anything horrible happens, it confirms your faith! Halleluja, you cry, there's the Old Villain again! The Cathars had cracked the whole Problem of Evil (which no monotheist can solve) in one bold hit! So it was no surprise to them when the Vatican's killers arrived. They didn't put up much of a fight because they knew what they were fighting. But I have wandered off course into an old obsession. I wrote a song about it called 'Massacre at Beziers', which you can see performed today on YouTube.

From the mountaintop of 2014, on which I write, all I can see of 1960 – 1964, the years of my first marriage, are misty valleys with a few peaks sticking up into the light. One of them is called the Mojo Folk & Blues Club, another is called hitch-hiking to Paris, but towering over all and balefully, frostily shining in the sun is that accursed Victorian nightdress.

In lieu of a holiday, Ann and I decided to hitch hike to Paris to see Wizz, who was busking there with the banjo player Pete Stanley. It was winter, and a cold coming we had of it. The only significant thing that happened, beside us seeing the Paris sights, was that Wizz told me about his planned trip down to St Tropez in the Spring, which description inspired me to write the song 'National 7' about hitching down the road to the south of France. Forever after, now for more than half a century, this song became the most frequently played and widely covered of all my numbers – which is embarrassing because I never hitched down to St Tropez.

The only other event worth mentioning occurred when our friend Richard invited me to show my paintings in the vestibule of an Edinburgh Festival theatre show, for which he was working as a stage rigger. The paintings went up to Scotland on the lorry with the stage props, while Ann and I hitched. I had the exhibition – which was not even reviewed – and the only memorable thing about the trip was when one of our truck drivers stopped for a drink at his favourite pub in Newcastle, and introduced us to his friends. They were all very friendly, but I could not understand a single word they said. So far, that was the most embarrassing few hours I ever experienced. You can only ask someone to repeat what they say a certain number of times, and

A Noose of Light

you can also only fake a head-nodding comprehension of what someone with a Newcastle accent is saying a certain number of times. After that, the only thing to do is crawl under the table and hide.

I now rather suspect that they were all exaggerating their accents to take the piss out of the Londoner, but that may just be belated paranoia.

Congo Big Stick

On the night of the Victorian nightdress, which ended my first marriage as finally and suddenly as the cut of a crusader's sword, I buzzed off on my rococo Heinkel scooter with no destination in mind. There was no room for destinations in the red mist, the furious outrage. After driving a few miles down the road, it occurred to me that I did not know where I was going, so I pulled into a lay-by to think about it. In one of my many attempts to stop 'prostituting' myself, my art, my creativity in the advertising industry, I had been working as an art student's nude model at Hornsey College of Art, and there at the roadside I remembered that the teacher, Beverley, had given me her phone number. I found the slip of paper in my wallet, and drove to the nearest red telephone box. And that's how I connected to my second wife and the mother of my children. That connection and its consequences never entered my head at the time. I did not feel attracted to Beverley, other than as a fellow artist. I just needed a place to stay overnight which would not involve obligatory explanations, and do-gooding phone calls to let my wife know where I was. Beverley and I had enjoyed a few conversations in the college staff room, and she had given me the phone number expecting that I would bring Ann over to meet

46

her. But that's not what the finger had written.

I arrived at her flat in Notting Hill at about 11pm on a Friday, and was introduced to her guests. Ivan was from Jamaica and John from New York. The music playing was Buchdehude, and Feodor Chaliapin. I was immediately included in the interrupted conversation about spiritual development, fed by tea and black bread and cherry jam supplied by our hostess. Ivan and John left at about 2am, and I bid my hostess a grateful goodnight before settling down to sleep on the studio bed, wondering what I would do in the morning. Some time later, and to my astonishment, I was awakened by my naked hostess joining me in bed, and demonstrating that some women, at least, were enthusiastic about sex. This was a revelation, a visitation: I welcomed it as a message from the gods that I was on the right path. The hero was continuing to progress towards the unimaginable goal through these challenging trials and sublime rewards.

During the following months of 1964, Ivan, John and (now resident) myself assembled at Beverley's Notting Hill flat at night to conduct exploratory ventures into the psycho-spiritual effects of Congo Big Stick, a Jamaican traditional blend of cow's blood and hashish, supplied by Ivan. Many interesting experiences were gained thereby, including my experience of marching up and down the room clapping my hands together for an hour to prevent myself vanishing forever into the furniture. This performance was watched, fixedly and silently, by my companions, and accompanied by Elizabethan love songs on the record player. When I felt safe enough to sit down at the table again, Ivan said, in his deep Jamaican voice, "I did that once, and I became a light hanging in black space, and the light got smaller and smaller and smaller, and then it went.....out." And also there was the experience of making a plaster mold of mine own hand, which stuck because I had forgotten to apply Vaseline to the hand, which then took two hours of careful hacking and squirming to remove from the mold. I did remember to smear Vaseline into the mold before pouring fiberglass resin into it, however, and we all sat around watching the resin harden. When we all agreed the time was right, I used a hammer to shatter the mold and reveal the rose pink transparent hand, shining in the table's spotlight like ectoplasm, or a voodoo juju. Beverley, awestruck, leaned forward and said, "Look, it's even got your hairs in it." And sure enough, there were my real hand hairs seemingly growing from the holy relic. Then there was the experience of submitting to a Jamaican 'pot-pilot' called Rupi, who actually taught us to fly. He stood at the end of the dining table and solemnly held out his arms, flapped them, and said, "We's all flyin'!" And we were. The whole room was shooting through the night towards Marble Arch, with us laughing inside it.

My new partner, Beverley, used to drive me to the art school in the mornings following such nightly sessions, and I wondered aloud how she could do so while suffering the after effects of Congo Big Stick. She said it was easy, all she had to do was realise that the car was standing still and the landscape was moving past it. At the art school, I had the easy job, reclining on the couch, naked, while Beverley put her elevated mental state to

A Noose of Light

good use by telling the students to realise that space touched the contours of my body like the sea touched the shore.

My wife Ann, having tracked me down, phoned several times to Beverley's studio, but I explained to her that I was on a new cycle, and that she should move on to the rest of her life without me. I think Ann had phoned Hornsey Art School to ask if I was still working there, and had been told Beverley's number. Soon after, Beverley was summoned to the Principal's office and questioned. Her relationship with 'a model' was not considered appropriate, and she was asked to resign. Ann also sent a friend, a Newquay associate called Arnold, around to Beverley's studio to inspect us. He arrived for lunch one day, and I discovered that a myth had developed among my old beatnik companions; a story that I had been stolen away from Ann by a 'black witch'. The explanation for my sudden break from Ann after four years of marriage was, and could only be, that I had been enchanted by magic powers. Arnold had recently converted to Catholicism, so was ready to see evil all around. At the lunch, he found that our knives and forks were satanic because they had black handles. He was also suspicious of Beverley's favourite black rye bread, and refused to eat any. This myth, that a 'black witch' had abducted me, spread around my erstwhile friends in a similar manner to the Tom/Mick myth. From the night of the intolerable Victorian nightdress, I never saw my wife again. She eventually sent around her solicitor: I agreed to divorce and to give her everything, and that was that. Her very nice Scottish mother, I heard later, had commented,

"Well, you lost him, didn't you?" I would love to know what she meant, but never will. Had she counselled her daughter to lay back and think of Scotland? Did none of them ever realize that I had abandoned everything and all of them simply to free myself from a frigid spouse?

Following our joint dismissal from the art school, I found a job at a theatrical stage manufacturer's factory off Shaftesbury Avenue, where, among other things, I helped to make the props, the spears and magic cave, for the London production of 'Camelot'. When Camelot opened in August 1964, my job ended and I quickly found another with the Dunhill company, repairing their customers' cigarette lighters in a small factory near Notting Hill. Beverley had her trust fund allowance, and I had a tolerable job. We were doing okay, and continuing with our explorations of spiritual development opportunities – sometimes with Ivan and John and Richard, and sometimes without.

My first contact with Beverley's Jewish Australian family occurred when her 'aunt' paid us a visit at the Notting Hill flat. When Beverley was a teenager, her mother had died of multiple sclerosis, so the 'aunt' was actually the sister of Beverley's stepmother, Edith, whom her father, Ben, had married a few years after the mother's death. I suspect the 'aunt' had been commissioned by the Australian family to inspect me, after Beverley had told them by letter she was in a new relationship. Coming from a dirt-poor south London family, I was impressed at the anxiety surrounding this visit. The flat was cleaned up to a wholly unnecessary degree, and some china I had never seen before was

50

displayed, ready for tea. The 'aunt' arrived dressed in a chic little Chanel suit with jangling jewelry, to conduct the meeting like a too-cheerful job interview, or perhaps more like a covert interrogation by an undercover agent? Whatever. Afterwards, Beverley told me the 'aunt's' verdict, "He's a nice boy, darling, but he's not a money-maker." How right she was.

We went to one of the London Buddhist centres and spoke to a genuine Indonesian monk, who told us about 'loving kindness'. We read many Theosophical books by Annie Besant, Corona True, and Madame Blavatsky, and came into contact with Monica Merlin – an elderly lady with a large greyhound – who took us down to the Theosophy centre at Tekels Park, Camberley, and introduced us to some of her Theosophical acquaintances, all old ladies. One of them looked at me through her blue tinted sunglasses and said, quite clearly, as if I wasn't there, "Oh, he's been *burnt!*" Monica explained that they often got reincarnated martyrs, like me, visiting the centre. I noticed and commented on the extraordinary atmosphere in Tekels Park. I said it was as if a delicate tiny crystal vase was balanced on every molecule of air.

We studied the Jewish mystical system of Kabbalah, and attempted 'Journeys on the Tree'. We read the Catholic mysticism of Teilhard de Chardin, and the Hindu mysticism of Kundalini. Our studies were regularly augmented by occasional Congo Big Stick sessions in which we discussed our research results with John and Ivan, and sometimes with other explorers introduced by them. One of these, an Haitian Voodoo exponent, attempted to gain power over Beverley by sending her a series of letters in the post. These were each an A4 sheet covered edge to edge with intricate but random scribbles in red ball-point pen – quite the most scary artworks I have ever seen. It was a delightful, if rather dangerous, time – which I now see came sometimes perilously close to episodes of psychosis, with lucid dreams and hypnopompic hallucinations – but we maintained a good level of stability within the whirlwind, because we were looking for a path to which we could commit, but finding the candidates inadequate. So inadequate, in fact, that we started to think about emigration to New York, where the cutting edge was really cutting.

Beverley knew a curator at the Museum of Modern Art, a man she had met through her art school activities. She wrote to him explaining our position, and asking him to be our sponsor for immigration to the USA. He replied, agreeing to sponsor us and to underwrite our initial accommodation. We got the forms from the American Embassy in Grosvenor Square, filled them in and sent them off. Three weeks later, I received a letter from the Embassy inviting me to an interview. On the designated date, I smartened myself up with a dark suit, white shirt and solemn tie, and arrived at the waiting room for emigration applicants. I wondered why I, alone, had been asked to attend, but I soon found out. I was conducted into a small room equipped with a desk and two chairs. On the desk was a large microphone, which was pointed at the interviewee's chair. I sat in this chair, and waited to be interviewed. Eventually a tall, crew cut, young American man entered. He did not greet me. He sat down and placed a beige file on the desk and opened it. Then he switched the microphone on, and said, "This interview is with Alan Alfred Tunbridge on September four 1964. Mr. Tunbridge, what is your purpose in applying to become resident in the United States?" I replied that I was an artist and that I saw New York as the right place to be for someone who wanted to participate in the latest developments in art. He said, "I see from your application that you are cohabiting with one Beverley Judith Green, and that you both plan to travel together to the United States." I said that was correct.

"You and Miss Green are not married?"

"No, we are not."

"And you intend to live together in the United States?"

"Yes, we do."

"Thank you, Mr Tunbridge. You will receive the results of your interview by mail."

He then stood up and gestured politely toward the door. A week later I received a letter saying that my application had been declined on the grounds that I intended to live in the USA immorally with Beverly.

I simply must just slide in here a time-warp insert taking the narrative a few years forward to 1969, when Beverley and I applied for a tourist visa to California. By that time we had our son Gabriel, aged three. Once again I was summoned to the American Embassy in Grosvenor Square, and once again I was interviewed – but this time by a female official. She reviewed my application and opened my file. I realised then that

I had been 'blacked' by the CIA, and that the report of five years ago had passed down to this officer. She confirmed all the points of the tourist visa application, including that I would be travelling with my wife and son, and then announced that my application had been successful.

She stood up and ushered me to the door, and as I passed through it, she said, "Congratulations, Mr Tunbridge. You've come a long way in five years."

Forty-four years later, at the time of writing, I still trace my antipathy to the CIA, and indeed to the American accent, to this unforgivably smug comment. Up to then, I believed they were the defenders of Western culture. After then, they were the 20th century version of the Spanish Inquisition.

Gurdjieff

Following the disappointment of our thwarted emigration, the moving finger and Ivan brought to us some books by and about a new exponent of spiritual development: George Gurdjieff. Compared to the pianissimo tones of the ancient lore and fossilized traditions we had been studying, Gurdjieff's stuff resonated like a struck cymbal. He didn't talk about grace or blessing or repentance, he talked about Work. He didn't talk about submission or prayer or self denial, he talked about super-effort and dancing and discipline. He didn't talk about guardian angels or spirit guides or gurus, he talked about greater and lesser accumulators, and how they can be accessed to blast your mind into higher consciousness.

We learned that Gurdjieff had died in France in 1949, but that a major community centre for Gurdjieff studies existed at an estate called Coombe Springs in Kingston Upon Thames, Surrey. We telephoned, made an appointment, and went there to meet John Bennett, the Director. In 1922-23, he had been a pupil at Gurdjieff's study centre at The Prieure, near Fontainbleau, France, and in 1946 had started his Institute for the Comparative Study of History, Philosophy and the Sciences at Coombe Springs.

Mr Bennett invited us to attend the community's Work Sundays, when non-residents visited to work in the ten acres of grounds, participate in a group exercise, and have lunch together. We attended a number of Work Sundays, and liked 'Mister B' and his wife Elizabeth, and the community's ambience of quiet concentration – but it took an unexpected and dramatic event to nudge us toward applying for residency.

One Sunday afternoon at Beverley's studio, we were discussing Coombe Springs with Ivan, John and Richard, when our friendly young Jamaican pot pilot Rupi dropped in for tea. He was in an expansive mood, as usual, walking about, peering out the window, doing little impromptu dances. He said that we were, "the people of the room", and he liked us so much that he wanted to give us a party.

"Right here in the room!" He said, "It's *such* a nice big room."

We wouldn't have to do anything, he would supply all the drink and snacks and music. We could invite our friends and he would invite a few of his, and everyone would have a great time – all at Rupi's expense.

"No holds barred!" He said, spinning slowly around, arms extended, gazing up at the ceiling, "*No holds barred!*"

We were surprised that Rupi had the money to fund such a project, but felt that it would be rude to refuse. Also we were interested in meeting some more of the Jamaican community in Notting Hill. Also Beverley and I had never hosted a party together, and it could be a sort of celebration of our relationship – like an engagement party. So we told Rupi to go ahead, and asked him when it could happen.

"Next Saturday night!" Said Rupi, "leave it all to me!"

So next Saturday evening, 'the people of the room' – plus Richard, the Edinburgh stage rigger, and Bill and Meg, our neighbours from the next floor up – tidied up the studio, and sat around the table with a bottle of wine and some crackers, waiting for Rupi to arrive. After 9pm passed with no arrivals, we suspected that Rupi had been stoned when he promised us the party, and had forgotten all about it, so we opened another bottle, and Beverley brought out some bread and chicken liver dip, and we settled into a quiet evening at home, as usual. At about 10.45pm, however, the doorbell rang, and I went down the two flights of stairs to open the street door. A young man and woman, two friendly faces, beamed at me from the darkness.

"Is this Alan and Beverley's place?" Said the young man.

"Yes", I said. "Are you friends of Rupi?"

"Rupi, yeah yeah!" Said the young woman.

"It's two flights up, number six," I said, and stood back to let them pass. About 15 to 20 people filed past me and clattered up the stairs. I had not seen them lined up there in the dark street. The last were two smartly dressed Jamaican men. The first was carrying a crate of bottles. He said, "Good evening, sir". The second had a walkie-talkie, and he said, "Good evening, sir. I'll look after the door from now on. You go ahead and enjoy yourself."

"Where's Rupi?" I said.

"He'll be along shortly, sir. You go on ahead."

The man nodded and smiled at me reassuringly, then turned away to speak quietly into his walkie-talkie. I moved to shut the street door, but he held up a gentle hand.

"Everything's taken care of, sir. You go and have a good time."

In a daze, I went back upstairs, thinking that Rupi must be some sort of Jamaican prince, or something. No sooner had I stepped back into the studio, and seen Beverley's shocked face, and the chattering crowd of visitors gathered around the guy with the crate, than yet more people came up the stairs and through the flat's front door. There were about ten more party people, and three more dark-suited, white-shirted Jamaicans, who carried in more crates, and an expensive sound system and some folding tables. The sound system guy swiftly set up his gear against a wall, produced a stack of long playing records, and soon had a Jimmy Smith jazz organ track blasting out. The crate guys displayed an astonishing array of plastic glasses, soft drinks, beer and expensive liquor bottles on their table, and proceeded to serve all comers with whatever they wanted. As if choreographed in a stage show, all the visitors started drinking and dancing like crazy. There were about 40 people, none of whom we knew, but who all seemed to know each other, dancing and laughing and smoking and knocking back booze. Beverley and I felt invaded and usurped, and were unable to participate. We marooned ourselves on the day bed at the end of the room like shipwrecked sailors, and watched the smartly dressed, stony-faced 'management' handle everything.

The sound system man stood with his back against the wall, arms folded, surveying the crowd expressionlessly, never moving unless to change the record. The bar staff never took a drink themselves, but served all comers with quiet efficiency. Twice, a disturbance occurred among the dancers – raised voices and scuffles – and both times a couple of the bar staff slid into the crowd to keep the peace. All they had to do to achieve this, apparently, was stare calmly at the combatants. They all knew what was going on, and we did not. No one spoke to us. John went through the noise and whirling dancers to the bar, and brought back drinks, and Richard had a go at joining the dancers – without much success. It was very strange. If it had been someone else's party in someone else's flat we could have had a good time. It was also too strange for our neighbours Meg and Bill from upstairs. They excused themselves and went home.

Around 12.30am, Richard came to tell us that he had just looked out the window and seen two big black American cars parked in the street right outside. It occurred to me that I should check up on the only other room in the flat – which was our bedroom. I went out of the big studio and along the hall to the bedroom door, which was closed and guarded by a giant darksuited, white-shirted Jamaican man. When I reached for the door handle, a big brown hand descended gently on my wrist, and a big brown voice said, "I'm very sorry, sir, the room is occupied for a while."

I said, "Look, I live here, mate, it's my bedroom!"

"I sincerely apologise, sir, and hope you can be

patient for a little while longer."

"Is Rupi in there?"

The giant smiled,"No, sir – Rupi will be along later."

I looked into his eyes and saw that he would sincerely regret having to restrain me, but also that no power on earth was going to make him step aside from that door. I returned to the daybed, and reported to Beverley – more or less shouting to make myself heard. She just looked a little bit more shocked, and continued to stare at the gyrating mob. There was nothing else we could do. There was only us left on the day bed, now.

One by one, or couple by couple, the dancers slowed down, and when they stopped swaying they slowly descended to the floor, curled up and went to sleep. By 3.30am the entire floor was covered with recumbent bodies. When the last had subsided, the 'management team' switched off the music, packed up the sound system and the remaining unopened bottles, and the folding tables and the crates, and quietly carried them all out. One of the barmen sent us a solemn salute. Perched on our little day bed island, now in a sea of bodies, we watched, half-asleep, as one of the bodies, a fat man, staggered to his feet and pissed copiously over his nearest neighbours before collapsing into the puddle.

After a while, we heard the bedroom door open and some quiet voices in the hallway. The giant bedroom doorkeeper entered the studio, and stood with his back against the wall, gazing at us calmly. This heralded the entrance of a very tall and thin older Jamaican wearing a beautiful dove grey silk suit, an elegant apparition which tip-toed between the bodies over to our island, and solemnly shook our hands one after the other.

He smiled upon us, and said, "Thank you for your hospitality. Rupi will be visiting soon. God bless you both."

As soon as he and the doorkeeper had gone, we went to see in what state they had left our bedroom. If anything it was a bit tidier than we usually left it. I searched the place thoroughly, but all I found was a single empty glass vial, a popper, under the bed. We were too tired to talk, or to worry about the unconscious guests in the studio, so we lay on the bed and went to sleep.

It was Richard who woke us at about 10am. He explained that he had slept on the couch, and awakened in time to somewhat supervise the departure of the guests, who had now almost all gone. We made some coffee, and moved to the studio to review the damage. It was much less than we feared, and the 'managers' had left us a valuable row of half-full liquor bottles lined up along the skirting board. We offered coffee to the few remaining party people, and asked them how they had been invited here. They said they had been in a local pub, about closing time, when a friend had told them there was an open party starting nearby. When the pub closed, they had headed to the designated address with others. The word had been, "Just say Rupi sent you." To account for the number of arrivals, we assumed that this invitation had also been made in at least one other pub. Mysteriously, none of the few guests we questioned knew anyone called Rupi.

Fortunately, Ivan and John returned to help us

clean up, and by 2pm we were all, as normal, sitting around the table having lunch, and talking about the very weird event when, lo and behold, the doorbell rang and Rupi walked in. I've never seen anyone happier. He was tossing a tennis ball about, and bouncing it off the wall, and chattering away, ignoring our solemn faces and angry questions.

"We didn't like the party, Rupi. We know you invited anybody from the pubs. Who were those guys in the big American cars?"

"Dey my good frens! Din they look after you? Din they take care of every-ting?"

"Why weren't you here! We didn't know anyone!"

"I's sorry I couldn't come, but I had some-ting else I had to do!"

"We felt invaded, Rupi. You should have been here!"

"Okay okay okay. Maybe this lil present from my frens will make up for it."

He leaned over the table and carefully placed the tennis ball in the exact center. Then he said, "See you later!" And was gone.

It was not a tennis ball, it was a tennis ball sized lump of raw opium – scraped straight off the poppy. Richard said, "Fuck me dead, that's opium!" Anyone might think that we habitual Congo Big Stick users would have welcomed the gift with enthusiasm, but we did not. Hash or pot or weed or speed was one thing, and opium was another. We had all seen Frank Sinatra in the movie 'Man With a Golden Arm', and read Sax Rohmer's Dr Fu Manchu stories, so we all believed that opium and heroin was an irresistibly addictive poison, which would destroy our souls. Richard was the only one brave enough to try it out. He pinched off a tiny piece of the rubbery substance, mixed it with tobacco, and rolled it into a cigarette. We watched him inhale deeply, and blow out a fragrant cloud – half expecting him to turn into a drooling junkie before our very eyes. After a while I asked him how he felt, and he said he just felt very cool and calm. So we all agreed to let Richard have the ball of opium. It was probably worth some thousands of pounds sterling, but we didn't care. We wanted it out of the house.

Over the next few days, a mutual commitment developed between Beverley and myself, a commitment to leave behind our current life, and to become resident members of the Coombe Springs community. Our discovery of the mechanisms surrounding Rupi's party only served to harden our determination to abandon and renounce the slap-dash style of our spiritual quest to date, and to undertake a far more disciplined and austere regimen.

Ivan made enquiries in the Notting Hill Jamaican community, and brought us inside information about the local drug trading system in which we had become naively involved. Rupi's 'frens' – the men in the big black cars – had commissioned Rupi to set up the next trading meet. For Rupi this was a promotion devoutly to be wished within his cartel of allegiance. The system was for a cartel acolyte, or trainee student such as Rupi, to identify a 'clean' venue, such as Beverley's flat, and to persuade the inhabitants, such as us, to accept the gift of an all-expenses-paid party – to celebrate something or other. Rupi had performed this task to the letter, and then happily submitted to the second stage of the system, which was a period of enforced seclusion for himself. In between our acceptance of the party and the party itself, Rupi was shut away in a safe house under guard, to minimize any chance of him revealing the location and time of the meet to Police or to rival cartels. The third stage – the task of inviting the party crowd to the designated address – was completed by more senior and trusted cartel officers who casually circulated the news of an 'open party' to the Saturday night crowd at several pubs in the area of the venue. The polite security guard I had met at the front door was there to ensure that any overkill of invitees would be barred entry. That is, if more than a certain number of invitees turned up, they would be politely told to piss off. The other sections of the management team were charged with music supply, and serving booze, and maintaining order. The entire enterprise was set up to enable two or three 'godfathers' of the London illicit drug industry to meet and trade at an unsurveilled one-time-usage venue: namely our bedroom.

After several more Work Sunday visits to Coombe Springs, Beverley and I were accepted as residents, together with Richard. Ivan and John decided not to join us. The move was a far bigger decision for Beverley, who sold most of her furniture and effects, than for me, who had already surrendered all my stuff to Ann. In 1965, we moved into the community with next to nothing but our clothes and a few books. Beverley was 28 and newly pregnant, and I was 24. We lived in separate accommodation on the Estate for a few months, until our marriage at Kingston upon Thames Registry Office, after which we moved into a little flat on the top floor of the Estate's 18th century Coach House.

For those interested, Google can provide a full history of the Coombe Springs Estate. Suffice to say that it comprised a large Manor House in 11 acres of well-tended grounds, together with a number of other large buildings – including a beautiful 16th century spring house, built by Cardinal Wolsey to supply water to his Hampton Court Palace three miles away. This walled and gated community of about 70 residents was our home for over two years, during which we lost track of world events. Like most residents we chose not to have a TV or radio in our living quarters, and there was no media-equipped common room, so we remained ignorant of many events that later became icons of the 'sixties':

> Moors Murderers Hindley and Brady sentenced.
>
> First Moon landing by Surveyor 1.
>
> Mao Zedong Launches the Cultural Revolution in China.
>
> Debut of Rowan and Martin's Laugh-In TV show.
>
> USA bombs Hanoi for the first time.
>
> England beats Germany to win the World Cup.
>
> Debut of StarTrek TV series.
>
> Rolling Stones perform on US Ed Sullivan TV show.
>
> China, USA, France and USSR perform nuclear tests.
>
> Release of Beatles' Sgt. Peppers Lonely Hearts Club Band.
>
> Ronald Reagan elected Governor of California.

6-Day War in the Middle East.

Martin Luther King assassinated.

In addition to the political, sporting, and entertainment events, we also missed out on the cultural explosion of the 'swinging sixties'. It all went by outside the walls, as distant from us as events in the Middle Ages. Indeed, I knew more about the Middle Ages than I did about the contemporary events of 1965-1967. This unworldliness was certainly not part of the Gurdjieff curriculum, which contrarily advocated knowledgeable mastery of mundane affairs. No, it was more to do with our determination to concentrate on 'The Work', in order to transform ourselves as soon as possible. Transform ourselves into what? Well, that was the whole point, wasn't it? We could not know what we would be transformed into until we had been transformed into it.

At that time, the Institute for the Comparative Study of History, Philosophy and the Sciences, under the direction of John Bennett, was working with two very different spiritual disciplines: Gurdjieff and Subud. The former was based on practices of willful control of everything, the latter on the complete opposite. Nevertheless, the core ethos of the community remained Gurdjieffian. We used to play host to a group of Subud-only practitioners on some weekends, and came to call them the 'helpless helpers', because senior practitioners were called 'Helpers' despite their inability to organise anything whatsoever. They used to hold group meditation sessions in the kitchen to decide who would peel the potatoes, and we would have to rush in and do it for them in order to get lunch on the table. In addition to the two

A Noose of Light

community activities of Gurdjieff 'movements' and the Subud 'latihan', Mister B had a third effort underway with his 'research fellows': three young men who were studying his concept of 'Systematics' – as defined in his book 'The Dramatic Universe' – which was far too complex for us to understand. Here's a sample comment from one of the fellows:

> *"In a multi-term system, in contrast with the more commonly known 'system' of systems thinking, the number of terms or self-autonomous components of the system determines the attribute of the whole system as well as the character of its terms."*

There's a reason why YouTube videos feature many fine examples of Gurdjieff movements, but no demonstrations of Subud latihans. It's because latihans can be either lots of people sitting perfectly still (which is not visually interesting), or lots of people flinging themselves about like monkeys in a cage. And if the latter was shown, then the participants would not wish for their crazy antics to be made public. Also, lots of viewers of these antics would get angry and deny that flinging yourself about is anything to do with Subud. Indeed, when the Indonesian founder of Subud, Bapak, visited the UK and Coombe Springs, he was dismayed to see that somehow the latihan had become a bizarre spectacle of people shouting, crawling, marching about, doing hand stands, swinging from the rafters, singing, etc. In Indonesia it was conducted in a far more sedate fashion.

When Beverley and I came to Coombe Springs, we found that group latihans were scheduled for two evenings a week in the large nonagonal exercise hall called the Djamichunatra – or Jami, for short – the first evening for the men, the second for the women. We were told that to do the latihan, we should simply let go of all restraint, drop the reins, let go, do anything that comes into our minds. On ladies' night you could hear the screams from the other side of the grounds, and Beverley told me that most of the women went berserk. She didn't, though, and could not see why the other women did. She thought it might be that she wasn't 'getting it', whatever it was. I attended the men's evening and felt similarly restrained. It was rather like being in the locked ward of a psychiatric hospital, though certainly quieter than the women. I decided to stick to the Gurdjieff stuff, and practiced my 30 minutes meditation exercise in the Jami every morning – along with whatever movements or group exercise was going that day.

During the first few weeks as resident, I noticed something disappointing. I had half-expected a broader, grander group interaction version of our 'people of the room' sessions in Beverley's studio, but found that no one, nobody spoke about the Work. There was no discussion among residents of any aspect of meditations, exercises, movements, latihans, study books, whatever. The only opportunity to ask questions or air views about the curriculum was in weekly House Meeting sessions, over which Mister B would sternly preside. Very few attendees of such meetings were brave enough to reveal that they did not already know the answer to their own question. Sometimes we heard that someone had made an appointment to speak to Mister B in the Lodge –

the cottage by the gates where the Bennett family lived – and it was understood that such consultations were for crisis situations only. Throughout our residency, the only occasion we thought to be important enough to consult Mister B about was our son Gabriel's naming ceremony. Not being Christian or Jewish or anything else, we nevertheless thought it proper to have a ceremony. At that time, Mister B had come upon Idries Shah's book 'The Sufis', and he was exploring the idea that Gurdjieff's concepts originated with this Muslim mystical tradition. So he suggested we conduct a Sufi naming ceremony for Gabriel. We were asked to supply a wooden begging bowl, a wool shawl, and a gold coin. So in October 1965, the simple ceremony happened in the lounge of the Lodge, with Elizabeth Bennett attending. We thanked baby Gabriel for choosing us as parents, wrapped him in the woolen shawl, and gave him his begging bowl with the gold coin, a sovereign, in the bottom.

But this was after Gabriel's birth at Kingston Hospital. I was among the first husbands in 1965 to break the taboo and venture into the delivery room – to be glared at by nurses and rammed into walls with trolleys pushed by resentful elder Matrons. It seems strange to today's minds, but in those days many midwives and nurses considered that the husband's attendance at the birth was an abomination – like priestesses of some sacred society suddenly overrun by tourists. More enlightened spirits in the hospital, however, allowed me to sleep under the doctor's desk during the 36 hours of the delivery, and also to stay with Beverley during the gruesome forceps-aided birth. When Gabriel at last arrived, shrivelled and bloody and screaming, I felt in my heart that this was an important moment of my life, as do most new fathers. What I did not know was that little baby Gabriel was a ticking time bomb that would take about 20 years to explode everything in which I then believed.

Much later on, when Gabriel was about five, and I had become friendly with Idries Shah, I told Shah the harrowing story of Gabriel's birth. In return, he told me the story of his own birth. At the hospital, his father, Ikbal Ali Shah, had been taken aside by the attending doctor and told that the prognosis was not good, and that he should prepare himself for a grievous shock. Ikbal Ali took the doctor by the throat, and said, "You don't know me very well, but you should know that I have a revolver at home, and I am now going to get it, and when I return, if you do not tell me that my wife and baby are well, I will shoot you in the head!" When Ikbal Ali returned with his revolver, the prognosis was much better.

So there we were. Within six months of joining, Beverley and Gabriel and I had become a conventional little family living upstairs in the coach house, and participating in every aspect of the community. During the day, Beverley looked after the baby and helped in the Institute's office, while I worked at local building sites, wheeling barrows of wet concrete. I got tired of that when the snow started to fall, so I drew some sample designs and illustrations as specimens, and took a job at a local advertising agency. It did not surprise us that I so easily made the switch from laborer to graphic designer. We both knew that we were now 'on the path' and that invisible forces were aiding us. We were faithful students, practicing the Gurdjieff movements at home, as well as with the dance groups in the Jami; assiduously studying the written material; religiously performing the morning meditation exercise, and working hard in the garden on weekends.

My mother and father came to visit, and I introduced them to Mister B, who towered over them like a fairy tale giant. They were most impressed by the lovely gardens, and walked about rather self-consciously. It was very odd seeing them there – like visitors from the old world to our new planet. I had previously taken Beverley down to Kent to meet them, and my mother had welcomed her warmly. But then she had liked Anne, too. My dear parents did not think much about philosophy or spirituality, but at heart they were stoics. The war had taught them how to do that.

But the most important thing was that The Work started to work! The daily discipline and new fatherhood combined to alter my consciousness. I felt I was becoming more real, and the more concentration I channelled into my meditations, movements and studies, the more real I became. The following series of anecdotes may serve as snapshots of our two years at Coombe Springs. I must be forgiven for focusing on my own experiences, because I did not know how events were affecting anyone else. The tacit rule was that no one spoke about their own responses and thoughts regarding the curriculum. As Mister B put it, "Your inner life is yours alone, and not to be chattered about." Even

Beverley never discussed hers with me.

'Special Exercises' were sometimes posted on the notice board outside the kitchen in the Big House. One day, a notice advised all residents that next Thursday would be a 'Fast Day'. On Thursday morning, before dawn, I abstained from breakfast, and trudged through the deep snow down to the Jami to do my usual morning meditation exercise. Then I set off for the building site, where I spent all morning in a snow storm, wheeling barrows of wet concrete up an icy ramp and tipping them into a large steel skip, which was then hoisted forty feet up to the open mouth of the giant steel pile driver tube. At lunchtime, all the workers assembled in a tin hut to eat their sausage sandwiches and drink their thermos's of hot tea, while I stoically studied Gurdjieff's book 'Meetings With Remarkable Men'.

Observing my grim solitude, one of the specialist pile driver team (who came from Liverpool) decided to make game of me. He said he needed my help at the top of the tube. After my foodless lunch, he took me to the bottom of the twin steel ladders flanking the tube, and we both looked up through the whirling snowflakes. He looked me in the eye and said, half mockingly, "Are you okay with this?" Not to be outdone by this scouser git, I started the upward climb, and he followed up the other ladder. At the top, the ground was forty feet below, and we sat either side of the tube, astride wooden planks – seemingly suspended in one of those snowball paperweights. The scouser then gave a great shout, and looked across at me. I could tell he was worried I might fall and die. I was worried, too, but determined to employ my concentration training to remain calm. I think the expression this created on my face made him even more worried. He thought I might be a right nutter, glaring at him. In response to his shout, a further element was added to the terrifying scene. Out of the whirling snow, the giant steel skip swung towards us, suspended on the crane cable operated from below. Our job was to grab the skip and tip its contents, a ton of wet concrete, into the yawning mouth of the tube. This we did several times. It was a scene from Dante's Inferno. My scouser mate was just doing his job, but I was doing my concentration and sensing exercise. What with the fasting, the cold and the perilous situation, I achieved an enhanced state of consciousness: something similar to that which mountain climbers mean when they say, "I've never felt so alive." The enhancement stayed with me when I descended from the tube. It was very similar to the state I had experienced earlier when I and some other male residents had enjoyed a sauna one night, and then walked naked through the deep snow down to the Spring House. Inside the elegant building was a 3-metre wide circular pool covered with ice, and we all jumped through the ice into the pool together. After these and similar adventures, I felt I understood better why all religions advocated physical austerities as a path to 'revelation'.

At the end of the pile-driving day, however, I returned to Coombe Springs to learn that a mistake had been made regarding the fasting notice. Whoever had written it had left out the instruction that a bowl of yoghurt and oatmeal was allowed. The notice had been corrected, but not before I had trudged off to my rendezvous with the pile driver. That evening, while I wolfed down my bowl of yoghurt, Beverley told me about the day's scandal: a middle-aged male resident called Ronald had also missed the yogurt amendment and had been caught cheating! That afternoon, Mister B's wife, Elizabeth, had been walking through the snow in the garden with her young daughter, Hero, when she had noticed this man sitting in a tree. In true Gurdjieff style she had asked him what he was doing sitting in the tree, and he had confessed that he had hidden a hamburger there – in preparation for the fast day. Why he chose to hide the hamburger in the tree, and not somewhere less public, will never be known.

On Work Sundays, exterior members of the Coombe Springs community joined with the residents to work in the garden and among the buildings. Sometimes Mister B would devise an exercise in which all could participate, such as a memory exercise involving touching your ear when anyone gave you something, or perhaps maintaining a continuously repeated prayer in your thoughts as you were working. I still remember one of these after all these years. It was in Arabic: *Ishkinaa siraat al mustakeem,* or 'Show me the true path'. Another one was the 'Stop Exercise' when Mister B would walk around the grounds and yell 'Stop!' at a group of workers, causing them to freeze in their tracks, and empty their minds to receive any available illumination, or perhaps Mister B's projection of *'baraka'* or blessing. On one such 'stop exercise' Sunday, I was working with a group trimming and weeding the drive, when a Telegram delivery man wheeled his bike through the gates and headed passed us towards the Big House. Just then, we heard Mister B call "Stop!" and we all froze – like a group of human statues, holding hedge clippers, brooms, wheel barrows and armfuls of leaves. The Telegram man froze, too, looking around at us in bewilderment for a very long 30 seconds, until Mister B called "Continue!" We all resumed our work, and the Telegram man resumed his delivery. Heaven knows what he told his Post Office mates. That was funny, but on another Sunday 'stop exercise' I did stop, and I did feel the descent of a delicate sweet infusion into my mind.

The next event to be described requires some preparatory information: Since early childhood I had suffered from a severe speech impediment. It was known in the family that my stutter had begun when I was three years of age in the summer of 1944, when one of Hitler's last V2 rocket bombs had gone astray and exploded near our home in Welling, Kent. I have no memory of this event, and for many years into adulthood I thought that the explosion had buried me under a falling wall or fence, but then my mother told me that it was just the sound of the bang that had shocked me. She said that I had been playing in the garden when the bomb landed, and that I could not speak when she ran outside to get me. She said that I continued to be unable to speak for about six weeks thereafter, and when I did speak again, it was with an extreme stutter.

Unlike the earlier 'doodlebugs', which announced their slow approach with a dreadful droning sound, the V2 was the ancestor of NASA spacecraft. It arrived from the stratosphere travelling faster than sound, so instead of going whoosh–bang, it went bang-whoosh. That is, you heard it arriving *after* the explosion. I don't remember the event, but my current theory is that it was the unearthly strangeness of this sound that shocked me into a PTSD silence, and later into the lifelong stutter that filled my schooldays with fear and shame.

Whatever, during the 22 years between the bomb and Coombe Springs, the stutter had improved – but my speech remained nowhere near good enough for public speaking. So I was surprised and rather filled with dread one Saturday when Helena, Mister B's secretary, asked me to do the lunchtime reading on Sunday. These readings were a semi-monastic Work Sunday tradition, when visitors and residents sat down to a silent meal while listening to a reading from a book selected by Mister B. Helena gave me the chosen book, with the selected chapter marked, to practice before the performance. The Gurdjieff ethos was to boldly accept any challenge or task, but nothing at Coombe Springs had frightened me so much (not even the pile driver) as the prospect of reading aloud to over a hundred silent people. An hour before lunchtime, I returned to our flat from the garden to clean up and prepare, and found one of Mister B's research fellows, Ken Pledge, waiting for me. Beverley was on cooking duty, and Ken had seldom visited us before, so I wondered why he was there. He awkwardly explained that he had heard I was due to do the reading, and he rather felt like doing it himself, so perhaps he could do it instead of me. I thought this was obviously a set up designed either to let me off the hook, or to spare

A Noose of Light

the lunchtime crowd from an hour's painfully stuttered reading, so I politely declined.

It was customary for the reader at such lunches to eat before everyone else, but I was too nervous to do that. I carried the book into the dining hall, where the seated guests were quietly conversing, and saw that an empty chair had been reserved for me at Mister B's table. The book was a translation of some discourses by the Sufi sage Jalaladin Rumi, and when I opened it the dining hall became silent. While lunch was quietly served and quietly eaten, I read aloud for about half an hour, without a single stutter – even putting some emotional expressiveness into Rumi's robust statements, such as, "Anyone asking a question must first come to the awareness that their knowledge is incomplete, and secondly that there is wisdom they know nothing about. Hence, the saying, 'Asking is half of knowing.'" I didn't know what to ask after the reading, or who to ask. I just knew that I had never before been able to read aloud without stuttering, and that I had somehow been helped to do it.

One of the Gurdjieff techniques for enhancing con- sciousness was called 'super effort'. The theory was that humans had access to three 'accumulators' or reservoirs of energy: the first was what we used in normal life, the second could be accessed when the first ran out (referred to by athletes as 'the second wind'), and the third was the Great Accumulator, which provided the energy of the other two, and which could be accessed directly by performing a super effort which drained the other two.

The point of accessing the big accumulator was that the blast of source energy would transform your consciousness. Again on a Work Sunday, I was helping to dig and fill a new stream channel across the grounds, when I decided to go for the super effort. Again, barrow loads of wet concrete featured heavily, and my effort was further enhanced by my feverish cold, an infection that had been lurking about for a few days. So there I was with the feverish cold and the wet concrete: I decided to go for it. As the afternoon wore on, the Estate Manager, Gilbert Edwards, became anxious about my manic activity, shovelling, tipping, wheeling, bashing and smoothing like a man possessed. He said, "Take it easy, Alan, Rome wasn't built in a day." But I had the bit between my teeth, and kept at it until the fading light stopped work. I went back to our flat in a rarified state, and Beverley reminded me that it was the night of Gurdjieff's birthday dinner, for which we all had to change into evening dress. So I had a shower and changed into my improvised black tie outfit, and walked over to the Big House for the scheduled cocktails. Beverley was, as usual, supervising the kitchen, so I walked into the reception room alone. A recording of Gurdjieff's harmonium music was playing, and there were all the residents in formal dress, standing about in island groups: rings of four or six people facing inwards, holding glasses, eating canapés, and conversing discreetly. When trying to describe it later, I said that I felt there should have been electric wires leading out from their trouser legs and skirts to wall plugs in the skirting boards, but I now think that was a bad metaphor. They were not machines, it was just that I could not

A Noose of Light

see where their energy was coming from. It seemed too strange to be true that it came from the material they were putting into their mouths, and they were clearly unaware of how bizarre it was to fuel themselves in this outrageously crude way. Nor could I see or imagine how they could stand there making inane small talk when they and the whole damned place was a miracle. I sat down in a quiet spot against the wall and just continued to look at the miracle. In his book 'Beelzebub's Tales to His Grandson' Gurdjieff wrote about "the organ Kundabuffer". I came to associate this putative human attribute with the concept of a cushion; an inbuilt psychological mechanism which acted as a layer of padding or protection between our perceptive faculties and reality. I also associated it with Jesus's comment about 'seeing through a glass darkly', and other descriptions of our blinkered normal state by a variety of religions from Zen to Zoroaster. In fact the whole idea of the need for transcendence, The Work, revelation, enlightenment, etc. could be encompassed by the assertion that humans are conditioned or programmed by normal life to not see things as they really are, but to view the world through a screen or cushion of assumptions, prejudices, fears, delusions, beliefs, desires, etc. My wet concrete super effort, apparently, had removed the cushion, ripped the veil, lifted the curtain – or to put it in more contemporary terms, had altered my brain chemistry to override conditioned responses to the environment.

Gilbert Edwards saw me and came over and squatted down by my chair and looked at me. I saw a crouched human animal looking at me, with a wise twinkle in its eye. I could tell he knew what I was seeing, even though he could not see it himself. He knew because he was an old Gurdjieff hand who had done super efforts himself. He asked how I was feeling, and I said I was okay. He didn't expect any further response.

A few years later, I read Mister B's book 'Witness', in which he described how he had a feverish cold when he performed a super effort while working in the grounds of Gurdjieff's community in Fontainebleau, France. Mister B had reported that he had indeed tapped into the Great Accumulator and had enjoyed a period of higher consciousness before Gurdjieff had popped out of the shrubbery to tell him that he would not retain the state for long because he was insufficiently prepared.

At the time of writing this memoir, I have seen a newspaper article covering the movie, 'Saving Mr Banks', made about Walt Disney's relationship with the author of 'Mary Poppins', P.L. Travers. The article focuses on Travers' "discipleship" to Gurdjieff, and emphasises Gurdjieff's lurid teachings about "Food for the moon" in which he maintained that the spiritual essences of people who did not achieve higher consciousness would, at death, be used to sustain the development of the Moon into a planet – while the Earth developed into a sun.

The article reminded me that Beverley and I always felt that this seemingly crackpot dogma was quite beyond our ken. Our focus was on working to *experience* higher consciousness. After achieving that, we might be enabled to understand the theoretical stuff.

The Sufis

One day in 1966, at a House Meeting where all residents were present, Mister B announced that he wanted us to read a new book by Idries Shah called 'The Sufis'. Along with the book, we were also asked to read a document provided by Shah, purporting to come from 'The Guardians of the Tradition'. Mister B explained that he believed Shah to be directly linked to and authorized by the ancient source of wisdom from which Gurdjieff himself had gained his knowledge. Further, Mister B implied that he would step aside to allow Shah to become leader of studies.

The Institute for the Comparative Study of History, Philosophy, and the Sciences Ltd., the organisation of which Mister B was chairman, had owned the Coombe Springs estate since 1946, and some of the residents had been there since that beginning. These older members had seen a lot of changes; not only the transitory switch to Subud and back again to Gurdjieff teachings, but also conflicts with other Gurdjieff organisations in the UK and overseas after Gurdjieff's death in 1949. Indeed, around that time, Mister B had even felt that civilisation was falling apart, and had travelled to South Africa to explore possibilities of initiating a sort of 'Noah's Ark' community there. This came to nothing, but such changes over the years had imbued older residents with a certain passive acquiescence that Beverley and I could not share. We were suspicious that some writer we did not know had turned up out of nowhere with these grandiose claims to maybe deflect our chosen course of spiritual development. On the strength of such suspicions I even drew a satirical cartoon and pinned it on the public notice board in the big house. It showed a pair of Arab carpet traders commenting on the price the gullible English would pay for Persian shawls.

But at the same time, we were attracted by the idea that it was no coincidence we had arrived at Coombe Springs at the very moment when 'The Guardians of the Tradition' were taking it over. It meant that some invisible influence was guiding our progress through the Work, and positioning us at the right place and the right time. We studied 'The Sufis' avidly, and waited for further communications from the mysterious Shah.

It's hard to imagine these days, but back in the sixties no one had heard of the Sufis, except dusty old academic orientalists in Oxford or Cambridge. The only prior reference to them I had was from Omar Khayyam, and he didn't seem to think much of them: one of his less understandable quatrains goes:

> *"The vine had struck a fibre; which about*
> *It clings my being – let the Sufi flout;*
> *Of my base metal may be filed a key,*
> *That shall unlock the door he howls without"*

Which, according to my translation (Fitzgerald's) meant that Omar's recipe of wine, women and song (his base metal) was more effective than noisy Sufi austerities in elevating the consciousness. And it should be noted by 21st century readers that my admiration for Omar was an aberration: virtually no one since late Victorian times had read him. He was a fossilised and forgotten oriental celebrity from the time of my great grandfather. Sobering, therefore, is it to reflect that today's Western hemisphere spread of interest and information about the Sufis, and indeed about any mystical tradition of Islam, was initiated back in 1966 by the work of one man.

But such reflections were denied me at that time, because it had not happened yet. The moving finger, the cosmic printing press, had not engraved it! We heard that a full Board Meeting of the Institute was scheduled, and that Mister B was going to move that Shah be appointed leader of studies. When the day arrived, I found reason to hang around the drive, hoping for a glimpse of the great sage. Some cars pulled up, and some people got out and started to walk down toward the Jami, where the meeting was to be held. I knew most of the Board members by sight, and did not spot any strangers in their midst.

Then I saw Mister B walking up from the Lodge accompanied by an animated figure who could not possibly be Shah: he was far too young and slim, and he was elegantly dressed in Western style, and he had shiny swept-back hair, and he was talking and gesticulating and laughing a blue streak – and chain smoking! Only last week, Mister B had declared at a House Meeting that "smoking was a pernicious habit"! I went back to our little flat in the top floor of the coach house, and told Beverley all about it. Our kitchen window over-looked the pathway leading down to the Jami, so after about an hour, we heard the Board members returning, and we peeped out to see them pass. Sure enough, there was Shah striding by, chatting cheerfully to the very Director I thought would most resist Mister B's proposal. He even had his arm draped, buddy-fashion, over the Director's shoulders. Clearly, this was a man of rare powers. But even after that revelation, I underes-timated what Shah could do. We had expected him to take over as Director, but he took over the whole Estate. He took over the whole Estate, lock, stock and barrel.

The next event was when Shah invited all residents and other members to a big meeting in the Jami. About 200 attended, all expecting some sort of resonant and stirring speech from this representative of the Guardians of the Tradition. Somehow, I was elected as stage manager and spent some time scuttling about acting, on reflection, rather like Basil Fawlty ushering a foreign guest into the dining room. What Shah said was that Mister B had already communicated the facts of the situation to us, and that he might as well stand on his head and whistle, rather than make any pompous speeches. There would be a new teaching, and those who could receive it would receive it. Any questions? A few in the audience raised their hands, and asked ir-relevant questions about aspects of Gurdjieff Work, and one even asked something about the Catholic Stations of the Cross. Shah answered all patiently, but it quickly became clear to all that no new revelations were going to happen. I felt ashamed at the response, at the pe-

A Noose of Light

destrian level of the questions, and felt desperate to ask something *relevant*, so I held up my hand and asked him if he had been born into the Work.

"Shah. Were you *born* into the Work?"

He dipped his head into his hand and paused for about ten seconds, then raised his head, looked at me, and said, "Yes".

What happened a day or so later was completely unexpected. Mister B called a House Meeting and announced that all residents had to pack up and leave. The Directors had approved Mister B's motion that the ownership of Coombe Springs would pass from the Institute for the Comparative Study of History, Philosophy, and the Sciences Ltd., to the Society for Understanding the Foundation of Ideas (SUFI). All residents were requested to vacate the premises as soon as possible, and to tell the Institute's office of their new address so that they could be informed of further studies and events when they became available.

Never had the stoic Gurdjieff training been more clearly evident. None of the residents made any fuss: most of us calmly set about looking for alternative accommodation, and had moved out within a month. The only drama I saw was when an old lady who had lived at Coombe Springs since 1950 was asked to leave. Her relatives had sent a car for her, but Mister B took Shah along to persuade her. I happened to be nearby when she attacked Shah, tearing off his glasses and stamping them underfoot.

Beverley and I and baby Gabriel moved into a basement flat in Kingston upon Thames. It was less traumatic for me than for Beverley: I had my job to go to every day, but Beverley was left alone with the baby. Never had the limitations of Gurdjieff training been more clearly evident, too. To my knowledge, none of the banished residents arranged to visit each other or to meet to discuss events together. We didn't even know any of their addresses. From living in a community, entirely dependent on a central authority for all aspects of daily life, we had been blown apart into a void. The Institute management was evidently also shell shocked: they did not even send us a list of other residents' addresses and phone numbers.

For a month or so we sustained ourselves with the belief that these circumstances were a test. This confusion and isolation, we surmised, was deliberately imposed as part of the transition to the new teaching. Those who became angered or dismayed would separate themselves from the emerging regime: they would exclude themselves as unsuitable students. We carried on with our morning exercises, and our book studies, waiting for contact. But then Beverley told me she spent her days walking up and down the living room, holding the baby. Our two years at Coombe Springs had left us with no friends outside the Institute, and no taste for normal social pleasures such as movies, fiction novels, TV or sports. In desperation we took regular weekend trips to the Zoo, and to the park, and to my parents' house. Then Mister B's secretary phoned us and came to visit. As well as running the office at Coombe Springs, she had been the leading Movements teacher, and admirable Gurdjieff exponent: always poised, always precise and cheerful. We hardly recognised her. She was now a shaking wreck, hardly able to maintain a conversation without weeping.

At last we had a phone call from Mister B, and he and his wife Elizabeth came to visit. They sat down to tea, and explained the situation: Shah was involved in complicated affairs and would be unable to move his family into Coombe Springs, as planned, for several months. Nor could he arrange further studies for the Institute members until his domestic situation had been stabilised. Shah had asked Mister B to recommend an ex-resident who could move back into the estate as caretaker while he sorted himself out. Mister B and Elizabeth had immediately thought of us as ideal care-takers. Would we do the task?

When they had left, Beverley and I just sat there silently under an invisible deluge of sweet relief. We thought we had been cast out like Lucifer into the void of gnashing teeth, but now we had been drawn back into the warm center. The Guardians of the Tradition had made us guardians of Coombe Springs.

I forget how we settled the terms of our lease, but it could have been no longer than a week before we were driving back through the familiar gates in our Morris Minor van, loaded with baby Gabriel and whatever household effects we still possessed. It was very strange. The entire estate was absolutely deserted. Mister B had given me a big bunch of keys, so we could choose anywhere to live – and enjoy all 11 acres of beautiful landscaped grounds as our private garden. We might have chosen the Big House, and lived like Lords of the Manor, or maybe the Lodge, where the Bennett family had lived with their sons and daughters. But there was never any question about it. We drove straight to the Coach House, and moved into the spacious ground floor, three-bedroom apartment beneath our old flat. This ground floor area had been reserved for unmarried female residents, and we had sometimes visited and coveted it in the past. Not that that was ever mentioned between us. No, we were there representing the Guardians of the Tradition, and could take no selfish pleasure from our stroke of good fortune. But secretly – secret even between ourselves – our hearts were singing: not only had we been found worthy of an important task, but we had also scored kick-arse digs in which to perform it.

As caretaker, I only had two duties to perform each day: I had to lock the gates at night, and unlock them in the morning. At night I would walk the 100 metres down the drive, carrying the giant padlock, and solemnly thread the chain through the iron bars and lock it. In the morning I would drive the van down to the locked gate, get out, unlock it, stow the padlock in the glove compartment and drive on to my ad agency job in Hampton Court. Beverley had the whole estate to herself and baby Gabriel all day. If she wanted to go shopping, she would call a taxi from the public call box outside the reception door of the Big House.

It was the glorious summer of 1966. The only disturbance that occurred to interrupt our month-long idyll was when our doorbell, the doorbell to the ground floor apartment in the Coach House of a large private estate, rang at about 8.30pm one dark and silent night.

A Noose of Light

I answered the door and found a small weasel-like man outside. He held out a piece of paper toward me, and said, "Mister Hampton?"

I said that I was not Mr. Hampton.

He said, "I got a bill here for Mr. Hampton."

I asked him to step inside, and led him through to the brightly lit lounge room, where I examined the bill, a very tattered and indecipherable document. Beverley came to stand beside me and we both gazed upon him. His eyes were flicking about in the shiftiest manner imaginable, and I realised he was casing the joint in preparation for a potential burglary.

He said, "I see the big house is all locked up… anyone in there?"

I explained that we were caretaking, and that everything had been cleared out of all buildings. His eyes looked at us as I handed him back his bill. He knew that we knew.

We continued to look at him, as if at an interesting rat.

He said, "Okay, it was worth a try." Then he left.

I don't remember how we were contacted to advise us to expect visitors. People we thought of as 'Shah's people' began to arrive: there was an architect who said he was going to make a scale model of the entire grounds and buildings; there was someone else who wandered around the grounds with a camera and sketchpad; there was a nice family called the McDonalds, about our own age, who moved into the Big House, and there were a few others. What impressed us about all 'Shah's people' was their relaxed openness and savoir faire – quite unlike the withdrawn and solemn general character adopted by most of the old residents. But most of all there was the Shah family, who moved into the Lodge. Beverley met Mrs Shah, Kashvi, in the Coach House yard soon after they arrived, but my outside job delayed my meeting with Shah until the weekend after their arrival. I went down to the Lodge, rang the bell, and was ushered cheerfully into the kitchen by Kashvi. She introduced me as 'Beverley's husband' to the Appointed Envoy of the Guardians of the Tradition, who was sitting at the kitchen table in a tattered old cardigan, pouring brandy into a medicinal glass, and smoking Peter Stuyvesant cigarettes. I was so nervous I could hardly talk or move, and was in that truly terrible state when you try with all your might to be relaxed and casual, but instead remain as fixed and stiff as the Tin Man meeting the Wizard of Oz. Shah held up his glass and said, "Medicinal use only: doctor's orders", then downed the brandy in one hit, and lit another cigarette. He was making notes on a writing pad, and pretended to be as nervous as I was. He dropped the pencil, and knocked the pad onto the floor, and made a silly fuss about picking it up. Kashvi said, in the fish-wife's voice she sometimes employed, "Shah! I swear that's the sixth pack of cigarettes you've smoked today!" After several more such pleasantries, I had calmed down enough to pass as human.

Shah said, "Kashvi tells me you're an artist."

"Yes, he is," interrupted Kashvi, "Beverley showed me some of his art – it's beautiful!"

"Well, it so happens that I need some artwork

done," said Shah. "I wondered if you might look at it for me?"

He strode out of the kitchen, returned holding an old leather-bound book, opened it and showed me the engraving on the title page. It was a rather faded monotone portrait of Jalal ad-Din Rumi, the 13th century Sufi poet and teacher.

"This is not in very good condition," said Shah, "and it was done hundreds of years after his death, so it isn't really a portrait – but it occurred to me that you might be able to copy it for me."

I said I would have a go, and Shah gave me the book to take away. I produced an enlarged copy in Indian ink wash on tinted paper. This portrait later appeared as the jacket illustration for Shah's book 'The Way of the Sufi', and began my working relationship with Shah that lasted twenty years.

It became known that Shah was planning a large party, for about 300 guests, that would last for three days. It became known that Shah was unhappy with the vibrations, or ethos, or spiritual ambience of the estate, and that the party would shatter this undesirable ambience, preparing the estate as a venue for the new teachings.

We learned that Shah already had a large group of followers or students, based in France, and that many of these would be attending the big party – along with celebrities and a host of entertainers, including an Afghan folk music band, belly dancers, several magicians and gypsy fortune tellers. There would also be hot air balloons, a nightly discotheque, fireworks and unlimited food and drink. The fancy dress theme of the party would be Shah's new book, 'The Exploits of the Incomparable Mulla Nasruddin'. Beverley and I did not fully grasp the scale of the thing until, while passing through the Big House, we observed a team of happy builders dismantling the very large window at the North end of the dining hall, and constructing a broad stairway rising from the dining hall floor, through the window aperture and down to the lawn outside. The builders cheerfully explained that it was to assist the free circulation of guests.

Clearly, this new teaching was more aligned to the jet-set than to the staid, rather Edwardian style we were used to. Our tranquil private domain had turned into a fairground, with large gaily-coloured marquees on the lawn, and even a covered stage equipped with a PA system. On the party's opening day, Beverley and I wandered about trying not to look awestruck. The hundreds of guests had spared no expense on their fancy dress: there were flowing Arab robes, and gorgeous turbans, and tailor-made troubadour and belly dancer costumes, and even two-person pantomime donkey outfits. Not to be outdone, Beverley and I had spent some time making a plaster mould of my face, lining it with Papier Mâché to make a mask, and painting it in lifelike colours. Shah was talking with a gaily-clad group on the lawn. He saw me coming, and turned away with a swirl of his cloak. I took off the mask. The swirl had told me it was a time to have fun, not to make creepy psycho-philosophical comments. I don't think I ever did learn how to have fun in the simple, open-hearted way that came so easily

A Noose of Light

to all the other guests. That, it was alleged, was what the party was for: to break up, disperse, explode the uptight seriousness, the 'Work Face' atmosphere of Coombe Springs. But that secure seriousness was what I was used to, and knew how to handle. Give me a 30 foot-high pile driver to climb in a snowstorm, and I'm your man. Tell me to wear a red nose and have fun, and I'm semi paralysed. Having fun didn't work for me, and it didn't work for Coombe Springs, either. It was not long after the party that Shah decided to sell the whole estate.

One of the major difficulties of writing this memoir is pinning down the dates of my memories, and sometimes I have to fix on a clearly remembered event, and construct a chain of evidence around it in order to pin it, like a rare beetle, on the calendar. In this case the clearly remembered event is composed of our son Gabriel sitting on the floor of our Coombe Springs Coach House home, playing the Beatles' new album, 'Sgt. Peppers Lonely Hearts Club Band', over and over again. Each time it came to the end, he would carefully move the arm of the record player back to the beginning, and settle down on the floor to listen to it all the way through again. He was born in September 1965, so it is not possible that the scene happened in 1966, and scarcely credible that it happened in 1967 – although he was a very precocious child, and may well have been able to do it toward the end of 1967. The album itself was released in June 1967, so it is possible that Gabriel could have been listening to it at the end of that year when he was two years old. Therefore, we were still living at Coombe Springs at the end of 1967. That's the best I can do to define the blurry period between the three-day party and the time when we were told that Shah had sold Coombe Springs to a property development company. This period is important because some other histories – now so readily available online – report that Shah bullied Mister B and the Board to give him Coombe Springs, and then kicked everyone out and sold it straight away. What I remember is that we were told that Shah would, for a specific period, make himself available to any of the ex-residents who wanted to speak to him about further studies. I don't know how many accepted this offer, but I do remember being surprised when I went up the stairs in the Big House to find that Shah had turned one of the larger upper rooms into his study, with an imposing desk, Persian carpets, and couches draped with oriental shawls. What surprised me most, though, was the enormous square picture hanging on the wall behind the desk. It was an octagonal symbol, about two metres square, black on white. In hindsight, I now see it as a rather typical corporate affectation of the 1960s to display a corporate logo behind the boss's desk, but at the time I just resented the fact that he had asked new arrival Tassilo Metternich to paint it, and not me. This and other signs indicated that Shah did indeed intend to use Coombe Springs as the HQ of his Institute. Other signs, however, indicated the reverse. We often used to see him strolling around the grounds deep in thought. If he saw us, he would raise his hand in a gesture that meant, "Hello, please don't bother me." We knew he was making up his mind, and it was when he began to refer to the Jami as 'Hitler's bunker' that we suspected what was to come. Looking back, I can see clearly that Shah was deciding that he could never adapt his style to the Coombe Springs environment, and that the environment could not be adapted to his style.

So the exodus repeated itself. Beverley, Gabriel and I moved out into another flat, this time in Putney, and exactly the same thing happened. I went to work each day while Beverley slowly descended into depression/anxiety. I can't remember anything from that period, because it was a void. It was an even emptier nothing than the first exodus. It never occurred to us to consult Mister B, or visit his new house. We had been granted access to the central fire, and then banished into the cold and dark again. It was harder for Beverley than for me. I was, at least, banished with a bit of booty: Shah had introduced me to his publishers Jonathan Cape, on the strength of the 'Way of the Sufi' jacket illustration, and Cape's was supplying me with fairly regular freelance illustration commissions – including that of Edward DeBono's first book, 'Practical Thinking'. I met DeBono and felt that he did not like my rather medieval engraving-style illustrations, but was obliged to accept them because they were certainly an example of lateral thinking.

I don't remember how long this void lasted nor what we did to fill it up, but the time came when I wrote to the address of the Society for Understanding the Foundation of Ideas, and received a typed reply from Shah. He said he was getting together a new center at Langton Green, Kent, and would be starting some real work soon. I showed Beverley the signature at the bottom of the letter, and we held it up to the light to confirm that it was hand written. We looked up Langton Green on the map, and saw that it was 3 miles from Tunbridge Wells. Of all places, Shah had picked the place with my name on it. Our faith was restored.

Langton Green

We purchased an old Volkswagon Beetle, and drove it down into Kent every weekend for a month, looking around Tunbridge Wells for a house. Eventually we found one in the old part of town, close to the historic Regency area called The Pantiles. Beverley's father in Australia gifted us a deposit, and we made the move in early 1967.

Shah's new home and HQ at Langton House, Langton Green, was indeed more suited to his style; its Regency proportions more spaciously and graciously horizontal than the vertical Edwardian primness of the Big House at Coombe Springs. When we first visited, we found that Kashvi had already furnished the house with her unique fusion of East/West décor, and that a team of carpenters were busy outside converting a large barn into a communal dining room, and a row of cottages into guest accommodation and office spaces. The 40 acres of surrounding grounds, with additional barns and workshops, also provided wider scope for whatever 'curriculum' the teaching might entail. And if that were not enough, the property also included Langton Green, the enormous village green, itself. Once again we were impressed with the difference in expansive energy between the new Sufi and the old Gurdjieffian regimes.

On our first visit, Shah took me into his study and explained that he intended to start a publishing house affiliated to his new Institute for Cultural Research, and that my graphic design skills would be useful. I said that I would be happy to help. He thanked me, but said that I had done stuff for him without charge in the past, and that this was no longer appropriate. I acquiesced, and agreed to charge the Institute as a normal client. He laughed and said I might let him have 'mate's rates', at least. With that we returned to the kitchen where Gabriel and Saira, the Shah's eldest daughter, were playing, and Kashvi was pouring Beverley a cup of tea. Shah rolled up his sleeves, and started throwing stuff into an already bubbling saucepan on the stove, while exchanging ironic complaints about women's privileges with Kashvi.

Kashvi said, "I hope you like pilau, because that's what's for lunch. Have you had pilau before?"

We said we didn't think wc had.

Kashvi shouted, "Shah! Don't put so much cardamom in this time, they're not used to it!"

"But it's not pilau without cardamom!" Protested Shah.

And so began our 20 year relationship with the Shah family. I still had my job in Hampton Court, so would drive there every weekday morning. On weekends or evenings, I might get a phone call from Shah's secretary Helena, arranging an appointment. Shah might ask me to design a book jacket, or to provide artwork for an Institute monograph, or to simply copy a rare piece of Arabic artwork someone had found for him. On weekends we would usually spend Saturday helping out maintaining the Langton grounds and buildings, and staying for dinner in the large converted barn named after one of Rumi's stories, 'The Elephant in the Dark'. Shah often attended these dinners of about 30-40 people, sometimes bringing along a guest – maybe a media person or university professor – who was not connected to the Institute. The dinners quickly adopted a certain style: the volunteer cooks would prepare the food, the volunteer waiters would serve it, and everyone would enjoy normal dinner party conversations until the dessert was cleared away, at which point some glasses were refilled with Langton's dreadful home made wine, and the general hubbub would slowly, slowly decline until only Shah's voice was left. He would continue whatever conversation he was having with his neighbours, effortlessly expanding it to encompass the increased audience. It was amusing to sometimes watch the unwitting guest slowly realise that everyone else had stopped talking to listen to Shah – who blithely carried on talking as if nothing was happening. The subject could be anything from Anglo Saxon history to the Russian occupation of Afghanistan: Shah could talk entrancingly on any subject. Sometimes he would say something related to Sufism, such as a new teaching story he had found, or a long 'harangue', as he called it, about cult behaviour and conditioned responses. Kashvi rarely attended these dinners, because she felt uncom-fortable with the ashram-like atmosphere. It was indeed singular to sit there among a rapt audience listening to Shah lecture at length, and contemptuously, about the mechanics of cult psychology. Shah used to say that if he wanted thousands of slaves he could get them, anytime, in India – but sometimes I would look around at all the rapt faces and wonder what the difference was between us and a similar gathering around a guru in Calcutta.

Beverley and I, with Gabriel, began to visit Langton Green on most Saturdays. Without intending to, or indeed realising it, we became the only Institute members who turned up without being invited. All the other people there every weekend were specially invited via a letter to their group leader. It simply did not occur to us to find out how the visitor's roster was organised, but we eventually realised that the Institute's employees, Sally and Helena, sent out invitations, and that the work schedules (gardening, maintenance, etc.) were managed by an older couple, Richard and Helen, who had purchased a cottage adjoining the Estate. We were vaguely aware that everyone else belonged to London-based groups, but we did not know how many groups there were, where they met, nor what materials or exercises they were studying. Here again, like Coombe Springs, no one talked about the Work. Sometimes we heard that documents and other materials had been distributed to the groups, but we never received any. In the 20 years, more or less, we continued to attend weekends at Langton Green, no one ever questioned us about our Saturday visits. In the first decade or so, Beverley always walked into the House with Gabriel, and later with our second son Nathaniel, to join a mother and child group – while I just wandered around outside and found something useful to do. Maybe Shah

A Noose of Light

was unaware that we were there most weekends? Maybe Sally and Helena assumed we had special dispensation from Shah? Maybe everyone else knew that I saw Shah frequently and produced some of his publications, so assumed I was in some sort of inner circle? On such thin ice we trod, all unaware.

The move to Tunbridge Wells caused our domestic and business situation to improve. At the Coombe Springs party we had met Pat and Mike McDonald, and I started doing graphics work for Mike's company Medical & Biological Engineering. Their leading product was an electronic muscle exerciser called Slendertone – marketed by Mike's partner Hermann Schaffer. Shah was a board member, and he asked me to do some designs for Slendertone magazine advertisements. Consequently I did all the ads and brochures for Slendertone UK for about 12 years. Similarly, another company associated with Shah, Medion, asked me to do ads and brochures for their ioniser – a device that electronically precipitated dust and bacteria out of room atmospheres. Meanwhile, I had quit my Hampton Court job and secured studio premises in a Tunbridge Wells building owned by a farming industry newspaper publisher called Agroup, for whom I produced artwork. So from pile driving in the snow while at Coombe Springs, I had ascended to running my own business within two years – and all largely due to my association with Shah. We even started a pre-school together in the main house's large garage block. The Shahs had two daughters and a son, the McDonald's had two sons and two daughters, the Shah's housekeeper had a son, and we had Gabriel – all aged between two and seven – so we pooled our resources, hired a qualified young teacher and started a day school.

And I had not stopped writing songs. Whenever the mood arrived, I would pick up the guitar and see what emerged from it – recording the result on a cassette, and posting it to my old Newquay friend Wizz Jones. In this way, over the years, Wizz and his muso friends recorded about 20 of my songs on his LP albums. We even got a double page feature article in the Melody Maker trade paper, called 'Wizz and Alan: the Moses-Aaron Syndrome' – because I was the Moses character who wrote the stuff but did not perform, and Wizz was the Aaron character who did. There came a time in 1969 when Wizz's producer, Pierre Tubbs, at United Artists asked me to visit his offices in Wardour Street, London. He said he had listened to some of the demo tapes I had sent to Wizz, and he wanted to offer me a singer-songwriter album of my own. I said okay, and that I would leave all the old songs to Wizz, and write a lot of new ones.

"Great!" Said Pierre, punching the intercom, "Now I'd like to introduce you to your producer!"

A very weedy-looking guy came in and shook my hand.

"Grahame will manage everything for you in the studio, and arrange the tour afterwards," said Pierre. "You can get in any musicians you want."

"What tour?" I said.

"You'll have to do a tour of all the folk clubs to promote the album – it's a routine part of the contract,"

A Noose of Light

said Pierre.

Now I had heard at length from Wizz how gruelling was touring the small venue circuit from Exeter to Edinburgh – sometimes sleeping in the back of a VW minibus; sometimes being drowned out by drunken crowds, etc., and I did not fancy it.

"I can't do the tour," I said. "I've got a four year old son, another baby on the way, and a business to run in Tunbridge Wells."

"Too bad, mate," said Pierre. "No tour, no album."

And that's how I probably became the first and last songwriter to turn down a solo album.

California

The years 1968-69 was a very busy time. I remember that Gabriel was three when we took him on holiday to California, so it was after September 1968 and before September 1969, so it must have been summer 1969, because it was very hot in Lone Pine. An American friend, Alixe, invited us to come to California, where she was managing an open-air concert venue. The 'concert hall' was a natural rocky amphitheatre in the Inyo Mountains, near the little town of Lone Pine, where Alixe was living. Classical music enthusiasts would think nothing of travelling all the way from Los Angeles or Las Vegas to perch among the rocks and enjoy a concert under the desert stars. We flew 10 hours over the pole from Heathrow to LA, and Gabriel was hyperactive all the way. We had dosed him up on a recommended sedative, Phenergan, but it had no effect. He ran up and down the plane for 10 hours, and even busted into the flight deck, diving between the legs of the stewardess when she took coffee in for the pilots. We arrived mid-afternoon totally wrecked, to find that we were a day early. There was no one waiting to pick us up. A phone call to Alixe in Lone Pine confirmed that we had got the time difference wrong, and that she was expecting us the next day. Half way through this call,

Gabriel at last flaked out, and went to sleep in my arms. Alixe phoned a friend in LA, who came to pick us up. Waiting for her to arrive, we took our first look at the Americans in the airport. When I got back home, three weeks later, I wrote a song called 'City of the Angels' – later recorded by Wizz:

> *"Over the pole by the light of the moon*
> *I never been to this city*
> *Don't want to come back soon*
> *Carried my case to reception*
> *Women and men standing back to back*
> *Maybe it's just for protection*
> *Women and men standing back to back*
> *Los Angeles, city of the angels*
> *What a place to be if you're looking for a friend"*

Alixe's friend picked us up and drove us to her home in the suburbs, where we were to stay overnight. All the way down Sunset Boulevard, the only pedestrian we saw in that bright, flat light was an incredibly obese man waddling slowly along in pink Bermuda shorts. We put Gabriel to bed, and had a drink with our hostess, Elaine, who couldn't wait to tell us about a recent 'incident'. Her husband was a chiropractor, and that night he had been at a chiropractor's conference in the city, leaving her all alone. She heard a noise outside the house, and turned down the TV volume. The noise happened again and she thought, 'prowler!' So she phoned the emergency number, and then got her husband's ex-army automatic from his desk drawer, and then sat facing the front door with the gun clutched in both hands. Pretty soon she heard a noise on the porch, and saw the solid timber inner door slowly open all by itself. She had forgotten to lock the door! She stared through the mesh of the screen door into the dark outside. Then a voice from outside said, "Is that Elaine in there?"

She said, "I've got a gun!"

The voice said, "Take it easy, Elaine. This is LA police department, and I am now going to show you my badge."

Then a hand holding a shiny badge flashed into view, and out again.

"Did you see the badge, Maam?" Said the voice.

"Yes, I did," said Elaine.

"Okay," said the voice. "I am now going to step in front of the screen door, here, and I do not want you to shoot me. Have you understood what I have just said, Elaine?"

Elaine said, "Yes", and watched as a burly policeman stepped cautiously into the porch light. He stood looking at her calmly through the screen door.

"Now, Elaine," said the cop, "I want you to remember this. I want you to remember what I will tell you right now. If I was a prowler, and you shot me with that forty-five, and I fell down out here on the porch, what do you think you should do, then?"

"I don't know," said Elaine.

"If you shot me and I fell down out here on the porch," said the cop, "I would want you to come over here, grab me by the feet, and drag me into the house."

"Into the house?" Said Elaine.

"Yes, Maam," said the cop, "right inside the house

106   A Noose of Light

– because if I'm out here on the porch, it's possible manslaughter, but if I'm inside the house it's justifiable homicide."

When the chiropractor came home, he said, "Hi, you're Brits, right?"

We agreed.

"Never did understand that cricket," he said. Then he got a tin of beer from the fridge, cranked up his Lay-Z-Boy recliner chair and settled down to watch a game of gridiron football on TV.

We excused ourselves and went to bed, and in the morning Alixe arrived to drive us up to Lone Pine:

> *"Went for a ride on the freeway*
> *Gliding along like a chromium ghost*
> *Everything real as a movie*
> *Fish in a network from coast to coast."*

Alixe had rented us a genuine old gold miner's cabin about a mile outside Lone Pine. I rented a genuine Ford Mustang, and bought a carton of genuine Tarrytown cigarettes and a bottle of Bourbon. We were all set to enjoy our US holiday, but a certain sensation of unreality persisted. For a start, we could not taste anything. We had stopped at a diner on the way up from LA, and ordered a tasty-looking lunch. Enormous quantities, and everything looked great, but everything tasted the same: a slightly salty, slightly creamy, slightly mustardy pap. We bought some fruit and vegetables, tomatoes and apples and onions. They looked great but also tasted of nothing! The only thing that tasted, slightly, of anything was Devil's Food Cake. We thought it was the exhausting flight and jet-lag, but the weird unreality persisted day after day. It was like being in a dream. On the first morning in our gold miner's cabin, Beverely thought she would gee herself up by walking into town, so she put on her straw hat and set off down the road in the bright desert light. She didn't get 50 yards before our next door neighbour started screaming. She had not even been introduced to us, but she came hurtling out of her front door and damn near wrestled Beverley to the ground.

"Oh my dear, my dear!" She cried, "Alixe should have told you that *no one* walks anywhere here! In the *street!* Oh my *Lord!*"

Eventually we understood from her that if a woman walked down the highway in California it meant only one thing, so I drove Beverley down to town in the Mustang. Here it was not much better. It was about 100 degrees in the shade, and the few people on the high street of Lone Pine were walking around so slowly that I thought they were actually pretending to do it. I went into a clothes shop to buy a proper cowboy's hat, a Stetson, and here again I was disquieted by the manner of the 'store clerk'. He ambled over in his Roy Rogers shirt and alligator boots, the very quintessence of a Hollywood cowboy, with a lopsided grin and a slow gravelly voice.

"Now you just let me guess," he said. "You must be that British friend Miss Alixe told about – come all the way from London, England?"

"Yes, I am," I said. "How did you guess?"

He chuckled a long slow chuckle, looking me up and down.

A Noose of Light

"Oh my lord," he said, "No offence friend, but anyone could tell you ain't from around here!" Then he chuckled again.

I felt like an actor in a movie who didn't know the script. The cowboy very politely showed me some hats, and then another cowboy entered the scene – a heavyset John Wayne type. The two cowboys started to have a slow exchange of views, while I tried in vain to shake off the feeling that they were secretly actors pretending to be cowboys. Their intonations, postures, lazy gestures, low complacent chuckles could not possibly be for real. I paid for my hat, shook hands with the cowboys, and walked away down the high street, now acutely conscious of my British sandals and khaki shorts.

Slowly we became acclimatised. We started to walk and talk slower, and to not be surprised when someone started up a conversation with us from 70 yards away. We had trips to the nearest big town called Bishop to pick up the art materials I needed to design Alixe's invitations and posters, and did some tourist trips Eastward to Death Valley, and Westward to Sequoia National Park. We had even resumed our regular Gurdjieff 'morning exercise': the simple relaxation and sensing exercise we used to practice in the Jami.

We first met Alixe way back when we were exploring the Theosophical Society, guided by Monika Merlin. Alixe had her own charming brand of Theosophical mysticism, involving spirit guides and reincarnation, but she never made a big show of it, and was always a considerate friend. Nevertheless she was always on the lookout for 'phenomena', and often spoke to us about the "power in the land". In fact, when we first arrived and drove up into the mountains to the West of Lone Pine, we reached a high viewpoint and looked back down and far away towards Death Valley, Alixe turned to us with a big smile and said, "Welcome to the land of Mu!" She believed California to be a remnant of a now vanished Atlantis-like Pacific continent. She also believed she was the reincarnation of the Egyptian Queen Hatshepsut, but we didn't hold that against her. She was a lot more interesting and generous than most people. Naturally, our Mister B-style Gurdjieff studies conflicted with her woo-woo stuff, but nevertheless we enjoyed her company. And anyway, who is to say that no similarities exist between Gurdjieff's 'Beelzebub's Tales to His Grandson' and Madame Blavatsky's 'Secret Doctrine'? Both are equally fantastical alternative scriptures; explanations of the origins and evolution of the universe and humans. Indeed, Blavatsky published in 1888 and Gurdjieff started writing 'Beelzebub' around 1924, so it is not impossible that he gained inspiration from the earlier opus – particularly as Blavatsky hailed from Russia, too. They may differ in the story they tell, but are arguably similar in sheer scope and audacity. I dare say Gurdjieff had a copy of 'Isis Unveiled' or 'Secret Doctrine' at hand when he was recovering from his first motor accident in Fontainebleau in 1924.

We might even add to the list G.R.S. Mead's 'Fragments of a Faith Forgotten' and Annie Besant's 'The Ancient Wisdom' – not to mention the works of Rudolf Steiner, and Oliver Lodge's Spiritualism. All these authors, and others, were truly formidable people who lived in the same epoch and who contributed to an unprecedented storm of novel esoteric ideas and histories – as if attracted by the dreadful gravity of the two world wars. Perhaps the only reason they are not officially gathered together into a literary genre associated with their particular era is that each attracted a cult following who either rejected the authenticity of the others, or who merely tolerated them as alternative 'paths'.

> *"Met a young girl California*
> *She driven mad by the power in the land*
> *Come to the end of her questions*
> *Going down South for a Mojo man."*

Talking about the power in the land, I think it may have got to me around the second week in the old gold miner's cabin – or perhaps it was thinking about Alixe's spirit guides, or maybe the Guardians of the Tradition had decided to stir me up a bit; either way, I woke up early one morning and became aware of a unique physical feeling spreading through my body. It was not alarming or pleasant or unpleasant, it was as if I was slowly separating into two states, one extremely dense and heavy, and the other extremely airy and light. Both sensations persisted for a while, and then a calm voice said right into my ear, "The living lode." I did not know what to make of it then, or now, but then it made me feel very happy. I got up quietly and went outside and climbed up onto the peaked roof of the cabin, and sat there watching the sun rise, reflecting on the homophone of load/lode, and the gold mining history of the location. Whoever had whispered in my ear, it showed they had wit.

We had just about started to enjoy ourselves, feeling that the trip was worthwhile, when Gabriel had his accident. We had been sitting in the shade outside our cabin when we heard a big crash from inside. We rushed in and saw three year-old Gabriel lying flat on his back on the floor with the kitchen table tilted over on top of him. The table had a heavy enamel top, and the remains of a towel rail – now just two broken spikes – sticking out of one side. Our little boy had tried to climb up onto the table and had pulled it over on himself. He was lying very still, and it looked like one of the spikes had gone straight through his eye. We righted the table, sat him up, and saw that the spike had just missed the eye but had gouged a deep cut beside it. Beverley phoned Alixe to find out where the nearest doctor was, while I improvised a towel bandage. To our massive relief, Gabriel woke up and started screaming. We bundled him in the car and drove to the small local hospital, where Gabriel continued screaming while a doctor sewed up his wound and talked about cricket. He wanted to know what the rules of cricket were. In my memory that was the end of our trip. It really scared us. The power in the land had nearly killed our little boy.

Tunbridge Wells

We were glad to get back to our house in Tunbridge Wells, and to resume our visits to Langton. My history seems to enter a plateau period around then. The course of our family life became relatively normal. I continued to do design work for Octagon Press, and book jackets for Jonathan Cape, the most notable being a series of scraperboard illustrations for Cape's editions of Herman Hesse books. But the backbone of my income remained the advertising designs I did for Slendertone, and the hack work for Agroup. Cape paid a fixed fee for the book jacket artworks, and I once calculated that the hourly rate the fee added up to was about three pounds sterling. Nevertheless, our lifestyle improved and we were soon driving around in a stylish red MGB GT with a Dalmation dog called 'Jongleur' in the back. The songs were going well, too (in the sense that I was writing more), and Wizz Jones sometimes visited, and showed me new guitar licks. It should be noted, however, that the highest annual royalty amount I was ever paid by the Performing Rights Society was 160 pounds sterling. The songs and the book jackets were truly labours of love.

I used to say that having kids was far too important to leave to choice, but that was profoundly stupid. Our second son Nathaniel arrived in September

1970, so he had to carry the terrible burden of being five years younger than his brother all the way through his formative years. If I could go back and do stuff differently, that would be one of the first things I'd change. But his birth was certainly memorable: it was of much shorter duration than his brother's, and when he came out he did not cry. His body turned from pale blue to pink as he took his first shuddering breath, then his new eyes opened and he looked into the eyes of each of us stood around the bed, the doctor, the nurses and me, each in turn. Then he squirmed his body around on the bed and looked up between his mother's knees at her face – and she said, "Hello cuckoo!" And after quite a long silence, the senior nurse said, "Well, there's an old soul!" Our improved circumstances at least allowed me to take some Champagne to the maternity ward, and to bully the giggling nurses into toasting my boy.

Trying to remember what happened after that is like doing the Hubble 'deep field' project, when the telescope was pointed at a blank, black area of space and the exposure left open. Slowly some events come into view.

Alixe came to visit, and while she was staying with us she visited Shah as well. Soon after, the Octagon Press assistant, Sally, told us that Shah was very worried that Alixe was our friend – because she was "poisonous". Sally said she had never seen Shah so worried, except when it was about his own kids. We were sufficiently committed to Shah to cease communicating with Alixe on the strength of this: a decision I now regret.

Beverley's father, Ben, and stepmother, Edith,

A Noose of Light

visited from Australia. Ben tried to persuade me to move the family to Melbourne, listing a number of material reasons why that would be advantageous. I could not present him with equally concrete reasons why we should stay, so was reduced to just saying no thanks. He did not understand our attachment to Langton Green, and we did not expect him to do so. Throughout our marriage, Beverley and I had maintained contact with our respective families, but neither of us was closely involved with our parents or siblings as some others are, so our familial connections remained peripheral to our lives. My own elder brother, Tony, for instance married an Evangelical woman and became a church Deacon. When he visited us in Tunbridge Wells, I asked him a Biblical question. I said, "If Jesus was crucified about 2,000 years ago, and thereby opened the door to heaven for us, and people had lived and died on Earth for at least 50,000 years before that, what happened to them?" He thought about it for a while, and then said, "In between him dying on the cross and being resurrected there were three days in which Jesus went down into hell and released everyone there." It's a very poor religious text that cannot answer every question put to it, but I did not ask him what the released people thought about the fairness of their hellish detention. After all, some of them had been there for at least 48,000 years.

It was about this time, also, that I decided to trace back my ancestry to discover the connection of my name and the name of the town. I already knew that Queen Victoria had so approved of the health spa status of Tunbridge Wells that she appended the 'Royal' suffix to it, and also that she had simultaneously ordered that the spelling of the nearby town of Tunbridge be changed to Tonbridge to futher distinguish it from her favourite. Nevertheless, my name of Tunbridge was the original, and indeed had been there since Roman times. It literally means the bridge made of tuns, large barrels, which spanned the river Medway at the point where the town now stands.

My family must have originated from this town, so out of sheer curiosity and sufficient disposable income I commissioned a research company to trace my paternal line back. The first thing they discovered was that my paternal grandparents were never married! There was no record of their marriage recorded at the register of births, deaths and marriages at London's Somerset House. I phoned my sister Wendy to tell her the news.

"You know, Dad's mother and father were never married?"

"How did you find that out?"

"I've got a team of researchers on it."

"Well, don't tell Dad, will you? We've been keeping it from him for 30 years."

It turned out that my paternal grandparents had been devout Spiritualists who were married in the Spiritualist Church, which was not recognised by the authorities. The researchers got all the way back to 1756, when Somerset House records began, to a William Tunbridge who was a cow keeper in Sloane Square. To explore further back would have involved the expense of paying a mobile researcher to examine church registers, so I gave up. Still, the spiritualist link explained, or rather illuminated, a childhood memory of my eldest sister Jean conducting a seance in the living room of our parental home. I don't think she knew about our grandparents – they almost never came to visit us – but I remember that Jean and her new husband lived with us for a while after their marriage, and that they used to have seances with their friends practically every Saturday night. I was 12 years old, so they allowed me to sit at the table and watch. They started out with an upended wine glass in a circle of alphabet letters and a pair of cards marked 'Yes' and 'No'. They each put a finger on the glass and waited for it to move. When it did, they asked it questions and it scooted across the polished table spelling out answers, which Jean wrote down on a pad. Naturally, I was fascinated, but I don't remember any of the 'spirits' saying anything interesting. Jean or one of the friends would often ask the spirits to describe where they were, but never got an answer. Then one night something interesting did happen. The glass spelled out that Jean had become so attuned that there was no need for the glass any more. Jean could just write down the answers on her pad. So Jean picked up the biro pen and we all sat there and waited silently, until someone realised that a question had to be asked. I don't remember what the question was, but someone asked something, and Jean's hand began to write all by itself. I've never seen that particular expression on a human face since: a mixture of delight and fear.

So over the following two weeks of seances, Jean filled up pages and pages with different handwriting.

Each time a new spirit 'came through' the handwriting would change – which, by the way, is impossible to fake. The odd thing is, again, that none of the spirits had anything interesting to say! There were a few events of interest, though. For instance one of them said she was called 'Grandma Innes', and she gave an address in the nearby town of Plumstead. One of Jean's friends took the trouble to go to the address and discovered that a Grandma Innes had indeed lived there before she died a few years ago.

And then the whole enterprise went a step further. One night, Jean's hand wrote that she, Jean, did not have to write answers out any more. She could *speak* the answers: she could become a *direct channel*. Her husband asked her if she felt okay about that, and Jean said she'd give it a go. She put down the pen, sat back in her chair and closed her eyes. We all waited, silently. Still and silent for a long time, and then Jean gave a sudden cry, and sat up, making us all jump out of our skins. I fetched her a glass of water, and she described what had happened. With her eyes closed she had 'seen' a little golden oval shape, and wondered what it was. It got bigger, and she could see little dark blobs around the outside, like a jewelled brooch or something. Then it got bigger, and she realised that it was not getting bigger, it was she who was getting closer to it. And then she was really close to it, and realised that she was looking down at the polished wood oval tabletop, with our heads and shoulders all round the edge. Then a really loud voice said something, and it was all too scary, so she broke away and opened her eyes.

A Noose of Light

In 2013 I visited Jean at her home in Canada, and recounted this memory. She was over 80 then, and did not remember the tabletop view, but said that she heard a loud voice and became scared. She and her family still occasionally do seances – but apparently nothing of use or interest continues to be delivered by them.

Back in 1970, Jonathan Cape's asked me to do a jacket for Doris Lessing's novel 'Briefing for a descent into Hell'. I visited the psychiatric wing of the Tunbridge Wells hospital, and took a photograph of the door leading into the 'Patient's Day Room', and that door became the jacket illustration. I took the artwork to her London home for approval, but she did not like it. She said she would have preferred something more "psychedelic". Just then, a young woman came to visit her, and Doris jumped up from the couch where we were, and started talking animatedly to the girl. The girl gestured towards me, and Doris said, "Oh, never mind him, he doesn't matter." I picked up my artwork and walked out. The door jacket got published, and I have maintained an antipathy to the author ever since.

With the arrival of the new baby, we decided we needed a bigger house and found one at the other side of Tunbridge Wells. Soon after, I made a very stupid business decision, and moved in with a local small advertising and print agency who offered me a bigger studio and better facilities and a company car and London's famous Café Royal as a client. But the clincher was their assurance that they would handle all the boring accountancy and invoicing and income tax work – which I truly loathed to do myself. Honestly, I used to hyperventilate when I had to check the bank account and invoices and tax figures. Within a year or so this new business relationship went very sour, and the sourness splashed over into everything else. The plateau period shattered into emotional instability, exacerbated by our feeling that our association with Langton Green had grown stagnant.

Beverley became so distressed that she asked me what she could do (a very rare request). I said, from the heart, that she should drive herself into a lonely spot in the nearby Ashdown Forest, and walk deep into the forest, and when she was sure there was no one else around she should *howl, howl, howl like a she wolf!* To her everlasting credit, that's exactly what she did – and she returned to say that she felt a bit better. In those days postnatal depression was relatively unrecognised, so my impromptu prescription may well be of use nowadays to others. I don't know what I was suffering from, but circumstances had conspired to make me feel like a rubber band wound up to snapping point. I hardly ever saw Shah any more. He was always on mysterious trips or lecture tours overseas. We were turning into ordinary people! I was spending my days with associates who thought of nothing but the material world and how to get rich in it. Something had to be done. As Rumi said, "The lion of The Way bursts his cage asunder!"

Andalusia

A dear friend, John Walker, came to dinner with his wife Eva one night and we confided our feelings to them. John said that we needed a change of environment, a long holiday, and that his mother, Sheila, had a farm in Andalusia, and that she would be delighted to have the Tunbridge family come and stay with her. He phoned his mother, and we spoke to her. So right then and there, we decided to sell or store everything that did not fit into a car, and to go to Spain.

We sold the house, and I introduced my business associates to another local graphic designer, who could step into my role at the agency. Within a couple of months, everything was arranged for our departure. We told everyone plainly what we were doing, but many disbelieved us. They thought it could not be true that we were just selling up and going to Spain because we felt like it. Some suspected that Shah had instructed us to do it, others thought I must have been offered a job by a multinational ad agency in Madrid or Barcelona. I got tired of people saying, "Oh, I wish we could do that." A secret I kept to myself was that I saw this trip as my chance to develop a series of paintings of consistent style. I wanted to stop doing commercial art, and start doing fine art. I did not confide this to anyone, because the whole concept of 'going to Spain to be an artist' was such a platitude. We purchased an apple green Renault 5 and put our two boys, aged seven and three, in the back, and drove to Portsmouth to catch the ferry to Santander.

Our first stop when we drove off the ferry into Spain was the Paleolithic cave paintings at Altamira – about 30 km west of Santander. We arrived outside the reception building to find we were too early. The official guides told us that the day's first busload of tourists was due in an hour's time. Then, for no reason at all, the chief guide said, "Today your lucky day – you have private view – venga!" He led us along the timber walkways deep into the cave. We were luckier than we knew, because the number of visitors per day was strictly limited, due to the erosion of the artworks caused by the carbon dioxide exhalations of tourist's breath. If we had not been granted a private view, we would not have seen the paintings at all. For the same reason – tourist's breath – the Altamira cave was completely closed to the public in 1977, and only reopened for very limited access in 1982. When the paintings were first discovered in 1879 they were thought to be forgeries by experts, and the anthropologists waited until 1902 before acknowledging them as genuine. Accurate dating had to wait until 2012 to confirm that the oldest painting dated to 35,000 years ago, and that the rest had been completed over the following 20,000 years. 'Cave people' had been touching up the frescos and painting new ones for 200 centuries, and yet their hand prints on the walls were exactly like my own. We did not know any of this at

A Noose of Light

the time, and were simply gobsmacked by the quality of the art. Such delicacy! Such strength! Deep in the back of the cave where daylight never enters, there was a chamber that originally had been only a metre or so high from floor to ceiling. Modern trenches had been cut into the rock floor and electric spotlights installed, allowing tourists to stand upright and look up at the drawings above them. The guide pointed out how the ancient artists had used the contours and cracks in overhead rock to emphasise the anatomy of the animal subjects.

I asked the guide, " This part of the cave would be pitch dark, and the artists would have had to lay on their backs and use a burning torch to see what they were doing. And anyone who wanted to see these paintings would have had to squirm in on their backs, holding a burning torch. So why are there no smoke marks on the paintings or ceiling?" The guide shrugged in a very Spanish way, "Nobody knows!" He said.

The Altamira visit was the very best way to start our Spanish 'retreat'. Beautiful 'modern art' paintings were being done 20,000 years ago! Nobody knows anything! Mystery rules! Our faith in our own destiny and quest was restored. We drove on South with our boys in the back, all singing 'Viva Espagna!'

We took our time driving south through the middle of Spain, using the national Parador hotel chain for overnight stays. At each town we participated in the 'passeggiata', when all the nicely-dressed families come out in the evening to parade pleasantly up and down the main thoroughfare, greeting each other, stopping to have a chat and a glass of Montilla: a very civilised custom. Sometimes we would stop en route when we saw a 'Piscina' sign, and have a dip in the municipal pool. All had juke boxes, and I quickly learned how to get approving nods from the locals by selecting Paco de Lucia flamenco numbers. The only place we stayed for two nights was Madrid, and that was just to see the Goya, Bosche and Velasquez stuff in the Prado gallery. I felt a deep affinity for them all. They, too, had perforce worked for people with money: merchants, aristocrats and priests! They and all the classic Renaissance artists were just an underpaid ad agency for the royals, bankers, warlords and clergy – churning out pictures of Princes and Madonnas like photos of hamburgers! It made me feel much better, and by the time we arrived at Sheila's finca I was overflowing with serenity.

Sheila's home was a citrus fruit farm of about 5 acres, and her house a graceful two-story hacienda – by far the largest building in a tiny hamlet of about ten typical Andalusian cottages. The whole top floor was ours, a rustic paradise overlooking the fragrant carpet of orange and lemon trees outside. In the distance was the nearest town, Alora, a speckle of white houses over the top of a tall hill. The road to the town spiralled upward around the hill as if in a Dr Seuss book, and we told the boys that it must be where the Cat in the Hat lived. Just beyond the hill was the main highway going south – 70 km to Malaga and the Costa del Sol.

I got my Spanish name on our first shopping trip into Alora. The market was a row of stalls along one of the main streets, all managed by women. Tourists *extranjeros* – rarely came to Alora, so we were something of a novelty. We nodded and smiled as the women fired questions at us – *Ingles? Americanos? Aleman?* – and complimented our boys – *Hermosos ninos!* We silently vowed to improve our Spanish, and looked for a butcher's stall – but there was none. Miming for the women, I asked them where we could buy a chicken. *Pollo! Pollo!* They cried, vastly amused by the mime, and pointed down the road to a residential street at the end. We went to the house indicated and knocked on the door. A Spanish lady opened it, and understood our apologetic request – *Pollo por favor muchas gracias* – and led us through the house to the back door, through which we could see several dozen chickens pecking at the ground outside. I confirmed to the lady that they were indeed chickens, as requested – *Si si, POLLO! Gracias senora* – not knowing what to do next. Then I noticed that the lady was smiling and politely offering me a big hatchet. I must have looked confused, because she went into the yard and pointed at a tree stump, which was stained black with the blood of many pollos, and charmingly mimed a chopping action with the hatchet. I don't remember how, but I eventually made her understand that I did not want to decapitate a chicken, so she led me to a large fridge which contained a couple of already headless and gutted and plucked pollos. Sheila told us later that the locals would never dream of buying a chicken they had not killed themselves (how could you know it was fresh?) and that the ones in the lady's fridge were probably ready for her family's dinner that night. We returned to the market with our chickens in a bag, and Beverley wandered off with the boys to buy some vegetables. I noticed some green plum-like fruits on one of the stalls, and picked one up. "Hmm," I mused, "hairy plums?" I put it down, and resumed my walk, but then noticed that the women on the nearby stalls were staring at me. At the same time I felt a tingling in my fingers, so I raised them up for a close inspection, and brushed them off with my other hand. The tingling got worse. The more I brushed, the worse the prickling grew – and I could not see anything wrong with my fingers! My attention was distracted by a sudden outburst of laughter from the stall holders, and I turned to see what they were laughing at. They were all laughing at me! One of them pointed at me and shouted, "*El Chumbo! El Chumbo!*" Which made all the others laugh harder. Later, Sheila could not believe I was so stupid as to pick up a prickly pear (chumbo) with my bare hands.

Sheila introduced us to Pepe Rossa, the leader of Alora's flamenco group. Just about every village in Andalusia had a group, and all took part in an annual competition held at a big hotel in Marbella. Pepe's group was one of the best. He allowed us to attend a few rehearsals held in Alora's village hall. We sat at the back and watched the Spanish girls swirl and stamp and clap. I fell in love on the spot, and determined to paint a picture called 'Verdiales', which Pepe explained was the name of the Malaga version of flamenco the girls were dancing. After that we became flamenco fans, and often travelled to whatever Fiesta was happening in the surrounding towns. Pepe introduced us to his mother, a formidable

A Noose of Light

Spanish matriarch. With Pepe translating, she asked what my name was.

"Alan", I replied

She frowned, disapprovingly. "What Saint's name is that?" She barked.

"Alehandro!" I cried, quick as a flash.

She nodded, and offered out her hand, palm down, as Pepe shot me a doubtful glance.

The months passed. Life became very pleasant, and we could see no reason why it should not continue indefinitely. We explored the Costa del Sol from Malaga to Gibraltar in one-day tourist trips, and also went further afield for overnight stays in Granada, Cordoba and Seville. We visited little villages where donkeys provided transport, and millionaire resorts such as Marbella and Puerto Banus, where the harbour foreshore sparkled with Ferraris and private yachts. At the height of that summer we noticed that the local river had dried up. So just for the hell of it, we drove up the river bed into the mountains, up and up, jolting over gravel ridges and around boulders. I let the boys take turns at steering. After a while, we noticed little homesteads on top of the bank on either side. White painted wells with donkeys standing by. Women in black dresses, white aprons and strange hats, standing there staring at us. We waved and shouted Hola! Some waved back, and some did not. There were no roads up there. We had driven into the Middle Ages. When we returned, we told Sheila, and she said there were many families up there who came down into Alora only once a year, their donkeys loaded with chickpeas. After selling to the market women, they would buy the stuff they could not make or grow themselves, and vanish off back up the mountain.

It was October, and I happened to be reading Sir James Frazer's 'The Golden Bough', and had come to the chapter about the 'October Pig'. Coincidentally, Sheila told us that Pedro, her farm manager, was very unhappy because this was one of the times of year when he had to fulfil his duties as 'El Melono' (the big melon) of his village. The title of El Melono is not bestowed by election, nor is it inherited. People just *knew* which man in the village was El Melono, and Pedro had been El Melono ever since he grew to manhood. He didn't mind it, except for what he had to do at this time of year, which was to kill the October pig. Not just one pig, but each pig that had been fattening up all year in the back yards of all the cottages in the village: a total of ten big fat pigs.

I couldn't believe it. I was reading that this Autumn ritual dated back 3,000 years to Ancient Greece, and was a pagan sacrifice to Demeter, the goddess of the corn – and here it was still happening! The day came, and we leaned out of our upstairs window to watch a solemn-looking Pedro lead a parade of women up the street to the first cottage. The women were all singing as he went in the door, and they sang louder when the pig started screaming. Pedro came out, spattered in blood, still holding the long knife he had used to cut the pig's throat, and some of the women rushed into the house. There and then they were going to dismember the pig into handy joints, and even make sausages of the rest.

A Noose of Light

Pedro marched grimly to the next house, and the women started singing again to cover the screams. And so it went on until the last cottage, by which time Pedro and most of the women were covered in blood. In the evening there was a street Fiesta. Sheila told me that Pedro's family was called the *Ranas*, because they all looked like frogs, so I asked her to tell Pedro that I admired his performance with the pigs, and that I was going to paint a special Ranas painting as a house sign he could display beside his front door. It was finished a week later: an oil painting on a wood panel about 30cm square, showing a family of frogs sitting near a reedy pool on a moonlit night. Pedro and his wife were very pleased with it, and for weeks I looked for it to be installed by his door. In the end I got Sheila to ask him where the painting was. He said it was far too valuable to leave outside, and he had hung it in their *interioso*: the inner, windowless, cool room that Andalusian families live in all summer.

Practising the occasional pagan custom, however, did not interfere with their Catholic rituals – as was demonstrated by the next event. I noticed that another local *hombre* was always working – either around his house or zooming about on his little moped with sacks of stuff on the back – so I called him *El Trabajador* (the worker). Sheila told him and he was very pleased. He had an extremely obese wife, Maria, and a teenage daughter, Anna.

One afternoon we heard a terrible commotion issuing from Maria's house, and from our high window saw Maria and Anna clutching each other and screaming in the street. The neighbours, including Sheila, rushed out to help, and everyone fussed around for a while. Then Sheila called up to us that Anna had found her father's cutthroat razor in the bathroom, and had tried to shave her legs – with gory results. *El Trabajador* soon appeared, wrapped up his daughter's wound, loaded her on the back of his moped and zoomed off to the local doctor's house. A tearful Maria was led inside by the other wives, and we returned to our peaceful occupations. After about an hour, another commotion erupted outside. *El Trabajador* had returned with a stitched and bandaged Anna, and all was well. But Maria was now screaming her thanks to God in the street, arms raised to heaven and tears falling. Even this was not enough. She rushed into her house and reappeared wearing a black headscarf. The other wives seemed to know what was happening. They just stood in a row, solemnly watching, as Maria, all 110 kilos of her, set off across the fields at a brisk trot. Sheila told us that Maria was doing penance and giving thanks by running in a straight line across country to the local church, about two kilometres away.

The killing of the October pig marked a seasonal change for us as well as the villagers. We realised that our boys could not continue to hang about playing with the local kids: they needed to go to school. All the international private schools catering for *extranjeros* like us were established along the Costa del Sol, so we obtained a list of likely places and began our inspections. The one we liked best was in Estepona. We liked it because we got on okay with the New York Jewish couple who ran it, and because it was associated with University of Cambridge. The boys liked it because it was slap bang on the beach, and everyone seemed to be having a cheerful time. What could possibly go wrong?

To complicate the issue of the move, we began to receive letters and phone calls begging us to get out of Spain fast. The death of Spain's dictator General Franco had just been splashed across the British and Australian media, and our friends and relatives thought the country would descend into anarchy. We thought this was funny, because we had never given Franco a thought during our stay, and he had never been mentioned by anyone we had met. In Andalusia it was as if he didn't exist. Anyway, Franco's demise serves to date precisely the beginning of our next Andalusian adventure to November 1975.

We moved into a large villa in a holiday resort complex just up the coast from the school. The boys were happy to walk along the sand to their lessons every morning, and we were happy to potter around painting pictures and visiting markets, and making friends with parents of other kids at the school. We spent most of our social mixing time with an Israeli family, Gabby and Katti and their two boys, playing backgammon, chess, and doing car trips to Ronda, Seville and Gibralter. A high spot was when the finals of the annual Flamenco competition occurred at a big Marbella venue, and we took our new friends along to see the show. Pepe Rossa's group was the outright winner with a sensational production called La Novia (the bride) featuring a wedding scene and scandalously erotic dance moves by the bride and groom.

All very pleasant, but our new friend Gabby was a

restless entrepreneur. He got bored and purchased a run down café near Marbella, and turned it into a Japanese garden restaurant, specialising in Mai Tai cocktails. He had his whole family working on it, and asked me to do artwork for the logo, menu and signage. Sampling the cocktails one night, Gabby asked me to go partners with him in the restaurant, and I said I'd rather keep him as a friend. Katti laughed and hugged me. She understood.

A Noose of Light

Morocco

Things were jogging along pleasantly, but it was when we went to Gibraltar that it occurred to us to take the opportunity to pop across the Straights and do a quick tour of Morocco. When the school closed for Christmas, we caught the ferry from Algeciras to Tangier, and drove down the coast highway to Rabat, where we stayed overnight at a cheap pension run by a terminally miserable French couple, who must have forgotten to move out when the Moroccans took over in 1956. I've never been to anywhere more saturated with hopelessness. It was like staying overnight in a Samuel Beckett play. We drove on to Casablanca in the morning, but things didn't get much better. We were shocked by the ladies in Gucci shoes stepping over beggar babies in the gutter, and discomforted by the groups of men in nightshirts, who just stood and stared at us. We didn't bother with Marrakesh, but turned inland and drove towards Fez. The roads became country lanes, and turning a long corner I just managed to avoid running over a strip of spikes placed across the road. As soon as I stopped, a little uniformed man in a gendarme-style cap stepped out of the shrubbery and walked slowly around the car. Then he came to my window, asked for my *papiers*, and studied my passport as if he'd never seen one before. I lost patience, and tried out my French – which unfortunately got mixed up with my equally bad Spanish.

"*Vraiment monsieur, nous sommes Anglais touristas! Que deseas?*

He didn't say anything. He just stood there staring at me through the windscreen. Then he gave up, dragged aside his spiked belt, and wearily waved us on. About a kilometre up the road I realised he had been waiting for a bribe.

A couple of kilometres outside Fez, travelling in at about 60 kph, we were talking about where we were going to stay in the ancient city when a head popped in my open window and said, "I be your guide!" It was a teenage Berber boy on a moped, hurtling along beside us. I pulled over and heard that his name was Mohammed, and that he knew all the best places in Fez. The irresistible thing about him was that he spoke very bad English with a pronounced Oxford accent. Impressed with his enterprise, I hired him. He took us straight to a hotel in the old town, which I suspect was owned by a relative. It must have been built a very long time ago because the timber treads of the stairs were almost worn through. Following Mohammed, we ascended them into a very large open barn-like area at the top, strewn with enormous shapeless cushions, and nothing else.

"Very nice family room!" Said Mohammed.

We stood and stared uncomprehendingly until Beverley said, "Ooooh, they're mattresses!"

I explained to Mohammed that we wanted an English-style hotel. He rather sulkily led us to one in the old *el Bali* district, but did not come inside with us.

A Noose of Light

In fact, he hid around a corner and gestured us on, into the reception hall. We checked in and went to a very pleasant second floor suite with windows overlooking a courtyard. It was quite late by then, so we ate dinner in the hotel and went to bed. At about 8.30 in the morning, we were awakened by a piercing Oxford accent calling from outside. "Helloooo! Hellooo!" I got out of bed, and went to the window. There below was Mohammed. Somehow he had found out which window was ours. He saw me and waved. "I hope you sleep well, sir!"

"We're not ready, yet, Mohammed!" I called.

"Excellent, sir. I will wait for you here!"

After breakfast, we walked outside and sure enough there was Mohammed. We set off walking at random along the narrow alleyways of the old quarter. Sometimes Mohammed would stop outside a building and recite a description.

"Here we enjoy one of the many bakery in the old city el Bali. Why is there many bakery in Fez? Because we enjoy population of 60,000 peoples and bread must be new each day."

We walked on until Mohammed stopped again outside another building, and grandly gestured towards a doorway.

"Here we enjoy property sellings where peoples come to find houses."

I stuck my head in the door and saw a small empty room with an old man sitting on the floor in a corner.

"He knows all houses for selling in ancient city," said Mohammed.

It soon became clear that Mohammed had memorised bits of a guide book, and was quoting from it more or less at random. It also became clear that whenever a policeman appeared he would vanish, and reappear when the policeman had passed. I asked him why this was, and he said, "I like to be lucky." Mohammed was an unofficial guide, a pirate, and what he was doing was illegal. The official guides were dignified, smartly dressed, older men with large, shiny brass badges hanging around their necks. I gathered that if they or the police caught Mohammed 'freelancing', his punishment would be immediate and very painful. Nevertheless he made himself useful in the intricate maze of narrow streets, showing us the famous fabric dyers vats, and the alley of brass beaters where one of the stall holders noticed that our four year-old Nathaniel was fascinated by the young boys hammering intricate patterns into the plates and trays. The workshop owner, a burly merchant wearing a Fez, nodded at Nathaniel and said something to Mohammed.

"He say he like your boy," said Mohammed. "He say he buy him for 50,000 Durhams."

I still don't know if the owner was joking.

Someone at the hotel told us about a famous shrine called Moulay Idris in the hills outside the city, and we decided to see it. We drove into the large square where some cars were parked, and found that it was some sort of holiday. There were hundreds of people standing and sitting, and they all stared at us when we got out of the car. The whole town was standing there staring at us silently. I tried a friendly wave, but they just stared harder, as if to see what the alien would do next. Eventually a guide with a guide's badge around his neck walked over and offered to help us for a small fee. He guided us away from all the interesting places, around the backs of houses, and up winding steps, pointing out the green roof of the mosque or palace or shrine from a long way away. It became obvious that he did not want us to go near the 'sacred' places, so we went back to Fez, and decided to head back to Spain in the morning. We had seen enough of Morocco, and had enough of being treated like aliens.

Next day, about 1pm, we paid off Mohammed, and set off North towards the ferry at Ceuta. It was further than I thought. The N13 road went on and on, and I kept looking for a petrol station. I should have filled up at Fez, but thought there would be a station en route. There was not. The petrol gauge got lower and lower, and the sky got darker and darker as the clock passed 5pm. Eventually we were driving along a deserted country road in the dark with an almost empty tank. All we could see ahead in the headlights was the scruffy road vanishing off into the darkness that wrapped itself around us on both sides. There wasn't even a tree. I said to Beverley that I would have to stop at the next town or house or farm – whatever. At last a light appeared ahead, and we saw a car parked outside a couple of dilapidated houses. I pulled up beside it, beeped the horn and got out. All was still. No traffic, no people. I called to the nearest house, and saw a curtain move in one of the windows. Then a man in a turban came out and cautiously moved towards us. I patted the bonnet of the car and said, "*Excuse moi, monsieur, gasolena niente!*" He looked at me blankly. I went to the petrol cap and unscrewed it and pointed down the hole. "*Nada!*" I held out my hands palms up, and shrugged. "*Petrol rien…zero!*"

He understood. He performed a series of gestures which I interpreted as meaning, 'Calm down, stay here, I will get help'. Then he walked off into the darkness. While this pantomime was going on, a woman and an old man and some children had emerged from the house and sat down on the ground near our car. They had brought something to eat with them, some bread and nuts, and they sat there calmly passing the food around between them. Beverley and the boys got out of the car, and smiled at the 'audience'. The old man nodded at me, looked at Beverley, and said, "*Anglais?*" Beverley said, "*Oui, Anglais.*" The old man smiled knowingly, and cracked a nut between his teeth. By the time the turbaned man returned, another couple of locals had appeared out of the darkness, spread a small carpet they had brought, and sat down on it. The old man told them we were '*Anglais*'. They expressed polite interest, and unscrewed the cap of a large plastic bottle of orangeade. The turbaned man said something to me in Arabic or Bedouin, and gestured that I should follow him. I hesitated and looked at Beverley. The turban said something else, and gestured that she should stay there. The audience observed this exchange and made comments. What else could I do? I told Beverley to get back in the car with the boys and wait, and followed the turban into the darkness. He led me up a black track and

A Noose of Light

around the back of a large barn-like building, through a yard, past a starved-looking tethered goat, up some wooden stairs into a long, low sitting room in which sat an old man with a long beard, and two younger men in western clothes. Between them on the floor was a large car battery, which they were apparently discussing. They hardly acknowledged me. The old man just gestured for me to be seated, and waved at the turban, who departed. A woman holding a brass teapot thing came in from the other side of the room, gave me a brass cup and poured some mint tea into it. One of the western guys turned to me and said, in perfect English. "I won't be a minute, please wait."

I had not realised how adreniline-pumped I was, but when he said that, a plug was pulled in my chest and all the tension drained out. I interrupted the discussion about the goddamned battery.

"Please excuse me," I said, quite loudly. "My wife and children are down there in the car and I think they may be worried."

The English speaker nodded, and said something to his associate. The associate looked rather annoyed, but got up and went out. Beverley reported to me later that she and the boys had been waiting in the car and watching the audience grow ever larger – god knows where they were coming from – and she had been telling the boys to wave at the children outside. By the time the associate arrived, there must have been about 30 people camped around the car, chatting and sharing their goodies. The associate ignored the audience and brusquely ordered Beverley and the boys out of the car. Then he wound up all the windows and brusquely gestured that they should follow him. Trying to sound cheerful, Beverley followed him up the black track, through the yard, past the tethered goat, and up the stairs.

Sipping my mint tea, I heard a little voice say, "Is Alan in there?" And saw Beverley's terrified face appear behind the glowering associate. I realised later that he had been deeply offended at being sent to fetch a woman – and an infidel woman at that. Whatever, we all sat together on the couch and the lady of the house appeared again – this time with a tray of spicy sardines as well as the mint tea. I still remember the taste, and thinking that it would be too strong for the boys. They sat there as good as gold, eyes like saucers.

I still have no notion of how a discussion of a goddamned battery could last so long, but eventually it was over. I expressed my proper gratitude to the old man, who just nodded, and we all trooped back down to the car. The audience was still there, and they greeted the appearance of the English speaker with enthusiasm. They apparently knew him, and liked him, and they commented on and encouraged every move he made. The parked car we had stopped beside was his, and he immediately set about transferring a gallon of petrol from his tank into mine. He produced a jerry can and a tube from the boot of his car, and unscrewed his petrol cap. Immediately, a man in the audience jumped up and remonstrated, then rushed off and came back with a wider tube. "Aaaaaah!" Cried the audience. The English speaker then fed the tube into the tank and sucked, getting a mouthful of petrol, which he spat out –

to the vast amusement of the crowd. The audience man then took over the sucking job, and skilfully syphoned a measure of petrol into the jerry can. The audience applauded. The jerry can was then carried over to my car, and several attempts to pour the petrol directly from it into my tank failed. "Aaaaah!" Cried the audience. What was needed was a funnel. It was the associate guy, the sulky disgruntled glowering one that solved the problem. He dived into the back of the English speaker's car and emerged with a glossy brochure. He tore off the front cover and wrapped it into a cone and stuck the cone into the filler tube. The English speaking guy then emptied the jerry can into my car. The audience cheered. I hesitantly offered to pay for the petrol, but he said, "That's okay, I do it for the blessing!"

Waving to the cheerful audience, we drove on and stayed overnight at a big hotel in Tetouan. Gabriel and Nathaniel had a wander round the gardens, and had rocks thrown at them by the local boys. Gabriel was outraged. I think it was the first time he had been physically attacked.

It was good to get back to Estepona, and to start the boys in their new year's term at school. Beverley heard that her Father and stepmother were on a cruise ship that would be docking briefly at Malaga, so we drove there and met them for lunch on board. Beverley's father asked us what we were doing in Spain, and again tried to persuade us to move to Australia. It was difficult explaining to him that we did not know what we were doing in Spain, but that we still wished to carry on doing it. I found it difficult to adjust my responses to the overt paternalism that was a cultural fixture of Beverley's family. No such hierarchy had existed in my own childhood: everyone was allowed to go their own way without comment from my father, and only expressions of concern from my mother.

The pleasant life resumed, with trips to Seville for flamenco shows, and especially to our favourite place high up in the hills, Ronda. The boys loved coming back to Estepona from there, because I would switch off the engine and do 'The Ronda Roll', silently swishing along down the twisting road for 20 kilometres through the forest, all the way down to the coast road.

We got to know the husband and wife who were Dean, Headmistress and owners of the international school, and visited their very modernised house in the old pueblo of Estepona. On one of these visits, the headmistress asked me if I would chair a meeting of all the parents. Apparently a dispute had arisen regarding the proceeds of a fund-raising campaign that had been completed just before we enrolled our boys. The proceeds had, as planned, been spent on building a new school playing field, but now some of the parents were objecting to this because the improvement increased the value of the property, which was wholly owned by the principals. Not knowing the level of resentment, nor its history, I cheerfully agreed to be the chair. At the meeting, held in the school hall and attended by about 50 people, I realised that it was the majority of parents who were bringing the action. Apart from myself and the principals, the only other person sitting on the stage was a very old retired English Judge. I tried

A Noose of Light

to keep order but the hecklers were quite adamant that they had not raised the funds to increase the value of the property, and that the school should be formed into a trust in which all parents should have shares. The meeting ended in deadlock, and threats of legal action. After, I was taken aside by a more reasonable couple of parents, and advised that I was out of my depth, and that I had not been around long enough to know what was going on, and that I was being used as a naïve patsy by the principals. The next day I drove down the coast to see the old Judge at his home, hoping that he could tell me the background to the dispute. His daughter answered the door, and told me that the old Judge had just heard from his solicitor in England that he, the solicitor, had received a document listing irregularities in the Judge's income tax statements stretching back for several decades. The old fellow was now near collapse because he stood to lose everything if prosecuted for tax evasion. The Judge, apparently, knew exactly who had dug up the dirt on him. The Costa del Sol was a haven for retired criminals of one sort or another – and several of these were parents or grandparents of children at the school. Things got worse over the following weeks. The teachers were being solicited by the parents to quit, and to testify against the principals. The headmistress summoned her heavyweight lawyer brother from New York. It became apparent that whoever the retired crims were, they could not find anything historical with which to threaten me. Nevertheless, my commitment to the school did not outweigh my fear of physical intimidation of my family, so we packed up and went back to

Tunbridge Wells – arriving almost exactly a year after we had departed.

Somewhere in this period – I think when we returned to Estepona from Morocco – I wrote to Shah at Langton Green to resign from the Institute, severing the connection between us. I had become agitated by our perceived lack of progress in the Work – as well as by the other business and domestic factors which lead to our trip to Spain – and wanted to toss everything overboard and make a fresh start. Beverley must have agreed to this, though probably by acquiescence not assertion. What also played a part in the resignation was my unease caused by the Robert Graves/Omar Khayyam affair, which even today casts a dark shadow over Shah's legacy.

Here's what Wikipedia says about it on Robert Graves's page at time of writing in 2014 – 47 years after the event:

> *In 1967, Robert Graves published, together with Omar Ali-Shah, a new translation of the Rubaiyat of Omar Khayyam. The translation quickly became controversial; Graves was attacked for trying to break the spell of famed passages in Edward FitzGerald's Victorian translation, and L. P. Elwell-Sutton, an orientalist at Edinburgh University, maintained that the manuscript used by Ali-Shah and Graves—which Ali-Shah and his brother Idries Shah claimed had been in their family for 800 years—was a forgery. The translation was a critical disaster and Graves's reputation suffered severely due to what the public perceived as his gullibility in falling for the Shah*

brothers' deception.

Beverley and I attended a book launch party at Langton, some time after the publication, and I saw Graves, a noble but somewhat bemused old lion, sitting in an armchair while Shah and others hovered. How strange that Omar's book should follow me through my life like that.

Why did Shah and his brother do it? Why did they risk the reputation of an aged and revered English poet, entangling him in a dodgy publishing scam involving a putative 'original manuscript' which was never produced in evidence? The best interpretation is that the Shah brothers wanted to correct the popular Fitzgerald translation because it did not reflect the Sufi nuances of the Persian original – in which, we were told, the metaphor of 'wine' was used for 'baraka', or blessing. Thus:

Fitzgerald's

> *Awake! for Morning in the Bowl of Night*
> *Has flung the Stone that puts the Stars to Flight,*
> *And Lo! The Hunter of the East has caught*
> *The Sultan's Turret in a Noose of Light.*

becomes Graves/Ali Shah's

> *While Dawn, Day's herald straddling the whole sky,*
> *Offers the drowsy world a toast "To Wine",*
> *The sun spills early gold on city roofs-*
> *Day's regal host, replenishing his jug.*

Fitzgerald's

> *The Moving Finger writes; and, having writ,*
> *Moves on: nor all thy Piety nor Wit*

> *Shall lure it back to cancel half a Line,*
> *Nor all they tears wash out a word of it.*

becomes Graves/Ali Shah's

> *What we shall be is written, and we are so.*
> *Heedless of God or Evil, pen, write on!*
> *By the first day all futures were decided;*
> *Which gives our griefs and pains irrelevancy.*

Was it worth it? Was it worth clouding an old man's last years for? I did not think so back then, but now I allow that Graves wanted to do it, so who am I to say he should not? As for Shah's involvement, I say that some mistakes are made with good intentions. I think I understand why Shah wrote and published all those books under phony names. He said he had a job to do, and he used every legal means to do it. After all, if you were commissioned by the Guardians of the Tradition to introduce a broader understanding of Sufi history and ideas into Western culture, why would you allow that culture's rules of etiquette to impede the effectiveness of your campaign? But in the Omar Khayyam case, I think he was led by his brother Omar to involve Graves in what is now generally recognised as a literary scam, and he regretted it. After all, Graves was the man who helped Shah produce his seminal book, 'The Sufis'. As Mister B is reported to have said in his last days on Earth, "I may indeed be a spiritual guide, but I still make mistakes!"

Personally, I think the "moving finger" which started writing on the first day, when "all futures were decided" is a predestination element of Sufi lore which Shah's brother chose to emphasise, but which is not a prominent feature in most Sufi studies.

The other notorious black mark against Shah's name is the affair of his brother Omar and the famous film animator Dick Williams. Shah told me that Dick needed someone to design a fancy brochure about his business, so I made an appointment to see him at his Soho Square studios. I had much admired Dick's illustrations for the Mullah Nasrudin books, and also his big movie animation work featured in 'The Charge of the Light Brigade' and 'Roger Rabbit'. He was an Oscar-winning artist, so I was thrilled to meet him. He met me at the entrance, and took me on a tour of the building, starting off in the windowless back hallway where he displayed his 'Trophy Wall', as he called it. The wall with all the golden statues and framed awards was brightly spotlit, so it was not immediately that I realised that this hallway was also the office of Omar Shah, Dick's business manager. Backed against the darkened opposite wall was a desk illuminated only by a small halogen light, and behind that desk sat the shadowy figure of Omar. I waved a salute, but Omar did not acknowledge it. I am not an insensitive man, and I felt a distinct atmosphere of seething resentment in that room.

At the tour's end Dick ushered me into his projection room, and showed me some footage from his amazing animated masterpiece-in-progress, which was based on the Mullah Nasrudin books, but later retitled 'The Cobbler and the Thief'.

Dick is the most gifted artist I have ever met, and a delightful person as well. I was very sad and mystified when I heard that his relationship with Shah and Omar had ended in bitterness. No one seems to know why, but there are rumours of draconian copyright claims and crooked dealing. Saddest of all, whatever the cause of the breakup, Dick's masterpiece suffered. The beautiful animated film of Mullah Nasruddin stories became mutilated by Dick himself into another story featuring an animated Dick Williams as the hero cobbler, and a composite Shah/Omar character called ZigZag as the evil villain. To this day it has never been shown in completed form.

I did a design for Dick's brochure, and was paid for it, but the brochure, I think, became another casualty of whatever that disaster was.

It was these memories and impressions from the period before the Spanish trip that accumulated in Spain into the decision to make a clean break from my Bennett/Shah history. The shadow of doubt and confusion had fallen on what was once clear and certain. I wanted a fresh start at everything.

Snapping Back

We rented a house on the outskirts of Tunbridge Wells, and entered Gabriel and Nathaniel into the local primary school. Although my Spanish attempt to develop a grand theme of painting had failed, I still wanted to stay out of commercial art. Beverley became interested in a new style of knitting machine, which featured a punch card programming facility. I punched out a few patterns, and produced some interesting knitted fabrics. Beverley found some patterns for sweaters and waistcoats, and away we went with our knitted fashions label 'alanbeverley'. We toured around the local Kentish boutiques and sold some to shops wholesale, and some to friends retail, but nowhere near enough to make a living.

Then our friend John Walker asked me to design a Mihrab – a sort of framed Islamic niche to hang on the wall facing Mecca – but as a mirror. I did my best using Arabic geometry patterns and Persian miniature-style illustration. John thought they could be mass produced, but they were far too work intensive for the price he could charge for them. We also produced some mirrors with mosaic patterned frames. I've still got the prototype of the Mihrab on the shelf over the TV, with the old photos of my parents, and the Minoan snake goddess statue in front of it.

All that occupied us for about six months but then a real thunderbolt hit out of nowhere. John phoned to tell us he had been diagnosed with leukemia. The following six months were overshadowed by the steady decline of my best friend.

His wife Eva was a doctor, and she was actually supervising his care at the Royal Marsden Hospital in his last days. He was put on a heart lung machine, with Eva monitoring his vital signs, and she staying at the hospital many nights in a row. I became concerned that their little boy, Miro, who was in the care of a relative, was missing his mummy, so I drove one night to the hospital. I knew they wouldn't let me in to see John on the machine, so I pinched a white coat off a peg and a clipboard from a desk, and marched around looking official until I found where he was. He was wired up with the works: a tube down his throat, drip feeds and monitor straps on his arms, and catheters to remove the waste. A male nurse was attending the wheezing electric pump, and Eva was scribbling on a clip board. She was surprised to see me. For some reason I became very angry, I walked up to the bed, took off the tape over one of John's eyes, and lifted the eyelid to see if he was still in there. He was not in there, his eyeball was just a grey jelly, like cold porridge. The male nurse twigged that something irregular was happening, and moved toward me. I told Eva that John had gone, and she should look after the baby, not hang around the corpse. I knew I was speaking for John: he of all people would have told Eva to snap out of it.

A Noose of Light

She did, and after the funeral she, being Catholic, asked me to be godfather to Miro. John would have laughed – he knew that I thought all religions were variations of the same psychosis. Nevertheless, there I was in a church near Hampstead listening to a deranged-looking priest, who was asking me, seriously, if I renounced the Devil and all his works. I said I did, and water was dripped and the deed done. I have in no way been a useful godfather to Miro, but he's done okay anyway, and I think he understands and excuses my neglect.

I acquiesced to a similar occasion in 1969, when Shah's father died. I was asked to drive the Institute's Vauxhall station wagon to the funeral from Langton Green. Inside were Shah, Kashvi, Omar, and Amina, Shah's sister. The whole family knew that I was nervous as hell, and excused my silence en route repeatedly as "He's concentrating on his driving." Then we got to the venue and watched as some Iman conducted the ceremony, after which we, some Institute members and relatives, had to hold out our hands while Omar dropped some coins into them. I just remembered that and put it in before I forgot it again.

But I can't let John and Eva go without telling you the best story about them. They met when John was driving a van around in France. She and her girl friend were Polish, and hitch hiking around Europe. John liked the look of them, and drove them where they wanted to go. En route, he fell in love with Eva, took her back to England and married her. Then they developed a little business together. Eva told John that her whole family and neighbours in rural Poland habitually bred Nutria in their back yards, and made warm winter fur coats from the hides. Entrepreneur John immediately purchased a large van and adapted the inside with a false wall. That is, a double lining to the inside enabling contraband to be stuffed down the gap. Then they started smuggling nutria skins from Poland over the East German border, across France into England, where they sold for a tidy profit. On the return trip, they would pay Eva's folks their percentage, and load up another shipment. Everything went well until, on one of the trips back across the East German border at night and in winter, with the van stuffed with nutria (and don't forget the Berlin Wall was still up, then), they hit a nasty guard post. The van was stopped and they were asked to show their papers. Usually they were just waved through, but this time they were asked to get out of the van and to step inside the guard post – a corrugated iron hut. Carrying baby Milo, John and Eva walked into the icy hut and faced the commandant, who took a long time examining their passports. He was just about to order that the van be searched when little Milo burst into tears and screamed the place down. On and on the screams went echoing off the corrugated iron walls. The commandant lost patience and stamped the passports and wave them out. Safely over the border and driving down the road, John said to Eva,

"Jesus, it was lucky Milo started screaming then."
"What you mean lucky?" Said Eva, "I pinch him!"

Around the same time as John's death, things were

getting a bit desperate. The knitwear wasn't enough, the Mihrab was a loser. I even tried to write a pop song, but I played it to Wizz when he visited, and he didn't know what to say. He was so embarrassed he was polite! He said, "It's not like anything you've done before, Al. I don't know what to say!" What he didn't want to say was that it was crap.

Then Beverley blandly announced that she had visited Langton Green, and talked to Shah's secretary, sounding out the possibility of resuming our regular attendances. It was a return to the fold, and this sheep was in no mood to resist.

No one knows what would have happened thereafter if I had refused to reconnect with Shah, but Beverley's chat with Helena spread the word through the network, and almost immediately I received a phone call from the sales manager of Slendertone. He said that he had heard I was back in England, and wanted me to take over the advertising again. He said that they had used up all my old ads, and tried out some new ones, which had not worked. Would I do some new ads and brochures for them?

It was one of those times when I could actually feel the pressure of the moving finger. I resumed being the creative director of Slendertone advertising. I went to see Shah, and noticed hanging on the wall of his study my portrait of Rumi, the first thing I had done for him.

"I'm sort of surprised to see that there," I said.

"Why shouldn't it be there?" Said Shah.

The letter of resignation was never mentioned. It was as if we had travelled to Spain anchored to a length of elastic, and at the end of the year had snapped back to exactly where we had been before we left.

I do not remember our conversation, nor if he commissioned me to do some design work. It is very annoying that all I remember about our reunion is the asinine comment about that picture on the wall.

I know that we moved house twice after that, but cannot account for events in the period other than to report that the second house we rented after our return from Spain was a large old manor close to Langton Green, and that this house boasted a huge dovecot in the garden, housing a flock of at least 100 pure white doves. How gorgeous, we thought – and proudly showed them off to any visitors. Richard and Helen Rieu, the de facto managers of the Langton Green estate, came to visit and Richard declared that the dovecote and the oak-beamed living room were the most charming he had ever witnessed. No matter, when Spring came around I began to notice something undesirable occurring in the dovecote. This structure was hexagonal in plan, about two metres wide and one metre deep, with two floors or levels – each floor featuring a row of stylish entry holes all the way round, shaped like Roman arches. On top was a pointed roof, and the whole thing was hoisted three metres in the air on a stout oak post. The flock of doves, we were told by the estate agent, had been there since the house was built in 1805. One sunny Spring morning, I noticed a few tiny struggling bodies on the ground beneath the cote. They were little chicks which had fallen out of the cote. I erected a step ladder and tenderly shoved them back in one of the portholes.

Next morning, there were more struggling bodies on the ground, and I examined them more carefully, noticing that none of the chicks were without some tiny blemish: a fleck of grey on a tail or wing was enough. None of them was pure white. Each morning thereafter, my duty was to carry a bucket of water out to the dovecote, and to drown to death all the imperfect chicks thrown out by their eugenicist parents, holding their little bug-eyed faces under until the last bubble popped out of their beaks. I do not exaggerate: over the course of the season I must have drowned at least 50 chicks. I became very angry and wished to make a protest. I told Beverley that the white doves of peace were Nazis in disguise, and that I was going to make a large Swastika flag and erect it on top of the dovecote. Beverley cautioned that if the postman saw the flag flying there every morning, he might get the wrong idea. I had to concur, but was unwilling to face another 'Nazi Spring', so we moved to another house.

In this third rented house since Spain, Gabriel became a teenager. Unlike the educational system in most counties, Kent had retained the 11-plus exam which streamed pupils into either Grammar or Secondary Modern schools. Gabriel had done very well in the exam and had been placed at a prestigious Tunbridge Wells grammar school. On parent's day, the Head Master took Beverley and myself aside to say that Gabriel was "Cambridge quality", and years ahead of his class, and was going to get 'A-levels' in maths and physics. While not knowing from where Gabriel had received *that* sort of talent, we congratulated ourselves and thought that it was due to the varied and 'colourful' upbringing we had given him. By the time we moved into our fourth house in 1980, he had began to bring his girlfriend and her horse around to visit. This means that a period of about four years had elapsed since our return from Spain, about which period my memories are few. I have tried my Hubble 'staring between the stars' trick, but all I remember is that it was the early 1980s, when fear of nuclear war was so prevalent that the government subsidised building domestic fallout shelters under a program called 'Protect and Survive'. Many of our acquaintances were hoarding tinned food and other supplies in their attics or basements. Shah decided to install a proper underground family fallout shelter in the grounds of Langton House, and attracted some local publicity when he hired a helicopter to deliver the massive steel cylindrical structure. Our friends the McDonalds bought a small farm just outside Tunbridge Wells, and built chicken runs and other facilities – including a shotgun for defence against the hungry shelterless mob who would swarm out from the cities after the first nuclear strikes. Beverley and I felt no impulse to subscribe to this trend.

Indeed, I think it was while inspecting the hoard of tinned food in the attic of my friend Ivan (not the Jamaican Ivan) that the subject of a partnership arose. Ivan was an occasional Langton Green attendee who had started a design and artwork group in Hove, near Brighton. He offered me a partnership in return for bringing the Slendertone account into the business. I decided that it was about time I became a director of a bigger concern, and agreed. I thought it was the most sensible business decision I had ever made. Naturally, it was the most disastrous. I received a fixed salary, and Ivan took care of all the accounts stuff. I designed all the ads, and the small production studio produced the artwork. There were other accounts but the major money came from my Slendertone advertising. Much of the income went on maintaining the stylish offices, and paying the small staff, but I thought it was nice that I didn't have to do everything myself. Ivan and I bought matching company cars, and I drove from Langton Green to Hove and back every day.

It was all pretty humdrum except for three events. Shah asked us to design and produce his new book 'World Tales', a very big project involving many illustrators. I did a few of the illustrations myself, but Ivan handled everything else – including liaison with Shah. Ivan told me his memorable experience when he went with Shah to meet the American publishers in London to get the page layouts and budget approved. The publishers were a pair of arrogant twerps, who fatuously criticised Ivan's page layouts, suggesting meaningless amendments. Shah went berserk, transforming himself into a furious Pakistani – complete with accent – jabbering away about wogs and race prejudice, and so alarming the twerps that they signed off on everything, approved everything, including the production budget, there and then.

Around then, I must have mistook myself for a successful businessman, because I extended largesse towards my nephew – a young man who was having trouble finding his place. He joined the studio as a junior artist, but did not blend with the existing staff. I did not blend with the staff, either, but there was nothing they could do about that. I had yet to learn that the only way for a new Director to join an established team is for him/her to sack everyone and get them to reapply for their jobs. After a few months, the staff got Ivan to ask me to get my nephew to resign. The nephew did resign, but then developed an unexpected talent for making miniature fantasy figures, and established himself as an independent freelancer in a flat in Brighton. I thought everything was working out. Unfortunately, however, Brighton was notorious for its drug culture, and the nephew quickly became a heroin user. He overdosed and died within a year of quitting my company. His mother, my sister, did not blame me, but I knew that my interference in his life had led directly to his death.

On the heels of finishing 'World Tales' for Shah, Ivan and I decided to independently produce a similar illustrated book called 'Cat Tails' – a multicultural collection of ancient folk tales about cats. Beverley helped out by doing literature research, finding old cat stories in The London Library, and other repositories. She enjoyed the work, and became a professional literary and picture researcher from then on. Halfway through production, Ivan and I took the book to the Frankfurt Book Fare to find a publisher for it – without success.

One winter night, driving back home through the Ashdown Forest, a big stag jumped in front of my car. I hit it head on, bouncing it forward along the road, where it tried to stand up and run away, but all its legs

A Noose of Light

were broken. It was pouring rain and pitch dark in the forest. I got out of the car and tried to hold the stag down by its horns. I was stretched out flat there in the road, lit up by the headlights, holding the stag down, unable to move. I could not bear the thought of it trying to run away on its broken legs. After a long while, a little green Morris Minor chugged up, and a fat woman got out and looked down at us.

She said, "You should get a large *spanner* and hit it between the *eyes!*" She pointed between her own eyes to show me the exact place.

Still lying in the road, I said, "All its legs are broken! Go to the nearest house and phone the Forest Rangers!"

She gave a long-suffering sigh, got back into her car and drove off.

During what seemed the following very long time, a few cars drove slowly past in the rain, each driver winding down a window to hear me explain, from my soaked and supine position, what was happening. At last a Ranger arrived in a Land Rover. He got out, never said a word, came and had a look, went back to fetch a bolt gun, came back and shot the stag through the head. I stood up.

I said, "What happens to it now?"

He said, "All the Rangers get a venison dinner."

I managed to drive the car home, but it was wrecked. The whole event seemed to sum up my discontent with the partnership: my clients were paying in most of the money, but I wasn't getting any of it. Somehow, Ivan had turned me into an employee! I decided to quit, but did it in the wrong way, demanding that Ivan recompense me for the assets I had brought to the business. It turned into a dispute over the assets and the copyright of the Cat Tails book, which dispute Ivan had the patience and good sense to win.

Emerging from the ugly dispute, I set up an independent studio in Tunbridge Wells, and resumed my freelance business – with Slendertone the star client, as before. Simultaneously, Beverley became agitated with the intrusions and other annoyances of renting and moving, and wrote to her father asking for a lump sum from the trust fund as a deposit to buy a house. As was our wont, we went right over the top and bought The Old Rectory, a 19th century five bedroom house, with two acres of grounds, 5 minutes drive south of Tunbridge Wells. The phone number was 23524, which I remembered via the mnemonic 'two fleas fly too far'.

A Noose of Light

The Old Rectory

Landed property is both famous and infamous for carrying an emotional charge that generates nice things like family traditions, and nasty things like wars. Now, 34 years later, I don't care about any of the addresses I have called home – except The Old Rectory. Being neither sentimental nor given to nostalgia, I can now indulge in both of those emotions by just thinking of that place. It was unusual for me to feel strongly proprietorial when we moved in – but I felt it was where I *belonged*. The family had a cup of tea in the kitchen, gazing at the giant navy-blue Aga stove, and I fearlessly announced, "I am going to die here." No such luck.

I think it's important to note that I come from a dirt poor working class family living in a rented flat over a high street shop in a nondescript suburb called Welling on the old Roman road from London to Dover. I was shocked speechless in the Blitz, and I was fed powdered egg, cod liver oil, and food parcels from South Africa during post war rationing, and I didn't start to wear underpants until I turned 14, because they were an unnecessary expense. "We used to dream of underpants" is one gag the Monty Python team missed out of their 'Four Yorkshiremen' sketch.

At 14, however, I was working in a Dartford

factory which built buses. My father was an unsuccessful freelance carpenter who was clinically depressed in an age that did not acknowledge it as an illness. The only times he was happy was after he had enjoyed a few beers at the pub, and it was only then that my mother expressed strong disapproval of his behaviour. Things got a little better when my mother discovered a freak aptitude for calculating odds, and was able to get a job as a Clerk in a betting shop, and when my father grudgingly surrendered his proud status of 'self employed' to take a regular job with the town council. But I had left home before those breakthroughs happened. I also had an elder brother whom I hardly ever saw because he had been born with short hamstrings, and was semi-permanently housed in a country hospital, where he endured 13 operations on his legs before he was 12 years old.

People set great store these days upon 'spiritual journeys' of one sort or another, but I think 'material journeys' are equally important and far easier to measure. I look back from now, and see a scruffy kid with no qualifications or training in skills nor etiquette wandering into the future like a stranger in a strange land. From my impoverished home and my hard graft factory I journeyed to a messenger job in the West End of London, where I learned to catch taxis and fiddle expenses. From there I ascended to the status of a Junior Artist who observed and imitated Beatnik style. From there, the Joseph Campbell 'Call to the Quest' occurred, which placed me in Newquay and the psychodynamics of group hysteria – from which I retreated into a rebound marriage and a modest household furnished in the 60s

A Noose of Light

style. At each step along the way, our hero had been observing and comparing styles! Comparing them with the non-style of his familial abode. In the West End I had been an avid window shopper at Liberty's, Aquascutum, John Lewis, Selfridges, Harrods, Heal's – soaking up all that which the gods of style approved. So when I walked into Beverley's studio on that first night, it hit me: this is the stuff! Most of it Beverley had picked up cheap from the Portobello Road market: there was a solid square dining table, comfortably, authentically, pitted and patinated; there were the rush-seated dining chairs, each one different; there were the richly patterned Persian shawls on the daybed, and kilims on the floor; there was the hand made clay Spanish teapot, with matching sugar bowl and jug that Beverley had brought back from a painting holiday in Spain – together with the bright Majolica plates holding the black bread, and large bowls holding fruit. And there were the tall brass candle sticks with the tall white candles shedding the soft light of the angels over all. This was style as an expression of herself; disregarding the style of the times, such as my marital home's spindle-legged tattiness and garish chessboard fitted carpet. And the music: 15th century English love songs sung by a counter tenor; Mahler's 'Songs of the Earth'; Vivaldi's 'Four Seasons'; Chaliapin's earthquake Russian bass; Polish girls soprano folk choir. Maybe my beatnik friends were right? If a 'black witch' had set things up to ensnare me, she could not have done better.

It was a *material* revelation, not only in terms of my happy conversion to frequent sexual activity, but also to a domestic style that I adopted forever, and all our homes thenceforth accorded with it. Of all these homes, before and after, The Old Rectory was the house made for it.

Gabriel was doing well at his grammar school, but Nathaniel was not finding academic learning at his primary school so easy. The 11+ exam was fast approaching, and his teachers advised that he would not be streamed into grammar school. We visited the secondary modern establishments in our area, and did not like what we saw. What to do? Beverley and I sat Nat down and told him the facts, then we asked him how he would feel about becoming a Prep School Boy. That is, to go to 'Public School' – which in England, of course, means 'Private School'. Fortunately, Nat had read some of George MacDonald Fraser's 'Flashman' novels, and he took to the idea of the boarding school quite enthusiastically. Once again, his grandfather subsidised the Tunbridge family, and Nat was enrolled in the oldest English Preparatory School, Temple Grove, near Eastbourne, East Sussex. Nat was nine, then, so it must have been 1979 or 1980.

Our weekend visits to Langton Green carried on, but I met with Shah less than before. My ex-partner Ivan had taken over some of the work I used to do for Octagon Press. It is odd, I know we lived at The Old Rectory for about four years, but memories of specific events are few. I remember Beverley's father and step mother visited the new house during one of their global circumnavigations, bringing a friend of theirs who was an English Lord. When they arrived, we met them at the front door, and grandad Ben immediately asked where the boys were. He was slightly put out because they were not all lined up there to greet him. I just said that they were upstairs playing Dungeons and Dragons. Once again I had muffed the correct paternal ritual.

At Langton, after the fallout shelter installation came the Takia installation. It was decided that a certain room in the Alhambra Palace at Granada should be reproduced on the back lawn. I took no part in it, but heard that this octagonal room had been used as a Sufi meeting and worship hall. An architect went to the Alhambra and measured the room up, then reproduced it as eight moulded fibreglass segments which fitted together as a free standing fibreglass structure: the inside boarded floor about 10 metres wide, and the pointed ceiling about 4 metres high. Around the outside were 8 windows featuring geometric patterns of wood blocks sandwiched between sheets of transparent fibre glass. It is doubly noteworthy because I did not know anything about the planning nor the construction of the Takia, but one morning I woke up at The Old Rectory seeing a hypnogogic vision, sharp as a tack, of hands placing wood blocks into an octagonal pattern. About a week later, I was shown the Takia, and realised I had experienced an example of 'viewing from a distance'. I went inside with a few others, and we experimented testing the acoustics of the space, pacing around, clapping and shouting. So far as I knew, and now know, that was the only use to which the building was ever put. But then again, perhaps I was simply not included in the Takia group.

It was during this period, also, that Shah asked me to draw his portrait. He did not like how he turned out in photographs and thought I might be able to do an alternative image for his book jackets. He was sitting at his desk in the study while I sketched. After a while he said that he was "Seeing something", and seemed quite pleased. He said he "Hadn't had one of these things for a long time." He was calmly gazing at the wall while he reported what he was seeing. He was watching a 19th century family who lived in a big house. They were "well to do", with the mother in a smart gown and the kids in knickerbockers. They were active spiritualists, who often held seances with their friends. Unknown to them, however, their home was being used for "real activity". There was a Victorian style gazebo in the garden which was used as a meeting place for........Shah did not say, but I gathered that he was referring to people who were disencumbered by physical bodies. Then the scene he was seeing changed. Shah was now watching a man who was dressed as a tourist, with a beige jacket equipped with lots of pockets. The man had a camera and a satchel strapped over his shoulders, and he was standing with other tourists in front of an edifice, a sculpture shaped like a bull's horns. The man knew what to do, and ran forward, his bag and camera flapping. Then the scene changed again. Shah was seeing a young man, an artist. He was dressed in a sheepskin waistcoat, and he had made a sculpture: a beautiful head of an angel. Then a barbarian came and smashed the head to bits, and the sorrowful young man "went off to live out the rest of his life somewhere." Shah seemed in no way concerned about the fate of the young man, nor that of the Victorian family or the flapping tourist. I asked him

A Noose of Light

what the visions meant, and he said he didn't know. He didn't seem concerned about that, either.

32 years later, I told this story to Nat, and he immediately said, "The one with the angel's head: was he talking about Gabriel?" I said, "Maybe." If Shah was just candidly revealing to me that he sometimes accessed the dream state while awake, the various and conflicting rules of dream interpretation would apply – and one of the 'rules' has always been that of divination. Either that, or the Guardians of the Tradition were using him as a medium. Either that, or he just made it all up – but why would he do that?

My memories of this period are fragmented and non-linear so, for the sake of honesty, I'll just report them as they occur to me.

Beverley and I heard that all the group members had been issued with a little white drop-shaped object, like an elongated pearl. They were instructed to keep this artifact on them at all times, but to *not* put it on a string, or make it into an earring or bracelet or brooch; to in fact not do *anything* with it but carry it all the time, night and day. We were not issued with it, and it was only many years later that I heard of all the difficulties members had following the instructions. Some thought these difficulties were the purpose of the artifact; that it was an aid to self-remembering, a reminder of their connection to Shah and the Sufis. Like everything else about Shah, nothing was ever conclusively resolved. He was ever the embodiment of Nasruddin.

There was a fancy dress New Year's party held at Langton in the Elephant-In-The-Dark communal dining room. Once again we were outclassed by the standard of costume worn by fellow guests. There was a head-to-toe Ostrich outfit that slowly paced around all night. Whoever was in it must have been a professional because his body was bent double for hours. His legs encased in orange tights, he manipulated the neck and head to stare at guests for uncomfortably long periods. There was also a very tall 'monk' hooded all in black, and wearing a black mask with a flashing green strobe light in the middle of his forehead. He, too, liked to stand and stare at guests (especially me, it seemed) for long periods. I did not know how to respond, except to fatuously raise my glass and say, "Good evening, sir". I would rise to the challenge much better nowadays, I swear, and probably cause him some discomfort – perhaps by emptying an ice bucket on his flashing green head! Such were the emotions raised 35 years ago which linger still. And then there were the belly dancers: buxom disguised girls with veiled heads and unveiled bosoms, bent on embarrassing the unenlightened in other ways. There were several of these extravagant parties, and fares on Langton Green in these years, and the fact is that neither Beverley nor I enjoyed any of them. It seemed to us always that everyone knew what was going on, and how to enjoy it, but us. The best I could ever do was to contribute manfully to the management via sign-painting and leaflet printing, etc. Despite my creative usefulness in other arenas, in the company of Nasruddin, I was ever a drone. Mister B felt the same way: in 1969, he ruefully commented to one of his 'Fellows', "I am very serious about The Work, but Mr Shah treats it like a joke!"

A Noose of Light

Circulating among the tents and coconut shies, and donkey rides on Langton Green itself, during a fund-raising fare for Afghanistan, I thought to *join in the nonsense* by visiting a fortune teller's tent. I sat down before the veiled 'Gypsy' within, and dutifully held out my hand for divination. Halfway through the 'reading', the back fabric of the tent lifted, and Shah's wife Kashvi, closely accompanied by other giggling females, stuck her head in and asked the Gypsy, loudly, if my liking for "kinky sex" showed on my hand. It happened that I *did* like kinky sex, but how did Kashvi know? And how could I deal with at least six giggling women after such exposure? At another New Year's party I decided to unwind or liberate myself via alcohol, and ended up dancing by myself in the middle of the floor while everyone else pretended not to notice. I suppose we can't help being ourselves.

Then came the Saturday night when Shah held forth after dinner about his enthusiasm for the Afghans – who were then fighting the Russian invaders. About 50 dinner guests silently attended as he went on and on about the Mujahideen's resourcefulness and courage, until I felt obliged to put in a modifying comment. I interrupted Shah to mention the Afghan's terrible treatment of women, history of endless tribal warfare, and woeful infant mortality rate. In response, Shah contemptuously abused me for about a half hour, calling me a worm, not even half-baked, not even quarter-baked, any dog can bark, etc., etc. When Shah left, everything carried on as usual. Nobody commented on the explosion. Beverley was silent in the car driving home. I think we both may have been in a state of shock. We went to bed, and I switched off the light and lay there thinking about the event. Then I felt an impulse to lay on my right side and to do a simple breathing exercise in order to settle my thoughts. Quite distinctly, and without fear or fuss, I became aware that I was being helped to focus on thought suppression. I remembered Rumi writing that he envied the concentration of the cat staring at a mousehole, and recognised that I, too, was staring at a mousehole in my mind: the mousehole from which thoughts were emerging. Every time a thought began to emerge, I was helped to erase it: I was shown how to do it. There was a more powerful will than my own in my mind. Pretty soon, no more thoughts were emerging, and a grey mist began to gather, absorbing my awareness without fuss or fear. I vanished into the grey mist for a while, then slowly reemerged. Then, of course, I did the wrong thing: I turned my attention away from the mousehole and directed it experimentally toward Beverley. I wanted to see if the dissolution had left me with enhanced powers of perception. The 'helper' silently expressed disapproval and broke the connection. Make what you will of that. I've done my best to report it as straightforwardly as possible. Why did I not report it to Shah? Why did I not confirm the experience as authentic by making an appointment to see Shah, and telling him what happened? Because I thought the silent helper *was* Shah, and I did not know how to go to him and ask 'were you inside my brain last night?' There was the possibility that the torrent of abuse he had directed at me had desta-bilised me into an hypno-gogic hallucination. There is a level of Sufi development called 'Certainty', and I now think that this event may have been when I lost the chance of reaching it.

We were having trouble with our son Gabriel. He had become friends with a boy from his Grammar school, and we thought this boy was a problem. We thought he might have a degree of autism or Asperger's, because he would never make eye contact with us, and he virtually ignored everything we said to him. Gabriel and he, however, would spend hours talking and sniggering together. We could not understand why Gabriel favoured this boy over his other friends who were open, polite and intelligent. We told ourselves that this sort of thing should be expected at the onset of adolescence, and waited for it to improve. It didn't. Gabriel told us that he did not want to continue at the Grammar school, or to work towards a place at university. He wanted to switch to art school studies. His Headmaster and Form master were very disappointed, and asked me to meet them for a discussion. I told them I did not see how I could force him to continue if his heart was not in it any more. What I did not know then was that Gabriel's new friend had introduced him to cannabis, and the rot had set in.

Gabriel switched to an arts course at the West Kent College, and was there for a year, but then the council discovered that he lived in Eridge, just outside the Tunbridge Wells education area, so he had to switch again to a Sussex school, The Beacon at Crowborough, and then, for forgotten reasons, to a Foundation course at Hastings Art College. We found a bedsit for him in Hastings with other students. He was 17, a little younger than the age I had been when I hitched down to Cornwall, so I wasn't worried. I thought that he would get the start in the arts which I never had. But the trouble had just begun. Within a year we were hearing that he was not turning up at classes. He became interested in photography and film making, however, and we were given new hope when he showed us a short movie and a series of photographs he had made. The course ended and he came to live at home again and we talked about finding him a job. He wanted to get into film production, but he had no qualifications. So I suggested he get a list of some London film companies, and write to them offering himself as a student for work experience. It wasn't long before he had landed a job as a messenger boy for a small company in Soho. In between messages, he was allowed to watch how movies were made in the Editing Suite. I thought we had cracked it, but after six months they told him not to come in any more. Apparently he had been drawing unflattering cartoons of all the staff on the notice board.

Meanwhile Nathaniel had left Temple Grove Prep School and graduated to Sevenoaks School, continuing his public school education – thanks to his fee-paying grandfather, Ben Green. I hope that one day Nat will write his own memoir about this period, because I have a shattered recollection of it.

One of these recollections is of a tramp that turned up at the front door of the Old Rectory one summer Sunday afternoon. I answered the doorbell, and saw a bizarre creature standing in the drive, looking sideways at me. He addressed me in an exaggerated Irish accent, "Top of the mornin' to ya sor, and could yer spare a cop a tay?" I immediately recognised Omar, Shah's brother, dressed in a pantomime tramp's outfit, and said that I'd bring him a cup of tea right away. Bringing the tea, I sat down with him and gazed out at the road, trying to think of the right thing to say. Miraculously, I remembered that the right thing to say to someone you think may be a Sufi was, 'where have you come from, and where are you going?' So I said this, I said, "Where have you come from and where are you going?" The tramp gestured dumbly down the road, and then gestured up the road. I couldn't think of anything else to say. Here was Omar in disguise: what the hell was I supposed to do? I sat beside him silently for quite a while, re-observing his Shah complexion and Shah brown eyes, then I went back inside to discuss the issue with Beverley, but she was silent. I think she was confronted by it, and she always answered confrontation with silence. When I went outside, he had gone, so I jumped in the car and drove down the road toward Tunbridge Wells. Sure enough, there he was striding along, his trouser legs flapping. I did not like to interrupt his performance, so I turned and went home.

At the Old Rectory we had two Burmese cats, a blue and a brown, called Blue and Brown. Every night they would venture out of the cat flap in the back door, and go hunting across the Kentish countryside. In the mornings we would come downstairs to find the back corridor filled, end to end, with a butcher's shop of dismembered creatures: baby rabbits, all that was left were their eyeballs and kidneys; Rats, similarly; nameless voles. One night I was actually awakened around 3am by a loud banging which echoed through the house. I went downstairs and along the corridor to the back door, and there were Blue and Brown (I do not exaggerate) both tugging mightily on the neck of a full-grown pheasant. The head and neck was the only part which fitted through the cat flap, and both cats were trying to pull the whole fat pheasant through. Soon after, Blue and Brown did not come home. After a few days I went calling for them along the hedgerows and fields at the back of our property. There I was calling and whistling at the edge of a field overlooking some woodland, when a bucolic face and figure emerged from the shrubbery like a pagan pixie. I addressed him, asking if he had seen a couple of cats around the place. He smiled at me, as if wondering if I was serious, and denied all knowledge of any cats. Next day, the very next day, I drove home from my office in Tunbridge Wells, and I saw two bodies laying across the centerline of the road exactly outside the entrance to my house. It was Blue and Brown, dead, strangled. The wire was still around their necks. It was only then that we discovered that our garden abutted at the rear to the Estate of Lord Abergavenny, the Master of the Queen's Horse, whose gamekeepers had murdered our pussycats. There was nothing we could do. We buried them, amid tears, under the Giant Sequoia on our lawn.

Not because of this, but during the same three-year period, I became emotionally unstable. First I became anxious: I would walk up and down the living room wondering what I felt anxious about. I couldn't think of anything! I went through the list again and again: the family, the house, Shah, the bank, my parents – but everything was okay! I couldn't stand it any more. I jumped in the car and drove South, not going anywhere. Around Sherbourne I pulled into a hotel and checked in for the night, and ordered dinner. Halfway through dinner, the waiter brought a phone over. It was Beverley. She had tracked all the hotels on the A30 and rung them up one after the other until she found me. Then I became frustrated at Beverley's reluctance to make new friends. I wanted to go out and socialise, but she preferred to stay in glum retreat. The only people she wanted to see were people connected to Shah. I found her glum silence infuriating. I said she was poisoning my life, and threw a whiskey bottle at the kitchen dresser, shattering the majolica plates and traumatising the boys, who sat listening outside the kitchen. Then I became depressed: I would sit at the dining table motionless and silent while Beverley made the dinner. Beverley would say, "You seem very depressed," which made me more depressed. The power of depression is that it feels like the truth. You feel that all the delusions which sustained you have been removed and that what you are seeing and feeling is the real truth that was there all along. The real hopeless, staring, deathly truth. This is the difference between my 'super effort' enhanced awareness experienced at Coombe Springs, and this pathological 'version': the former did not engage the mechanisms of mood variation. I made an appointment with a psychiatrist, but the day before the appointment, the depression blew away like a dark cloud. I kept the appointment nonetheless, and saw a pleasant dark-eyed man at the local Nuffield medical centre. I told him my story, and he said, "You are the third person this week to come in here and say it all blew away like a dark cloud." I also saw the local GP, who prescribed some antidepressants and told me not to drink so much. Neither named the condition 'manic-depression', which later psychiatrists diagnosed as 'bi-polar'. Perhaps that was because naming scary illnesses to patients was considered unhelpful in those days.

I was awakened one night by a powerful dream: Beverley was being flushed away down a storm drain, and I heard her cheerful voice calling, "Alan, remember me?" It was the cheerful voice of our first years together. I got up and went down to the kitchen. She was sitting at the dining table. I said I was sorry.

Beverley and I decided we were suffering from stress and needed a holiday, so we booked a flight to Tunisia. We had a camel ride into the desert, and a coach trip down to an abandoned full-sized Roman arena called 'Gem'. It was the size of Rome's Colosseum, but standing all alone in the middle of nothing. I took along some Octagon Press books on Sufi lore. It was no good, we returned as estranged as when we left. We decided that part of the problem was that we could not afford to live in the Old Rectory. There was stuff needed doing to the floors and the roof and the old coach house around the back that was just about falling down. We could not afford any of it. I used to crawl into the cavernous roof space and push my penknife into the beams. They were like polystyrene, or I thought they were. I was no timber expert. We put the house on the market, and I started to show people around – always carefully pointing out that the great beam over the coach house doors was rotten, and in fact it was the doors alone which were holding the goddamned beam up. Despite this, the buyer was almost killed after purchase when he ventured to open the coach house doors.

We moved to a far more sensible and newer and cheaper house on the North side of Tunbridge Wells Common, and became regular hosts for the Langton Green Story Telling Club. This institute-inspired initiative encompassed a weekly group meeting to recite Sufi stories. A Langton member, Pat Williams, also managed a tape cassette recording series called Seminar Cassettes, for whom I contributed as a storyteller.

The house had a double garage, half of which I converted into a studio for me, and a space where Nathaniel could practice his drum kit. Once again I neglected my business whenever possible to come home and try to paint pictures.

But it wasn't enough. The guts had fallen out of everything. Everyone had heard all the stories, and there were no new ones. All the books were like convoluted labyrinths which led you on page after page and then left you staring at a blank wall. Why should we desire new stuff when Shah said that the old stuff was all we needed? Everyone else seemed content to jog along with the routine, but we were consumed with restlessness. Shah used to say, "My job is to bore you to death!" I felt he had succeeded, but now what? There came a time when I was sitting in Shah's study, talking about books of divination, and he gave me one such book – by Rumi, as I remember. He told me to open it at random and read the first paragraph I saw. I did, and the paragraph said that if I did not adopt the gentle nature of the dove, I would suffer the 'cauterie' (the cauterization applied to a severed limb). I thought this was true. I had become impatient and aggressive with the Work, with the system, with my family, with myself. Shah looked over my shoulder to see what the book had divined, but he didn't say anything. I remembered then that he had mentioned something like this a while ago. So far as I know, Shah never gave direct instruction to anyone about the Work, but that time he had specifically told me to "abstain from excitement." I was unable to abstain from excitement. In daily practice, excitement was creativity: I had to get enthusiastic about an idea in order to devote the energy and time required to realise it as a painting, a press advertisement, a song, whatever. I did not know how to work in any other way. But perhaps the truth was that I was not willing to try any other way. Later on, when I consulted a Sydney psychiatrist about my bipolarity, he prescribed Lithium. I wrote to him after I had tried it for a few weeks to explain that I could not take it as it killed my creativity. This is not an uncommon complaint of bipolar patients – even of relatively low severity, 'artistic temperament' ones like me.

And then came the time early in 1986 when Beverley and I were sitting in the 'Durbar' room adjacent to Shah's study. I don't remember why we were there.

A Noose of Light

Shah was at the other end of the room talking to another couple. I don't remember why we were waiting for him. Suddenly he looked over at us, broke away from the other couple, walked over and held out his hand to me. He shook my hand and said, "No hard feelings!.....No hard feelings!"

It was a dismissal, and we never saw Shah again.

In 2013, Oliver Hoare kindly sent me a copy of his memoir 'The Steganographer 6'. Published in 2011, it records his own and his mother's long experience as trusted group members and confidantes of Idries and Omar Shah. I had very little contact with Oliver at Langton Green, so receiving the book came as a pleasant surprise. A decade or so earlier I had developed a personal web site featuring my paintings and songs, and included a brief written account of my years with Bennett and Shah. I think it was this online mini-memoir which Oliver had stumbled upon and which had inspired him to send me his book.

Oliver's memoir confirmed that Beverley and I, though frequent attendees at Langton during the 60s, 70s and 80s, had been peripheral members, disconnected from the more intensive activities of the London groups, and from the even more intensive activities of the South American groups managed by Shah's brother Omar, called 'Agha' – with whom Oliver and his mother Irina were particularly involved. Oliver's memoir is a fascinating and revealing report on the Gurdjieff-Bennett-Shah transmission spanning his father's contact with John Bennett in Turkey in 1922, through the shocking split of the brothers and the groups into two mutually exclusive regimes, to the controversial continuance of the teaching under the aegis of Omar's son Arif in 2011, after Idries and Omar had died.

I can but wonder that while I was frequently meeting Shah in his study to progress his publishing design projects, and Beverley and I were peacefully attending Langton Green on 18 year's worth of weekends, deadly schisms were occurring in the groups, members were enjoying chaotic overseas tours to Sufi shrines, and intimate secrets were being whispered to favoured disciples at bacchanalian Brazilian parties. We knew nothing about it! If all that is what Oliver witnessed and reported, heaven knows what else was afoot behind the scenes and between the lines. I sent him this section of the text, and he mildly objected to the term "bacchanalian", so I herewith amend it to 'heavy drinking'. Further, as at Coombe Springs the rule was silence and secrecy about all activities. The group structure resembled a network of espionage cells, each 'controlled' by Shah or Omar, and none of which knew what the others were doing. I think it is significant that, despite this, Oliver has decided to break out and expose these goings on to the degree he has. I cannot decide if I am resentful or relieved to have been excluded from all the trips and theatrics and sudden transcendent states. Okay, I'm resentful. Beverley and I would have enjoyed that.

It is absolutely true that Shah spent a lot of energy decrying 'cult behaviour', and 'conditioning', and talking and writing disparagingly about 'gurus'.

He used to say that if he wanted slaves he could have got a million of them in India, and that he was only interested in teaching people who were well set up with stable jobs and families, so that they had 'spare capacity' for studying his ideas. But any outsider guest attending one of the Saturday dinners in 'The Elephant' at Langton House would be hard put to distinguish the behaviour of the assembly from that of any other cult leader. Indeed, Shah's wife Kashfi disliked the reverent atmosphere so much that she very rarely attended. Shah himself, according to Oliver, viewed his attendance at these dinners as an arduous burden, but acknowledged that they were necessary for the retention and sustainability (that fashionable word) of the group. As some wag quipped, "I know we should focus on the content, but it's nice to see the vessel once in a while."

As someone who saw the vessel quite often, I am convinced that Shah was as special a personage as any of the historical Sufi leaders he wrote about. Oliver's mother sometimes thought they, the Shah brothers, were more than human, and could disassemble themselves at will and switch bodies. But I hold that they were as human as any other group leader in this field – including religious leaders – who, while equipped with extraordinary abilities, were also subject to very human limitations and obstacles.

Shah's seminal book 'The Sufis' lists many of the revered teachers of 'The Tradition', along with their distinguishing characteristics. Further reading reveals just how different these teachers and their teachings were. There were Jelaludin Rumi's 'Whirling Dervishes' with their dance, Abdullah Shattar's 'Shattari' school and their 'Lightning Quick' method, Ahmad al Rifa'i's 'Howling Dervishes', who practised snake charming and self-mutilation, and many others. Following the style of this tradition, we might say that Idries Shah was the leader of the 'Story-Telling' Dervishes, and that his brother Omar Shah led the 'Partying Dervishes'. Certainly, even the quickest review of the Sufi schools reveals that just about every possible human activity has been employed as a method for achieving ecstatic states and/or transcendent consciousness. And I dare say we can say something similar about Christian saints, Hindu gurus and Buddhist monks.

As for 'supernatural powers', I know with as much certainty as I know anything that Shah possessed abilities which science has not categorised yet. These so called psychic or paranormal abilities are now subject to respectable scientific research, following general acceptance of the link between quantum mechanical theory and consciousness studies. Shah was extremely parsimonious with them, and indeed reluctant to expose his people to any. He told me that he had damaged someone once, so he had to be careful. I believe that this reluctance was the source of the split between the brothers. Shah was afraid of risking the mental stability of his people by involving them in energy-loaded Sufi exercises such as anyone can nowadays see on YouTube. Omar wanted to let it rip: to prescribe exercises and energetic exciting events, and let the chips fall where they may. It is not coincidental, I surmise, that he became an alcoholic at this time. So far as I know, the fibreglass copy of the octagonal Alhambra Takia, so expensively erected in the Langton House garden, was never used as a venue for such exercises, nor did Shah ever conduct the prolonged dhikr or dance rituals associated with Sufi exercises. But then again, I was only a peripheral member of the Langton assembly, so much may have been happening without my knowledge. Oliver Hoare is the only fellow student out of hundreds who has decided to write about his own and his parents' experiences with the Shah brothers. In this sense the whole movement was operated as a secret society, and most surviving members remain silent.

What we can say for sure is that Shah always claimed that his task was to introduce and distribute information and inspiration about Sufi history and practices across the Western world. This he achieved magnificently. What he achieved in terms of the personal development of his individual followers is in-finitely more complicated, and perhaps will always be impossible to define – because it's impossible for any of his followers (including me) to know what would have happened to them if they had not followed him.

What happened after Gurdjieff's death and Bennett's death and Shah's death was what happens after every death of every spiritual leader: the pupils either return to normal life, or become shrine keepers, or become second-hand leaders themselves (there's even a Sufi story about this, called 'The Soup of the Duck'). But these second-hand leaders are no bad thing, because each new generation rises up needing the support and visionary outlet that their parents needed, so it's necessary and good that the old story is rehashed in new ways. The noose of light continues to catch the Sultan's turret every morning.

Having been through all that I have reported in this memoir, I have humbly accepted the ultimate outrage: that I do not know what or whom I would have become had I not lived the life I have lived.

Like all of us, I must be content with that.

Australia

For a whole package of reasons we decided to emigrate to Australia in 1986. We needed a fresh start. The marriage and my business and our social life and Langton life had grown stale. Gabriel also needed a fresh start. He needed to leave all his negative experiences behind him. Nathaniel was the only one who might be disadvantaged by such a move, but we spoke to him about it and he complied democratically with the family majority vote. We told him we would get him into a Sydney school equivalent to Sevenoaks. We helped Gabriel to complete the application form for entry into the Australian Film & Television School. As part of the application, he had to enclose a sample reel of his work, and this was his short 'symbolist' movie called 'The Sorrows of the King' – featuring moody shots of his girlfriend. We waited for the Sydney school's response before progressing our emigration. The sample reel found favour, but Gabriel was required to be in Sydney for interview on a particular date. This meant that he would have to travel ahead of us, because we had the house to sell and other arrangements to make.

Then we found out that Beverley was no longer an Australian citizen! We were told by Australia House in London that she, along with every ex-pat Aussie in the world, had been notified in 1976 that they had to renew their passports to comply with a new system. Beverley had failed to do so, because prior to that date we had taken out a joint British passport, and she had not considered it necessary to renew her Aussie one. Unbelievably, our family position vis-a-vis emigration was that both boys could enter Australia and claim citizenship because their mother was born there, but their mother could not, neither could their father. The only way out was to apply f or Aussie emigration via the 100 point system. Fortunately we would have a bank balance in excess of $200,000 after the house sale, so we could be fast tracked. But we still had to attend Australia House and watch incredibly boring and blurry movies 'Introducing Australia' – sitting side by side with whole families from India, Yemen and Rhodesia. If I was not an elitist snob before that, I was after.

Beverley had an old school friend called Val, who had married a soldier who had ascended to the rank of Commander of the ADF force based opposite The Heads at Sydney Harbour. One of the perks was a splendid house at Camp Cove opposite the base, which had a private stair and gate access direct to the beach, which became a personal playground for the two teenage daughters and a son. This is where Gabriel stayed while awaiting his interview, and the arrival of his family. We too eventually arrived at this house on Boxing Day 1986, and we all stood on the balcony enjoying a million dollar view of the start of the Sydney–Hobart Yacht Race. Coming straight from an English winter into a blazing Aussie summer, we were a bit shell shocked with the ravishing

A Noose of Light

scene: the giant yachts racing by, the media helicopters hovering, flocks of gorgeous parakeets squawking in the trees, enormous crowds yelling their heads off. I sipped my champagne, and asked mine host, "Jeesus, do you get this all the time?"

"Aaaaall the time," said the Brigadier General, straight faced.

We decided to take a tour before we settled down. Our household effects were in a container on a slow boat, and would not arrive for many weeks. Gabriel would receive his interview results in a month, and Nathaniel was content to delay his return to school for a while. I bought a big Holden station wagon, and we set off on a road trip, first up to Surfers Paradise to visit Grandad Ben and Edith, then inland to Goondiwindi, then all the way down the A39, past Coonabarabran, Dubbo and all points to Melbourne, where we stayed with Beverley's brother and family in Toorak. We learned how big and empty was Australia, and how much we preferred Sydney to Melbourne as a home base. I did not like the purpose-built grid-pattern streets of the latter, and preferred the organically developed, goat track formation of the older colony – along with the harbour, of course.

When we returned to the Camp Cove house, Val had a quiet word to Beverley. It seemed that before our arrival Gabriel had tried to persuade the younger daughter to run away with him, up North to Queensland. Val thought it would be better for us to rent furnished accommodation while we waited for our effects to arrive. This we did, finding a large third floor flat in Rose Bay. From that temporary base we obtained an interview with Mr Mackerras, the headmaster of Sydney Grammar School. We took Nat along, and Mr Mackerras seemed a bit nonplussed at our direct approach. He politely told us that parents signed up their male offspring *at birth* for a place at the school. Nevertheless he talked to Nat about his Temple Grove and Sevenoaks schools, and then announced that it so happened there had arisen a vacancy in a form suiting Nat's age, and that he could start immediately.

Beverley and I celebrated by booking seats at Sydney Opera House to see a performance of 'Carmen' – my favourite opera. The opening scene looked marvellous, with the girls swirling and singing outside the tobacco factory, waiting, like us, for Carmen to appear. Then a veritable *coup de theatre* happened. Instead of sizzling Carmen making her entrance, a little dwarf walked on! Well, not quite a dwarf, but she could not have topped five feet tall. I was blown away. I laughed out loud. What a triumph of staging! My elation began to crumble, however, when the 'real Carmen' continued *not* to arrive, and the dwarf started singing. Oh god no! She's trying to do some flamenco steps! Yes, this dowdy little woman was supposed to be Carmen! I was outraged. I walked out, and poor Beverley had to follow.

Waiting for our slow boat to arrive, I rented a ramshackle studio space and spent every week day trying to paint pictures. I was on another side of the planet in a country I had never been to before, and in circumstances I had never experienced before, so I thought the

A Noose of Light

new environment might allow the magic to happen that would transform me into a professional and fine artist. As in Spain, it did not happen. Who was it who said that insanity was repeating the same thing over and over again hoping for a different result?

Gabriel's application to the Sydney Film and TV School was refused. I asked him what had happened at the interview, and gathered that he had been interrogated by the examining panel on his knowledge of and enthusiasm for the cinematographic art, and had been found inadequate on both counts. I was disappointed and baffled: one of the major motives for our move to Australia had been to provide a better career opportunity for him, and that opportunity had now been wasted. We had been prepared to pay the fees for his choice of college education, and now the college had rejected him. He was 21 years old, and yet had no interest or enthusiasm for anything, except passive listening to rock music. How long would this 'difficult adolescence' go on?

To add to our confusion, the Sydney property market started to boom, and we realised that we had to buy a house quickly. We settled for a four-story, three bedroom terrace in the inner Sydney harbourside suburb of Woolloomooloo. The purchase drained our bank account, so I had to get a job. I was 47 years old with no contacts or professional history in Australia, and no employment record with any UK employer, because I had been freelance there for the last 25 years. Fortunately, our slow boat arrived and delivered my portfolio, so I was able to take my graphic design and advertising samples around a number of Sydney ad agencies. One of them asked me to do a job which none of their resident artists knew how to do: a 2-metre tall fibreboard cutout display unit of the Opera House, with a bank deposit account rate attached. The agency offered me one of their empty desks as a rent-free freelance space, and within a few months asked me to join the staff.

So there we were again. We renovated our house nicely, installed our container load of furniture, and settled down to life in Sydney. I had a good job, Nat had a good school, and Beverley even got a job as a part-time picture researcher for the local Readers Digest office. Gabriel had decided he was interested in sound recording and had landed himself a job as assistant to the Manager of a local studio called 'The Paradise'. He learned how to operate the 38-track recorder and was soon promoted to manage the night shift, when amateur bands rented the studio at a cheaper rate. The moving finger seemed to have written us a nice little life. What could possibly go wrong?

Schizophrenia

It is quite impossible to convey the emotional content of the real events reported in this section of the memoir, so I am not going to try. Later on, I met many parents of sons and daughters who developed the illness called schizophrenia, and all of them said the same thing: they had never suspected that such a hellishly horrible thing could happen to any family – let alone their own family.

Gabriel got fired from his job at the recording studio because he had forgotten to lock the doors one night when he left. Consequently it was just luck that the million dollar equipment was still there in the morning. The reason why he had forgotten was that he had been smoking cannabis with the rock group using the studio that night. This dismissal was the start of a behavioural decline which eventually resembled a sort of autism. Nothing we said or did seemed to get through to him. He stopped talking to his parents and his brother. He slept all day and stayed up all night. He often woke us up when he ran up and down the stairs, intent upon some project he would not tell us about. One morning, in desperation after he had ignored repeated requests to get out of bed, I emptied a bucket of water over him. It did no good.

The crisis came when he took to giggling to

himself at dinner. Beverley repeatedly asked him to share the joke, but he just carried on giggling. His brother Nat lost his temper and lashed out at his brother across the table. That was the last straw for me. I told Gabriel I was going to put his stuff in a suitcase and throw him out of the house. He followed me up stairs to his room, and watched me as I stuffed clothes into a suitcase.

Suddenly he said, "You are not my father." I stared at him, and he said, "You used to be my father but you aren't any more."

As I stared at him, a breeze blew in the open window and lifted a lock of his hair, shaping it momentarily into a question mark over his head. It dawned on me then that my son was mentally ill. Up to that moment we thought the trouble was an expression of a particularly difficult adolescence. But everything changed when I realised he was not just *acting* crazy, he *was* crazy. I took him back downstairs, and sat him back at the table with Beverley and Nat. I asked him why he thought I was not his father, and it all came out.

He had been staying up all night receiving messages from the TV set in the kitchen-dining room. The messages came through the detuned white fuzz on the screen, and were being transmitted to him from a particular planet far away across the galaxy. On this planet was a committee of beings who were instructing him what to do. He had been born into the world to do a special job, which was to help save the world from the Devil. He gave detailed information about the planet and the committee and the task he was destined to complete. I asked him who the Devil was, and he said,

"Burt Lancaster."

We made an appointment to consult a psychiatrist, and took Gabriel along. The psychiatrist seemed to think Gabriel was pretending, and questioned him aggressively. He prescribed some medication, and gave us the phone number of the 'crisis team' attached to the local psychiatric hospital. We went home none the wiser, hoping that the crisis, whatever it was, had peaked. Gabriel did not want to take the medication, so I swallowed one of the pills to show it was okay. Gabriel took the prescribed dose, and an hour or so later became very anxious. He said he felt very weak and afraid, and begged me not to leave him. I said I would never leave him, and he drifted off to sleep.

I don't remember what happened after that, but Gabriel must have relapsed within a week or two. I remember phoning the crisis team one night, and being surprised when a police car, not an ambulance, arrived. The police stayed outside while a doctor and a male nurse came inside and interviewed Gabriel while we sat with him at the dining room table. His answers to the questionnaire satisfied the criteria, and I heard the doctor say that Gabriel had schizophrenia and must be hospitalised immediately. It was the first time the word schizophrenia had been used. Gabriel heard it, too. I saw him edge towards the stairs, and knew he was going to run for it. I stood in his way, and told him it wouldn't be for long. He was escorted to the police car and driven off. I can't remember if we followed to see him checked in to the hospital.

That night I went to bed, but could not sleep.

While I stared into the darkness, Gabriel came in the door and walked over to my side of the bed and put his little hand my forehead. He was about eight years old, and he said, "There, there. I'll just have to stay here now, that's all." It was a hypnogogic vision, but quite real for all that. It helped me deal with what was to come.

We went to see him in the hospital next morning. The staff had very little time for us, but said that he would be discharged in three days, and gave us a handful of pamphlets about the Schizophrenia Fellowship carers group. We learned for the first time that we had no power or rights over our son's treatment, because he was over 18 years of age. The psychiatric hospital treated the patients' families as little more than nuisances.

Thereafter followed 15 years of coping with florid psychosis, during which Gabriel was in and out of the local psychiatric hospital and police lockup scores of times. Parents bitterly called it 'the revolving door policy', which meant that patients were arrested, 'sectioned' (that is, they were incarcerated and treated against their will), and tossed out back on the streets three days later. There was nothing we could do, because Gabriel did not want us to help, and the psyche hospital had no spare beds. If we had locked him up ourselves we would have been guilty of kidnapping.

He befriended a gang of fellow patients and drug users, and struck up a relationship with a girl patient whose parents had bought her a small flat. Gabriel moved in with her, and we rarely saw him after that. Sometimes I would make the effort to find out where he was, but it was not a task I welcomed. He was usually found in a terrible state in a terrible place with terrible people. The law gave me no rights to intervene, and was reluctant to intervene itself. Sometimes the hospital would phone me to say that Gabriel had been arrested, but that was just for me to visit and fill in a form. One time he had been arrested for throwing a burning mattress into the street from his second floor flat, another when he broke into a shop, another when he collapsed in the street. One of his more stable friends called me to say he was walking up and down the middle of the busy road between Darlinghurst and Paddington. Nat and I drove over there, and saw him raving to himself in a sidewalk cafe. We grabbed him and he fought us. We dragged him across the road to my car with Gabriel shouting for help, and Nat calling out to the rubbernecking crowd, "He's my brother! He has schizophrenia!" Someone phoned the police and a police van arrived fast with sirens blaring. The cop took one look and said, "Oh, it's just Gabby!" Then they loaded him in the cage and drove him away for yet another three-day stay in the revolving door psyche ward.

Another time, I had a call from the local general hospital, St. Vincent's. They told me that Gabriel's girlfriend had called an ambulance to her flat. The paramedics arrived to find him almost dead in bed after a stroke had paralysed half his body. The girlfriend said he had been like that for a week, but she was frightened to call anyone because of all the drugs in the house. There were no drugs in the house except for the amphetamine injection he had overdosed with. I saw him in the hospital bed, a living skeleton. A hospital officer came in and stared at me, outraged, as if to say, 'How could you let him get into this condition?' I told him to contact the psychiatric hospital for Gabriel's records. He was three months recovering from the stroke, but eventually returned to his girlfriend's flat and the street life.

Next time, he got pneumonia and the hospital phoned me to come over and calm him down. I drove to the Emergency Ward and could hear him screaming from the car park. I went in and saw that someone had resentfully scrawled 'SCHIZOPHRENIA' across his clip board in bold red magic marker.

To illustrate the almost comedic state of mental health care at that time in central Sydney, I'll recount just one more event. I received a call from Gabriel's girlfriend one night. She said that her neighbours had called the police because Gabriel was tearing up the hallway outside her front door, and making a tremendous noise. He had been acting violently, so she had locked him out. I told her that it was good, because the police would arrive with a crisis team, and Gabriel would be sectioned and taken to hospital. I had been trying to convince the psyche hospital to do this for a week because I had received reports that he was seriously unstable. The police arrived with the crisis team, and the girlfriend called me back as requested. I asked to speak to the team's doctor, explained who I was, and asked her to take him to hospital. She calmly explained that she could not do that because he did not meet the criteria. I was familiar with the criteria necessary to 'section' a patient: it stipulates that the patient must be in danger of harming himself or others, or of damaging his own reputation. I said to the doctor that the neighbours certainly thought he was in danger of harming others and/or himself.

She said, "Yes, but he is not harming his own reputation." She had calmly, coldly inverted the meaning of the criteria to avoid having to take my mad son to hospital.

All the above is a folio of snapshots from 15 years of being father to a son with schizophrenia, While all that was going on, however, other dramas were unfolding.

Divorce

It might be annoying to some readers that I continue to return to my thesis regarding the moving finger, but I don't care. This is my memoir or autobiography and I'll write it like I see it. It seems to me that my life has proceeded from one crisis point to another, with relatively calm passages in between. The rather prosaic metaphor that comes to mind is of a ship; an 18th century British Royal Navy frigate, as portrayed by my favourite writer Patrick O'Brian. There she is sailing along with flowing sheets embracing the balmy breezes, when the lookout high up on the Mizzenmast spies on the horizon a dark line of cloud punctured with lightning flashes. Captain Jack battens down the hatches and furls the sails, but it's no use. The storm arrives and all hands struggle to stay afloat in the tempest. And when things calm down again, the ship is sailing on a different course in a different sea. The point is that Captain Jack could do nothing but stay afloat. Similarly, I have thought very carefully over all such crisis points in my life, and concluded that there never really was any opportunity or likelihood of me doing anything other than what I did. Worse, there never really was any chance of anyone else involved in the crisis doing other than what they did. This indeed is the moving finger in action.

From its beginning in Beverley's Notting Hill flat, our relationship had been anchored in our shared passion for the spiritual quest. We had explored the territory together, rejected much, and chosen the path we took. I say 'chosen', but our choice was inevitable after we had seen the alternative paths. There was never any possibility of us *not* applying for residency at Coombe Springs, and never any possibility of us declining Shah's invitation to join him at Langton Green. There we entered our paradise time when all was right with our world, and we were genuinely, ingenuously puzzled that other couples could not flourish as we flourished. It was so simple! I wrote my songs, and drew my illustrations, and developed my graphic design business. Beverley looked after the boys and helped out at Langton House. We drove around Tunbridge Wells laughing, in a red MGB GT with a Dalmation in the back. Oh dear, how happy memories can hurt.

Yes, the horizon was already darkening. Little by little we became discontent, restless. Sex deprivation occurred inevitably during Beverley's second pregnancy, and I did not refuse an opportunity to embrace our 18 year-old home help Rosalind. Not that it came to anything: I was so excited that I ejaculated before I got her knickers off. Honourably and foolishly, I felt obliged to tell Beverley of this misadventure. She sacked the slender Rosalind and hired a fat, ugly girl who secretly gobbled big bags of sweets like a gigantic chipmunk. Then we moved to a bigger house at the other end of town, and continued to be discontent. Maybe if Shah had insti-tuted a weekly group exercise at Langton: some sort of head-banging dhikr? It might have provided the anchor, the weight we needed to hold us down. But there was nothing to hold on to but witty little stories we had heard before, and convoluted instructions on 'learning how to learn', and repetitive weekends at Langton with Shah trying to "bore us to death". So we had to break away. The final sail-splitting gust was my disastrous business partnership – and then the storm blew us all the way to Spain.

After a year away, we returned to have another go, but the conditions were the same. There was even another business partnership which ended in disaster. I found myself thinking that I preferred Coombe Springs. There was always something to *do* at Coombe Springs. There were latihans in the Jami, there were special exercises every week, there were difficult movements to practice, and morning exercises, and house meetings, and visitors to look after every weekend. And most of all there was the super effort I had achieved, and the elevated view of reality it had generated. It proved that the Work *worked*. Shah might have said we were being paid off as we went along, but where was *his* payoff? Had anyone received it? At Coombe Springs we had opportunities and techniques with which to achieve periods of higher consciousness every day. At Langton we were told every Saturday that we were too stupid for the "penny to drop". These were my thoughts on leaving for Australia.

(28 years later I was to learn from Oliver Hoare's 'Steganographer' memoir that, in the years when Beverley and I felt we were stagnating, Shah's original European group members and new South American members were

taking group trips to Sufi shrines in Turkey, and having mass meetings in a newly built Takia in Arcos, Spain. But you know what my first thought was when I read about this? I thought that Shah must have known I would find out about it some day, and that it would inspire me to write this memoir. Such is the long-lived nature of discipleship. Such is the reluctance to relinquish the elitist belief that one is numbered among the saved, not the damned.)

When we arrived in Australia, the anchor of our marriage – our shared loyalty to a teaching – was dragging on the seabed. And then came the dreadful impact of Gabriel's illness. This was the biggest storm of all, and it blew us apart. Beverley went into her style of shock – which was to clam up and say nothing about it; to clam up behind a protective shell – and I went into mine, which was to start smoking cannabis again after a gap of 23 years, and to deeply resent all the years I had wasted with Bennett and Shah. What was the use or value of The Work if it did not protect my son from schizophrenia? What value to me was 'higher consciousness' if my son was destroyed by psychosis? How wise was Shah's secret committee of 'grey beards' if they did not know that my son was predisposed to go mad? How powerful were the 'Guardians of the Tradition' if they could not help my little boy?

Shah's sister, Amina, visited us. I don't remember why she was in Sydney, or indeed Australia, but there she was, chattering away cheerfully as usual. I had always liked her, and attempted to avoid any subject that would reveal my disenchantment with Shah. But she picked it up, and she sadly said, "What have we done to you?" I could not answer that, because it was my *expectations* that had been disappointed. In order to be disillusioned, I had to first be illusioned. Did Shah illusion me? Did Bennett?

I was promoted to Creative Director of the agency, and was working late hours at night, coming home and falling asleep in an armchair only to be awakened by Beverley shouting in my ear. I felt that she blamed me for Gabriel's illness, but when I asked her about that she stayed silent. I was making $120,000 a year, and she never asked about my work. My home was a vacuum of accusing silence. I brooded about our long years with Bennett and Shah, and became obsessed with the new French philosophical theory known as post-modernism. I read Derrida, Foucault, Lyotard and Baudrillard, and decided that here was a true new path. Away with all the quaint medieval Islamic mysticism!

I spent weekend days at the Boy Charlton swimming pool in The Domain, laying on my back reading Andre Frankovitz' 'Seduced and Abandoned: the Baudrillard Scene' aloud, the better to understand it. I collected a small group of listeners, Sydney boys, who thought it was 'cool': all that stuff about simulacra, and the map that had covered the real landscape.

One evening, Beverley's cousin came to dinner. We sat outside in our little Woolloomooloo back yard, and I waxed enthusiastic to her, the cousin, about post-modernism. She was genuinely interested. Then Beverley came out with the after dinner coffee and said the fatal words.

"I hope he's not boring you with all that post-modern stuff."

It was the jolly joking tone that got to me. I could take ribbing about my enthusiasms, but not that she could be jolly joking about me to her relative, while to me, her husband, she was the shouter in the ear, the silent accuser, the hand of frigid death.

I pointed at the moon. It happened to be a full moon in a clear black sky. I said, "By this moon and these stars, I divorce you, I divorce you, I divorce you." I had read somewhere that this was the ritual way to do it. Not that I had rehearsed it – it just popped into my mind.

"So you want a divorce, do you?"

I nodded, and that was it.

Her brother Geoff visited from Melbourne. He was a well-respected businessman, and he had come to talk terms. He said that our marriage had received financial help from the family trust over the years and that, under the circumstances of a divorce instigated by me, I should repay all such monies. I agreed, and eventually everything donated to us over the 22-year marriage was repaid to Beverley from the proceeds of the house sale. She got $280,000 and I got $30,000. Geoff invested her share back into her family trust.

I did not care. I knew that my own 22-years long donations to the household had not been considered, but I did not care. I could see 'the wolf's tail' on the horizon, heralding the arrival of the shining Hunter of the East. I could see my own rebirth free from Gurdjieff, Bennett and Shah: the hero striding off into new territory, leaving all behind.

So far we had used a single lawyer to handle everything on an amicable basis. It was an amicable divorce. I thought it was all over. But then Beverley hired a new lawyer to claim what she imagined to be my superannuation. I think her friend Val, the general's wife, had put her up to it. It was sheer female spite. As I had only been employed for a few years, the super sum was minimal, but nevertheless I was forced to spend $1,000 on hiring my own lawyer to refute the claims of her lawyer. I was disappointed and angry because I thought we had got through the nasty business like enlightened, reasonable people. In 1991 the divorce was finalised, and I was free, and Beverley travelled to England on purposes unknown to me.

With my job at the busy agency and the divorce proceedings and the house sale, I was left with one day, one Saturday in which to find a new home. I had agreed with Beverley to move everything into my new place and hold it there until she was ready to choose the items she wanted. I found a large two-bedroom loft in Chippendale, and moved everything in. Beverley had arranged the removal team, and picked the cheapest one: a couple of burly Russians who strung out the removal time and bed assembly so long that I eventually sacked them, paid them, and slept on the couch.

My younger son Nathaniel had sided with his mother, become estranged from me, and moved in with a friend. Gabriel was living in a succession of 'Halfway Houses', minimally supervised by the mental health authorities. One day I found myself sitting in a new

A Noose of Light

apartment, staring at a blank wall and my new life. Naturally, the first thing I did was phone a prostitute. That night, a little Thai girl arrived, and told me all about her family back home, and how she sent money there. About 12.30am her pager buzzed, waking us up in bed, and she said she was supposed to be somewhere else. I had already paid by credit card, but I gave her a $300 silver fountain pen awarded to me by a client for doing a successful campaign. She turned it over in her little hands, wondering what she could do with it. I realised she could not write.

I had resorted to prostitutes on only one other occasion, a year or so earlier, when I visited a brothel near Darling Harbour. I became so interested in the process and system of the new experience that I was unable to perform. There was a comfortably appointed bar room with some other customers having a chat and a drink. It took me a while to realise that all the young women present were employed by the establishment. Not knowing what to do, I went back to the reception room and asked the lady behind the desk. She said I should just choose the girl I wanted and ask her to go upstairs. I returned to the bar, and immediately noticed that a slim girl in a black dress was staring at me in an almost alarming manner. She was being spoken to in a jocular way by a large, noisy fat man who was dressed like a farmer. Her eyes said, 'rescue me!' So I waited for the farmer to turn away to order another drink, moved in, and held out my hand. She grabbed it like a life rope and we headed upstairs. I was pleased with this because it assuaged my moral guilt at being there: I might not be the knight in shining armour, but I could at least be the one with the shining credit card. When we entered her room, she asked me to have a shower while she "changed into something more comfortable". When she said that, I was gone. I realised I was caught in a process more ancient than the earliest pyramids, and from then on was as detached from events as any archaeologist was from the potsherds he was digging up. After the shower, I lay down on the bed and was administered to like a corpse at the embalmers. The poor girl tried everything, but it was no use. Eventually, I asked her to just relax in my embrace and let the clock tick out on our time together.

Dawn

After the night with the Thai girl, I decided I did not want to become a sleazy long-term customer of commercial sex. No, I wanted a woman to look after, someone I could take care of, someone I could come home to, someone I could love. I remembered that, just before the divorce, Beverley and I had attended a party given by a man called Jay, an illustrator I sometimes employed in my advertising work. At the party I had enjoyed a conversation with a girl called Dawn, and had spoken to her enthusiastically about Mary Renault's historical fiction books. At one point of the conversation, she had looked at me with a memorable expression in her eyes, a wishfulness. Some things are indescribable. What is describable, but of secondary importance, was that she had a delicate little face and body which I found attractive. A week or so before Jay's party, I had walked past a boutique shop window on the street outside my ad agency, and noticed a delicate little lady's blouse in the window. It was made of white cotton *broderie anglais* lace. I stood there staring at it, wishing that I knew a girl I could buy it for; yearning, like a secular prayer, for a girl it would fit. Dawn was that girl. She was 17 years younger than me.

The day after the Thai girl visit, I phoned Jay and

asked him who she was, the girl at the party with the wishful eyes. He told me her phone number. I called her and asked her out to dinner. She thought I wanted to employ her as an art director, but at the rendezvous in a Thai restaurant in Darlinghurst it became clear that the meeting was purely social. We spoke about our families, and I told her about Gabriel. She nodded understandingly and then told me that her brother had the illness. Something fell into place between us with an inaudible click, and thereby began our relationship which was to last until her death 22 years later in 2011. When we walked out of the restaurant together I felt her hand slide into mine, and I knew I had found my new wife. We went back to my place, and for the second time in my life I rediscovered the joy of sex with an enthusiastic and responsive woman. After all the tension of Gabriel's illness, the divorce, the house sale, the move, it was such a relief that I had a sort of seizure, laying there on the bed howling and choking with tears like a newborn baby.

Dawn worked as a studio manager and art director of a small package design company located quite near my own offices in North Sydney. Several times a week I would send bunches of flowers to her office, and every night I would pick her up outside in my car. She introduced me to her friends, and we became another couple in a group of other couples, all largely belonging to the Sydney advertising crowd of art directors, copywriters and photographers. She was living in a bedroom of a share flat, so it was not long before I asked her to move in with me. I had finished with marriage, so I designed a gold ring for her as a pledge of my troth. It had a dark red garnet stone carved into a St Andrew's cross: the shape of a kiss scribbled at the bottom of a letter, but embedded in gold. I had it altered to fit my finger after she died, and I wear it now. We visited her parents in rural New South Wales, and her sisters in Queensland. Somehow a year passed, and then I heard that Beverley had returned from the UK, and wanted to visit me.

I did not want Dawn involved in this meeting, so asked her to visit friends on the evening arranged for it. Beverley arrived accompanied by her friend Val, the General's wife. I served them tea and talked about Beverley's sojourn in England and the Isle of Mull. I arranged for Beverley to bring her removal team in on a particular day, and to take away any items of furniture or equipment she wanted for the new flat she had rented in Belleview Hill. I gave her a set of keys, and explained that I did not need to be there while the removal was happening. I bid goodbye at the door, and the last word was had by her friend Val, who told me to "Look after your money!" This may have been a satirical comment about how Beverley's brother Geoff had managed the terms of the divorce.

On the day of the removal, I did not even think about what was happening at home. I was quite prepared to see what Beverley had taken when I returned from my office. Dawn, however, had arrived home first. In the early evening the phone rang in my office, and a hysterical Dawn told me to come home straight away. She was terrified.

I drove across the Harbour Bridge to Chippendale as fast as possible. Dawn was waiting for me in the car park, shaking like a leaf, and we went into the flat together. She took me straight through to the studio, where I saw that one of my paintings had been placed on the floor. In the middle of the painting was placed a dead pigeon with a carving knife stabbed through its breast, its wings outspread and its blood dripping down off the edge of the canvas. Stuck in the blood was a photo of Dawn's sister, and stuck in the blood beneath this photo was a scrap of paper bearing a scrawled message about 'sisterhood' being abused by men. The whole thing looked like a voodoo death spell.

A quick glance around told me that Beverley had removed nothing from the flat. I called Val's phone number. Beverley answered and I berated her for terrifying Dawn, and acting like a character in a horror film. I could hear Val and her daughters giggling in the background as Beverley sneered at me. I hung up on these harpies, and called the police. While waiting for them to arrive, I searched the flat and found that only one item was missing: I opened the wardrobe and saw that Gabriel's naming ceremony begging bowl, wrapped in its woolen blanket, had been moved. I thought Beverley had taken the gold sovereign placed at the bottom of the bowl, and left the bowl and blanket behind – but it may have been the Russian removal men.

The police arrived quite quickly, a male and female constable. I explained that my ex-wife had visited and committed this vandalism. The male constable looked around the studio, and then down at the crucified pigeon.

"Artists, are you?" He said.

"Yes, we are," I replied.

He cocked his head doubtfully.

'Painting worth much, was it?"

"No. It had no value."

He looked around, hopefully.

"Any other damage...anyone injured?"

"No, but Dawn here was terrified."

He nodded sympathetically.

I noticed that the female constable was facing away, holding a walky-talky to her face in order to conceal her giggles.

"Okay, okay, let's just forget it", I said.

The cops left to tell their amusing story to the night shift in their canteen, and I poured us a couple of scotches. Dawn and I worked out what had happened. While going through the flat, Beverley had discovered a few of Dawn's things and realised she was living with me. She found Dawn's sister's photo and assumed it was Dawn. God knows where she had found the pigeon: I don't think she had caught and killed it. It was probably already dead and she found it on the balcony. The blood was red oil paint. It was a few days later that I found the family photo albums, and discovered that Beverley had carefully cut out her own face from all of the shots. It must have taken her several hours work with a scalpel.

I felt ashamed that Dawn had been subject to this nasty little drama, and decided to make it up to her by taking her to meet my mother and sister in England. Dawn had never been to Europe, so she was thrilled to bits. We flew to Nice, hired a car, and spent three leisurely days driving up to Paris, stopping overnight at random Hotels. I had smuggled in a number of ecstasy pills, which we saved up for our exploration of all the usual Paris tourist sites. Dawn was incandescent, and a little worrying in her ingenuousness. Outside the Pompidou Centre, for example, she spotted a group of very elegant, very tall, black Parisian young men, and walked in amongst them to tell them that they were very beautiful and to ask if they really did come from Africa. They did not know what to make of her, or of me – who was obliged to stand nearby and smile like the reluctant minder of a drug-affected celebrity. On our last night we decided to hit a famous nightspot, so I consulted our Montmartre hotel's concierge, who recommended a 'Club Badjos' in Place de Concorde. We popped out last 'eccies' and arrived about 11pm, but found the place closed. A friendly French guy noticed us, and told us that the club opened at midnight – but we could wait at a nearby cafe. He told us that the cafe was a popular hangout for Club Badjos members, and squeezed us in among the chatting throng – who sat shoulder to shoulder on the long benches provided, drinking Pastis and smoking Gitanes. The French guy said he was with Medecines Sans Frontieres, and he asked me about Australia. On the other side of him, Dawn had immediately started chatting to her neighbour, who was a very large German. After a while, the French guy leaned closer and whispered to me that the man Dawn was talking to was a German murderer, and that I should be careful. I looked at the German, who seemed harmlessly enchanted to be talking to Dawn, even if he apparently did not understand much of what she was saying. There was not much I could do, anyway. Nevertheless I was relieved when, at midnight, all the 'Badjos' stood up and walked across the road into the Club.

I immediately thought of the movie 'Casablanca': the misty atmosphere, the dim lighting, the circle of little tables around the central dance floor; even the music seemed to belong to that era, although I had never heard anything quite like that particular brand of heavy-beat saxophone jazz. We claimed a table, and I went to the bar to get some drinks. By the time I got back, Dawn was on the dance floor, tranced out, doing her speciality slow-shimmy. There were a few couples dancing, too, but they were holding each other in a sort of creeping tango. Dawn was all alone, shimmying, as happy as a clam. I glanced across the floor and met the urgent eyes of the French guy, who was at a table on the other side. He held my gaze, nodded towards Dawn, and slowly shook his head. This fresh source of paranoia erased the last dregs of fun from the MDMA in my system, and I lapsed into neurotic-defensive mode. After all, *somebody* had to be responsible. I joined Dawn on the floor and managed to keep up a pretty good imitation of a tourist having fun – while covertly scanning the shadows for muggers and white slavers.

We must have caught a very early plane from Paris next morning, or maybe it was the one after, because we arrived at Heathrow at about 7am on a Sunday, rented a car and drove toward my mother's place in Kent. After a few miles I noticed how empty were the roads, and decided to give Dawn a whirlwind tour of London. Delightfully, the roads stayed virtually empty all the way as we zoomed down Oxford Street, down Regent's Street to Piccadilly Circus – with Dawn pointing and hooting at all the famous names and places as they went by the window. She had seen it all so many times in books, movies and TV that she didn't believe it was all real. Then we cruised through Trafalgar Square, the Strand, Fleet Street, and up Ludgate Hill to St Paul's and the City, with me acting the part of a pompous tour guide. Finally to the Tower of London, and across Tower Bridge and down the Old Kent Road to my childhood home of Welling.

My mother answered the doorbell and looked at me. Just for a flash I saw that she did not recognise me, but I took her in my arms and everything fell into place. Much later I remembered that flash, and realised it was the first sign of her dementia, which steadily increased in severity until her death 18 years later. She loved Dawn, as she had loved Janet, Ann and Beverley: each very different women.

Next door to my mother's building was a restaurant called 'Avenida'. I decided to throw a big party there to welcome Dawn to the Tunbridge family and friends. About 30 people turned up, and it went well. I detected a few arch looks from certain friends and family members, but none overtly commented on the age difference. My friend Nigel Hinton, in fact, made a point of completely ignoring Dawn's youth and beauty, and telling me forcibly how wonderful was her character. The only other thing I remember about our stay is that

A Noose of Light

Dawn insisted on a train trip up to London alone, to buy a pair of boots in Kensington. I don't know how she fixed on this mission, but she returned very happy with her British boots.

PotatoHeads

The word 'method' comes from the Greek *meta hodos*, which means 'along the path'. It has not been my fate to stick to any path or method for very long. Now at the age of 74, I feel I have remained forever adolescent, and have grown tired of the perpetual state of instability and doubting. Gurdjieff writes of "crystalisation", and Shah of "conditioning", but I often envy those who have gained a gravitas and peace of mind from sticking to a method or path, and have often thought that open-mindedness is over-rated. Sometimes one wants to close the door, and just sit in a cosy and familiar room away from the wind. After all, in the end, what is the payoff of either state? Shah told me to abstain from excitement, and I think he was offering a recipe, a method for diminishing the volatility, the childishness of mind which is both my shortfall of character and windfall of creative talent.

Shah was one of the few people I have known who could simultaneously exhibit volatility and gravitas. I forget the cause of the occasion, but at a Langton lunch party held outside, all the guests were standing around in island groups, all facing inward like little fortresses of conversation. I think I was the only one who saw Shah crouch down as if ducking under a low ceiling, place his

A Noose of Light

hands together in front of himself like a snowplow, and scuttle around between the island groups with a devilish grin on his face.

They say a leopard cannot change his spots, but what if it's the spots that change the leopard? After Gabriel was diagnosed, I learned that schizophrenia is a neurodevelopmental illness. Apparently, the adult brain is formed during adolescence by thousands of new neurons being created in or released from the brain stem. During adolescent years these new brain cells swim up or *migrate* through the white matter, or *glia*, within the brain to thicken the blanket of grey matter wrapped around the outside. This wrapping is called the cerebral cortex, and it's where we do most of our thinking, and it's usually about 4 millimetres thick. The trouble in schizophrenia is that some of the migrating neurons don't make it through the glia, so people with the illness end up with an abnormally thin cortex. Somehow or other this makes them vulnerable to all the deficits of schizophrenia. Having a son with the illness, I have thought that I, too, might have a touch of it, and that this touch may account for my habitually mercurial behaviour, and that if a postmortem were conducted on me, all the little neurons which didn't make it up to the cortex would be seen stuck in the glia of my brain like shipwrecked sailors.

When Dawn and I returned from our trip to Europe in 1992, there began a relatively blissful period. I stress the word 'relatively', because not many would associate the word 'blissful' with the circumstances of my life. Gabriel was living in a succession of 'Halfway

Houses' under minimal patient supervision, but made no effort to keep in touch with me. Whenever I managed to arrange for us to meet, he simply didn't turn up – and when I, at last, managed to get him on the phone again, he was always airily unrepentant, clearly affected by street drugs and/or psychosis, telling me to "lighten up, old man". I assumed he was being regularly arrested, sectioned, treated and returned to the street, but had no way to track what was happening to him. Parents have no legal right to medical or police information about their mentally ill adult offspring. If I knew his address, however, I would sometimes just visit it at random. The first time I did this, the door was opened by a stoned teenager, who led me through to a filthy room in which about six teenage boys and girls were sitting around on the floor. Gabriel was there, but comatose, his head drooping, barely conscious. The second time was at another address. He saw me out of his second-floor window and refused to open the door. The third time, I tried calling at the same address at night, but was pulled over by a police car, breath-tested, found to be 0.06, arrested, fingerprinted, charged and summoned to appear in Court – where the Magistrate heard my story, dismissed the charge and expunged the conviction from my record. After that, I gave up trying to see Gabriel. At the arrest, I asked the cops why they had pulled me over. They said they had just decided to go for white cars that night.

Nathaniel still sided with his bitter mother, and had declined my offer of financial help, so I was pleased when he called me to arrange a visit. It was his first and only visit to my Chippendale flat, and he walked around looking at my paintings on the walls. I said he could take away any that he liked to have in his home. He picked out a few, and left with them. Later I learned he had sold them to help finance his departure back to England in 1997. Dawn always told me not to be so upset about Nat. She always said, "Just wait, he'll come around." It took more than ten years, but she was right.

What was blissful was my new life with Dawn. After all the drama, all the disillusion and heartbreak, there I was coming home to a beautiful, cheerful, loving woman every evening. And what's more, there was space in my life again to indulge the greatest luxury of all: uncommissioned free artistic expression.

I had taken to smoking a cannabis joint every evening, and experimentally drawing on a pad of Arches water colour paper with a fine-point felt-tip black pen. The experimental bit was that I would place the pen nib on the paper and watch with delighted interest what it drew. It was a sort of automatic drawing. My elder sister Jeannette had, at one stage of her life, been a spiritualist medium, and performed automatic writing in seances with a group of friends, so maybe I was exploring whether I had inherited any of that talent, and could apply it to drawing. Whatever. The drawings emerged onto the paper as wobbly faces and figures. One night, Dawn looked over my shoulder and said, "They look like PotatoHeads!"

From then on, having been named, the PotatoHeads grew in power. They were like genii released from a magic lamp. Soon after being named by Dawn, they demanded a voice! One night, the pen drew a speech balloon and inside the balloon it wrote, "This is important." I gave out a great cry of triumph, which startled Dawn in the kitchen. I shouted to her, "Dawn, our troubles are over!" I had received a lightning-flash vision of a series of paintings, very large oil paintings, featuring the PotatoHeads speaking to the world through their speech balloons.

I immediately produced a small prototype PotatoHead painting of the 'This is important' balloon. The balloon was black, the writing was red, and the background was green. I realised that the all-important outline drawn by the felt-tip pen on paper had to be a raised-up ridge, like cake icing, in the paintings. I found an engineer who made a series of different sized nylon nozzles to fit a particular brand of acrylic paint tubes. It had to be acrylic because these raised lines of paint had to dry fast. All I had to do was replace the paint tube cap with the screw-on nozzle, and then squeeze out the black paint like tooth paste. Then I wanted the colours bordered by the black lines to look like stained glass windows, which effect required an impasto underpainting, such as yellow, overglazed with a coloured varnish, such as red, to produce luminous orange, or other hue. So I experimented with a fast-drying impasto oil medium called Oleopasto, and a fast-drying glaze medium called Old Holland. Both worked fine, but I found the colour was intensified if I lightly brushed off some of the glaze with a rag.

Having established the production process, the PotatoHead genii took over our lives. I would draw the original 'cartoon' on paper, and perhaps enhance the

A Noose of Light

drawing with watercolour. If deemed worthy, the spontaneous drawing would be photographed and enlarged to the chosen size for the painting – sometimes two metres wide – and traced onto the custom-made stretched canvas. Then I would use the acrylic paint tube and nozzle to apply the black line to the figures, the balloon and the writing. Dawn wanted to help, so she enjoyed filling in the impasto under-painting, over which the final transparent glaze was applied.

Our flat soon turned into a factory, to which we joyfully returned every night from our 'day jobs'. The Chippendale studio room became too small for our aspirations, so we moved to a rental house in Mosman, which had a long and roomy attic space under the roof, with a skylight. Perfect. Pretty soon we had four or five finished PotatoHead paintings, and we decided to look for a gallery. One Saturday in February 1993, I took the pictures to the Rex Irwin gallery in Woollahra. Rex said they were not his sort of thing, and advised me to show them to Madame Scheinberg at the Holdsworth Gallery in Paddington. Mme Scheinberg looked at the pictures and said, "If you can do 20 by January, you can have a show." Her unpleasant daughter, who doubled as a gallery assistant, sneered, and said they were, "Just another Hip-Hop rippoff." I had to ask her what Hip-Hop was.

What had actually happened at this meeting was that Mme Scheinberg had asked us about our backgrounds, and learned that Dawn and I were graphic design and advertising professionals with lots of friends who earned above-average incomes. On the strength of that, she had been willing to bump another artist out of his exhibition date of January 1994, because she judged that more sales would result from our friends.

There are some high-rise buildings where you cannot ride a lift all the way up to the top, but must switch to another lift halfway. Thus it was with our delight at the prospect of the exhibition. The meeting at the Holdworth Gallery was the halfway floor, and what happened after was the second lift, which shot us into the stratosphere.

The date set for our show was 8 January 1994, which gave us about a year to finish 17 paintings. Mme Scheinberg had asked for 20, and we already had three, plus a number of watercolours. We had already moved to a bigger studio, so the second thing we needed was more free work time. Dawn quit her job at the package design studio, and I quit my creative director job. I looked around for a freelance space to rent in another agency, and found a good sized room in Zulu advertising, a small design group in East Sydney. I registered my own company called 'Marketology', got some cards and letterheads printed, and put the word out that I was open for business – business that allowed me to zoom off and do the PotatoHeads any time I could. The third thing we needed was an appropriate car to reflect our new status as hotshot fine artists. I traded in my Honda Accord for a brand new Mazda MX6. Why that car? It was gleaming white with smooth rounded lines. It looked like a peeled potato! I ordered a custom number plate for it. It said, simply, POTATO.

Things fell into place effortlessly. My host design

group, Zulu, leased their office space from a larger agency called BAM SSB, and received a steady flow of creative work from this agency – some of which they passed on to me. Zulu also employed a few staff graphic designers, who were naturally interested in the POTATO car and the work of its over-ebullient driver. One day, about a month after I started my design output there, one of the Zulu team stuck his head in my room.

"Are you a big fan of Mondrian?" He asked.

"Not particularly, why do you ask?"

"We just noticed that all your designs are in primary colours, red, yellow, blue and black."

"Oh, that's just because I don't know how to find other colours on my computer."

He looked at me disbelievingly, then saw that I was happily serious. Then he leaned over and touched a few keys on my keyboard, causing a whole spectrum of colour choices to appear on my screen.

"Gee, thanks!" I said.

I was doing brochures, ads, showcards, posters for Canon, Commonwealth Bank, CocaCola, NSW Police, and a host of others. It was all the same to me what colour they were, because my heart was with the PotatoHeads. The client's didn't care either, but the graphic designers thought I was some sort of heretic, and treated me with suspicious disdain thenceforth.

The Battle for Research

Gabriel must have met his girlfriend Heidi in early 1992, because my grandson Jack was born on 25 January 1993. They must have met in the Caritas psychiatric hospital in Darlinghurst, because Heidi, a fellow patient, lived in an apartment in Paddington, rented or purchased by her parents – so a meeting in one of Gabriel's scruffy 'Halfway Houses' is unlikely. I imagine that the moving finger had slid both Heidi and Gabriel into the hospital simultaneously, and they had found companionship in each other.

The first Dawn and I heard of this liaison was in late 1992, when the phone rang in our new Mosman studio. Astonishingly, it was Gabriel's girlfriend, who introduced herself as Heidi, and asked if she and Gabriel could visit. Gobsmacked, I asked them over for tea on the next afternoon, which happened to be a Saturday.

Sure enough, the next day, they arrived: a pleasant-looking pregnant girl and a neat and tidy Gabriel. I really did not know what to make of it. Dawn served tea and we all sat down on the veranda over-looking the back garden and had a chat – like normal people. Heidi explained that Gabriel was living with her in her Paddington flat, and that she was making sure he took his medication, and that she wanted to meet his father, having already met his brother and his mother. Dawn and she discussed the pregnancy, and I chatted with Gabriel. He seemed quite calm and coherent. I think I would remember telling him about our forthcoming exhibition. I don't, so the meeting must have been before our visit to Mme. Scheinberg.

Not knowing anything about Heidi's history, I dared to think that this nice, intelligent, normal girl had somehow taken Gabriel under her wing, and that I might not have to worry about him any more: with her support he would stop doing street drugs and living in filthy places with filthy dropouts and junkies. He would settle down with his partner and child, stay on his meds, and lead a relatively normal life. Alas, it was not to be. Unknown to me at that time, Heidi was exhibiting the effects of pregnancy-elevated estrogen levels in schizophrenia patients. Sometimes, as in her case, all symptoms of the illness disappear. I learned this later. After my grandson Jack came into the world, Heidi relapsed and steadily declined back into her symptomatically unmanageable, drug abusing and sometimes violent behaviour.

But it was nice to have a spell of stability and hopefulness in early 1993. Dawn was working on our paintings more or less full time; I was driving to my freelance office every weekday to churn out brochures and press ads, and returning to work with Dawn in the evenings and weekends; Nathaniel was paying us the occasional visit, and I knew that Gabriel was in a good place, and under regular supervision. Because of the new baby, Heidi and Gabriel came under the oversight of the Department of Community Services, so I knew that ongoing support was being supplied. Indeed, everything seemed to be going so well that I became vulnerable to altruistic impulses.

I was walking through the living room of the Mosman house one afternoon, when I heard the word 'schizophrenia' uttered by the TV. I stopped dead, and watched as a man called Dr. Stan Catts shook hands with the New South Wales Shadow Health Minister, Andrew Refshauge. The voiceover explained that the NSW Labor opposition had made an election pledge of funding for an Australian schizophrenia research institute to be set up in New South Wales, and that Dr. Stan Catts was to be its chairman.

I stopped Dawn as she walked past, pointed at Dr. Catts on the screen, and said, "I am going to help that man."

The TV then said that if the NSW Labor party won the next State election, the institute would receive four million dollars over four years – becoming the only institute in Australia entirely dedicated to schizophrenia research. The next State election was set for April 1995, so I considered that my advertising and marketing skills might prove useful during the two-year interim. I found out that Stan Catts was a psychiatrist at the Prince of Wales Hospital, Randwick. Over the phone, he told me that other parents of patients had rallied to the cause, as had many neuroscientists, psychiatrists and other mental health professionals. He invited me to attend a meeting of everybody involved in creating the new institute.

At the appointed time, I arrived at the Prince of

A Noose of Light

Wales Hospital expecting to join a hall full of people, but walked into a small meeting room. Seated around a table were three sets of parents, four or five neuro-scientists and psychiatrists, and a student nurse with a clipboard. Standing in front of the white board was Stan. To make things even more surreal, I had brought along a recent PotatoHead painting, which I thought might be appropriate. It was about a metre wide, luridly coloured, and showed a worm-like creature with heads popping up all along its body. The worm was pictured as entering the canvas from one side, and then doing a sharp reverse turn, while the front head said, "Uh oh, thinking about myself again!" The background looked vaguely like organic matter, or maybe a sunset. I propped it up on the white board, and it was imme-diately declared marvellous by Stan – though everyone else seemed dumbfounded.

The other parents present had been assigned roles as Directors and Board Members of the not-yet-existent institute. A chartered accountant called Jim had been made Financial Officer; Judy, the wife of a famous Rugby coach, had been elected as a fund raiser and spokes-person, as had Don, the Secretary of a major trades union coalition; Stan was Chairman and CEO, and a lady called Joy, the Chairperson of the local 'Schizo-phrenia Fellowship', was elected as 'Consumer Liaison'. After I explained to everyone what I did as a job, I was elected as Marketing & Development Director.

We discussed the name of the institute. One of the scientists not present had decided that the name should be Neuroscience Institute of Schizophrenia and

Allied Disorders (NISAD). I said it was too long and no one would remember it. But the scientist was apparently influential and had recently discovered something new about brain mechanisms, so we were stuck with it. Stan explained that NISAD would be a 'virtual institute' in that it would not own any building; instead it would fund and direct research units placed in other establishments all across Australia. Instead of paying for the expensive upkeep of a building and equipment, NISAD's researchers would utilise the laboratories and equipment of existing centres such as universities, hospitals and other research institutes. In this way, more of our funding would go to the actual research. It all sounded eminently practical.

Don had already raised a considerable sum through his trades union connections, and Judy said she would get the support of the National Rugby League (NRL) to stage a fund-raising event at the Sydney Town Hall. I suggested that I should design a logo, and a giveaway brochure, and also produce an illustrated newsletter about what we were going to do when Labor won the election and gave us our pledged money. I also said I would try to get a major ad agency to donate the production of a press advertisement, and a TV commercial to be broadcast without charge on the public service. It was so agreed. It was also agreed that it would be unwise to rely totally on the Labor Party winning the election, therefore the first task should be to put our case before the incumbent Liberal NSW Minister for Health, Ron Phillips. Stan said he would make an appointment.

So it was that I, who had expected to make a small

contribution to a cause supported by hundreds of far more influential people than myself, found myself waiting in the vestibule of the NSW Minister for Health's offices in Parliament House, Sydney, with chairman Stan, and fund-raiser Don. We put our case, and presented the Minister with a fat document forever after called 'The Purple Document', because I had given it a purple cover to make it stand out. This was the first document to carry the NISAD logo, and it set out every aspect of the institute's structure and research strategy, along with an accurate and sometimes lurid history of the illness now called schizophrenia, but previously called *dementia praecox* (youth madness). We did not expect Ron Phillips to support us, and we were right. A week later, we received a polite letter wishing us well, but no funding pledge.

While waiting for this government response, I had devised the title and format of NISAD's first news-letter. It was called 'HeadLines', and its first front-page article was titled 'LABOR WILL DELIVER!' It shame-lessly championed the Labor Party, and the shadow Health Minister Andrew Refshauge, and also explained the manifesto and structure of the future institute as if it already existed. Inside was a number of articles about brain science, and the brain areas suspected of being involved in schizophrenia symptoms. From the start, I tried to make brain research as exciting as an Indiana Jones or Star-Trek movie, with titles such as 'Into the Mysterious Amygdala', and 'The Brain Stem: Our Reptile History'. What this first edition also carried was a 'whistle-blowing' expose titled, 'Is the NHMRC Bigger

Than Democracy in Australia?' This because Stan had told me that the National Health & Medical Research Council – the key national research funding body – had redirected into Aboriginal Women's Health part of the funds raised by Don for our schizophrenia research. The NHMRC sent a very strong letter of objection to Stan about this article, and he blamed me as the "overenthusiastic editor of our newsletter". I didn't mind a bit. The newsletter had put us on the map, both publicly and officially.

From that point until the State Election of March 1995, the Directors of NISAD acted pretty much like an underground spy network – meeting at night in a variety of vacant rooms and halls to plot our next moves. Don continued to raise support with the unions, Judy organised a profitable 'Night for NISAD' at the Sydney Town Hall, and Stan recruited scientists, setting them up in theoretical research groups, ready for when the money arrived.

But it was hard going. Despite getting some awareness ads in the newspapers, and even a 30 second public awareness clip on TV, the general public's interest in the birth of Australia's first schizophrenia research institute had been minimal. Worse, despite the Schizophrenia Fellowship circulating our 'HeadLines' newsletter to its members, interest and support, even from families directly affected by the illness, was disappointingly low. We discussed this at out clandestine meetings, and agreed that the reluctance was due to the unique stigma carried by this illness. All mental illnesses carried stigma, but schizophrenia carried the most, because it

A Noose of Light

was perceived as the worst. At that time, and before, it was not uncommon for "paranoid schizophrenia" to be named in horror movies as the cause of the gory atrocities splashed across the screen. People did not want to be associated with it in any way. Even parents and siblings of sufferers were often so traumatised by the illness arising in their families that they disconnected from the sufferer: they washed their hands of their own son or daughter, brother or sister, cousin or friend. I told my fellow directors that I had felt the power of this trauma myself. When Gabriel had been diagnosed and started to decline, I was in shock: I had never imagined that I would be one of those people who were fated to look after (be burdened with, cursed with) a mentally ill child. On the contrary, I was always the hero of the quest, destined to aspire to the highest; to storm the very gates of heaven. For me, the hideous fact of my son's illness negated every belief and self-image I possessed, leaving behind nothing but betrayal and bewilderment. So I understood, I said, why so few rallied to our cause.

Driving with Stan back from one of these night-time meetings – this time held at the College of Psychiatry's building in the grounds of the Cumberland Hospital in Western Sydney – Stan confessed how disheartened he felt by the dearth of public response to all our efforts. He said it was not just the public response that was depressing, but the professional response was almost as negative. Some of his fellow psychiatrists called schizophrenia "the graveyard of research", and regarded it as a career killer. Many wanted nothing to do with it, in much the same way as families rejected their affected members. How can you help people who told you to go away and leave them alone? That's what they said about schizophrenia patients. Stan said that it had all got so bad, so hard, that he was thinking of 'giving it all away'.

I told Stan that what had counterbalanced the bewilderment and betrayal and despair I had felt about Gabriel was anger: pure, clean anger. While his mother Beverley had virtually abandoned Gabriel and veered into ridiculous new age nonsense, I had become angry at Bennett and Shah, who had pretended to be wise men but who did not even know that the most catastrophic event in my life would be my eldest son's illness. I felt outrage, contempt and anger – and that was the energy I was channelling into my work for the Institute.

Stan now says that it was that drive in the car with me that persuaded him not to 'give it all away'. Instead, he decided to wait until after the election: he decided to wait to see if receiving a big chunk of money would change people's minds about supporting the Institute. Eventually it did.

Labor won the March 1995 election, Andrew Refshauge delivered the money, and all of a sudden lots and lots of people became very interested in schizophrenia research.

Living Like Millionaires

O ne sunny Australian summer's day near Christmas in 1993, Dawn and I were driving in the 'POTATO' car to see some sliced up human brains at the University of Sydney. We had the windows down, so as we turned into the entrance and past a group of students standing on the corner, we clearly heard one of them say, "There goes my favourite number plate in Sydney!"

We laughed the carefree laugh of people in Hollywood movies who are just about to have a dreadful accident. In about a month's time, we would preside over the opening of our own exhibition, and nothing really mattered after that. We had discovered that the Mosman rented house was riddled with mold, so had moved to an even more expensive house near the harbour. It had a bigger studio and a garage for the POTATO car. We celebrated the move with a house-warming party for all our friends – at which our good friend Anmarie commented, in a worried sort of way, that we were living like millionaires. Like me, Anmarie was a freelance graphic designer, so she knew that Dawn and I were living way beyond our income.

Dawn and I were having a break from painting the PotatoHeads by visiting the brain bank in Sydney

University: a small research centre where human brains were stored and processed for use in research. I was going to take some photographs to illustrate the next issue of my HeadLines newsletter, and Dawn had tagged along out of morbid interest.

The brain bank was in a couple of rooms in a university building. One of the rooms was filled with large but ordinary refrigerators containing donated brains. The friendly technician showed us some deep frozen examples wrapped in plastic – more like Sunday joints from the freezer than the most complex and mysterious things in the universe. Then we were ushered into the other room, containing some tables and a slicing machine. One of the technicians was laying out some slices on a tray, rather like nibbly bits to have with a glass of wine. Dawn was in a state of delighted horror, and kept making unscientific noises. I took my photos while the technician explained how the slices were made to order. A cannabis researcher would, for instance, order sections from the frontal lobes of a deceased long-term user to study how the drug affected the number and distribution of neurons. One of the things NISAD would do when and if the money arrived was start up a brain donation program called 'Gift of Hope'.

I always say that 1993 was the happiest year of my life, and it was. If you could measure degrees of happiness from blood samples, the degree shown by my 1993 blood samples would be higher than any other year. Dawn and I were happily collaborating on the PotatoHead project; I was happily engaged in developing NISAD; Gabriel was happy and stable with

Heidi, and had fathered my little grandson, Jack; there was plenty of work flowing through my Marketology office, even though I was going home early most days to do PotatoHeads. I was working sixteen hours a day, and happy to do it. Then came the exhibition.

On the opening day of the exhibition, Saturday 8th January, 1994, the biggest bush fires ever recorded in the Sydney area had been blazing for three days. The smoky sky was raining embers all over the city. Friends and relatives overseas were phoning to check we had not been burnt in our beds. That afternoon, as we drove in to the gallery, the ash was thickly falling like grey snow. Halfway to Paddingtom from our house in Mosman, Dawn remembered that she had left a very large bowl of snacky chips and crisps and things on the kitchen table. She wanted to offer them to the exhibition visitors. She said we must turn back to get it. I said it didn't matter, and that getting it would make us late for the opening time. Dawn had a panic attack about the bowl of chips, and that was the end of my happiest year. We turned back, we were late, and far fewer people than expected turned up – either to the opening or during the week of the show – because of the bush fires.

We sold half the exhibited paintings, but there was no review in the press, and no interest from anyone except our friends. The proceeds from the sales added up to a microscopic fraction of the money we had lost by sacrificing so many hours producing the pictures. It didn't even cover the cost of all the custom-made canvases and oil paint, let alone the rent for the two houses. Dawn had quit her job, and I had neglected lots of Marketology work – all for the PotatoHeads.

The black chickens came home to roost, and the dreamers awoke in the cold light of the coop – to mix several metaphors. I had to sell the POTATO car back to the dealer I bought it from. We had to move out of the millionaire's house into an attic flat overlooking Redfern railway station. Dawn got a job as a graphic design teacher in a private college in North Sydney. I rode the train in every day to carry on with my Marketology business. The whole joyous year was swept away down the storm drain of history, and the moving finger began another chapter.

Fostering Jack

I remember a family picnic party in Central Park, Sydney. We all turned up, about 30 of us. It was well organised – I believe by Heidi's mother Julie – with a number of trestle tables and a barbeque and some outdoor games equipment. Gabriel and Heidi were there sitting at a table, but he was in a semi-catatonic state, staring at a paper plate full of smarties and jelly babies on the table in front of him. Heidi kept trying to gee him up, to no effect: he was hiding in plain sight. Everyone was making a discreet fuss of little Jack, who was about 2 years old. There were some other young kids there, but I did not know to whom they belonged. It was warm and sunny, so the event might have been Jack's birthday in January 1995.

There seemed to be two sets of every relative. There was myself and Jack's other grandfather, Bill. There was my partner Dawn, and Bill's wife Margie. There was my ex-wife Beverley, and Bill's ex-wife Julie (Heidi's mother), and there were a number of Bill's and Julie's adult daughters. Perhaps they were the mothers of the other little kids? Nat was there, and so were a number of other aunts and uncles. Strangers were strolling by on the path, nodding and smiling at us, the large and diverse family all getting together. I thought that, unknown to them, they were admiring the most dysfunctional family they would probably ever see, because there was even another layer of convoluted relations at the picnic. Jack's new foster parents, Liz and Greg were there, and so was the little girl, Asia, they had also fostered. I forget if either of Asia's biological parents were there, but I don't think they were. Greg had been married before, though, and I'm fairly sure one of his daughters was there. It was Liz and Greg, little Jack's foster parents, who had endorsed this united nations of dysfunctional parents, psycho offspring and busted marriages. Part of the fostering deal was that contact must be maintained between the child and the biological family. We all knew that, and that's why we were there.

What had happened was that the NSW Department of Family and Community Services (DOCS) had stepped in when they considered that baby Jack was in danger. Dawn and I, together with Bill and Margie (Heidi's father and step mother) and Julie (Heidi's mother) and Beverley, had visited Gabriel and Heidi's flat, and found it to be an unsuitable place for a toddler: his parents' chain smoking had stuffed up his nose with nicotine tar, and their addictions to street drugs meant that toxic substances were to be found around the home – not to mention an unusual degree of dirt and disorder. More, Heidi and Gabriel had been allowing some of their fellow schizophrenia patients to take Jack out in his push chair, and this had been noted by concerned citizens. After her 'remission' during pregnancy, Heidi had relapsed, and without her support Gabriel had also relapsed. They were now both thoroughly crazy, and they looked it.

I don't know if grandfather Bill and step mother Margie were approached as possible foster parents for Jack, or if his grandmothers Beverley or Julie had considered it. All such consultations were kept strictly confidential by DOCS, and we the participants did not discuss it with each other. We related to each other as if there was nothing wrong – each trying to outdo the other in expressions of cheerful optimism – rather like relatives at a hospital bedside. Dawn and I were certainly in no financial or domestic state to take on a toddler – so the DOCS team had concluded that little Jack would be better off with a stable, well-established family who had not been blown to bits by schizophrenia. For everyone involved, except the DOCS professionals, it was unbelievable and appalling that any of us should be involved in such a shameful transaction. Yet here it was, and there was no escape from the iron finger that was engraving this paragraph on our lives. Why didn't any of us take over the care of Jack, to save him being fostered out to strangers? After all the financial and domestic reasons have been considered, I think the rock-bottom reason, the basilisk stare reason was that we all sincerely believed Jack would be better off being brought up in a family not cursed by schizophrenia.

Both sets of grandparents and relatives attended a formal meeting with the DOCS team, and the fosterers Liz and Greg. Each of us spoke in approval of the fostering decision, and signed the papers. It was done. Outside the meeting room, there was Beverley and Nathaniel in solemn conversation, utterly ignoring

Dawn and I who were standing still, looking at them. Dawn took my hand and pulled me away. She said, "Nat will come around in time. You just have to wait, and he'll realise what she's like." It took about ten years, but Nat did come around.

Can people be blamed for exhibiting the effects of a severe trauma delivered to them by circumstances outside their control? I don't think so. As Mullah Nasruddin says, when real danger and disaster enters, *everyone* is affected. Beverley was simply unable to adjust to becoming the mother of a mentally handicapped adult. She would probably have been able to handle the physical disability of a child, but the mental disorder thing cut too deep. After all the years she had devoted to 'spiritual development', it clashed with her self image so violently that she fled the scene, and took refuge in various types of new-age spirituality – where no doubt she found an acceptable delusory reason why this disaster had happened to her. In times past, families used to lock mentally ill offspring up in the attic for the same reason – and many a gothic novel was born thereby – but nowadays it's all handled by government departments and underpaid nurses. The patients are crazy, not stupid, so they find ways of getting around any restrictions, and maintaining their delusion that it is not they who are crazy, it is the doctors and the civilised world who are crazy. In mental health parlance this is called denial. Beverley's long term response to Gabriel's illness was a form of denial.

While I felt the same betrayal and disruption, I did not have me to blame, as she did. Perhaps blame is the wrong word. Perhaps it would be better to say that the mother believed there was nothing wrong with herself, therefore it must be the father's fault. I read the literature and knew that almost all cases of schizophrenia arise in families with no history of the illness, so I didn't blame anyone. But I certainly did blame Shah and Bennett and all the gurus and savants among whom I had sought guidance. My son's illness exposed all their convoluted theologies and spiritual traditions as delusions. I blamed them and hated them for not knowing this would happen to me. I was murderously angry. I did not seek shelter in effete new-age therapies, I sought it in science: I worked hard to help create a research institute dedicated to erasing schizophrenia from the human race.

Rising from the Wreckage

The New South Wales Labor Party won the 1995 election, and the new Health Minister Andrew Refshauge delivered on his promise to fund the Neuroscience Institute of Schizophrenia and Allied Disorders (NISAD). At around the same time the Zulu design group, from whom I rented my freelance office, decided to move to a cheaper location. I went with them, but found that the amount of work they assigned to me steadily reduced over six months to nothing. Fortunately, my friend Anmarie told me that a freelance room was available in the North Sydney ad agency where she rented an office. So I moved there, and began to receive regular in-house commissions, writing and art directing for the agency's wide range of corporate clients, as well as for a few clients of my own.

Dawn became discontent with our attic flat overlooking Redfern railway station, so we moved to a house in the nearby suburb of Stanmore. It had a garden and a separate studio room that Dawn utilised for her fabric dying activity. She hand dyed swathes of silk and made slinky dresses from them. She arranged with her employing college to have her lecturer's salary paid to our company Marketology as a fee, thereby transferring responsibility for income tax payment to the company.

With her income and mine combined, and our accountant claiming maximum allowances, we began to rebuild our financial stability.

After rising from the wreckage for a year or so, however, I grew confident enough to imagine that I could write some more songs. So confident, in fact, that I purchased a $3,000 digital recording deck. This was a mistake, first because I discovered that my song writing days were past, and second because Dawn resented that I made the hefty purchase without consulting her. After all, the recorder was paid for with a Marketology cheque, and she was a Director of our company. The seed of discontent was thereby sown, but did not sprout until another incident occurred.

I came home from my office in North Sydney one Friday evening, unlocked the front door and stepped into the hallway. There on the floor in front of me was my hat, a stylish trilby. There was no way it could have fallen off the peg to the middle of the floor. Dawn was far away visiting her mother in the country town of Young, so it could not have been her who dislodged the hat. While I puzzled over this, a bald head popped out of the bedroom door halfway down the hall, and looked at me. We looked at each other until I had processed the information.

Then I said, "Are you burgling my house?"

The bald head said, "What you fuckin' gonna do about it?"

The burglar, a teenaged skinhead, then advanced up the hall towards me, causing me to leap sideways into my study, looking for a weapon. Before I found anything,

I heard the burglar run back down the hall, through the living room and out the back door. I followed cautiously, but was stopped dead by the chaotic scene in the living room. The burglar had picked up every piece of electronic equipment, one by one – the TV, record player, speakers, computer and radio – and carried it to the back door. He had, however, neglected to unplug anything, so the wires trailed across the room to where the loot was piled. Propped against the pile was a long iron crowbar. I seized this and ran out the back door, across the yard and into the street. But I was too late. I heard a car start up and roar away. Returning to the house, I phoned the police and reported the burglary and assault, then went into the bedroom to view further damage. All the drawers were opened and contents strewn everywhere. Dawn's jewellery and some other valuables were missing. I went outside and into Dawn's studio. There in the middle of the floor was a neat pile of human excrement, and beside it a besmirched piece of Dawn's dyed silk.

A male and a female constable arrived to view the scene of the crime. They asked what had been stolen and its value. They pursed their lips and opined that I'd been lucky.

"Aren't you going to arrest him?" I asked.

The male constable looked philosophically at the wreckage.

"Well," he said, "We could dust for prints, but it's Friday, see? So you would have to leave everything just as it is until Monday, when the print squad gets back on duty."

A Noose of Light

I said, "So if I do that, and they get some good prints, what are the chances that you'll be able to track him down?"

Quick as a flash, the male constable said, "Seventeen per cent. We arrest seventeen per cent of all reported burglars, mate."

"So if I live in this bloody mess for two days, and if the print squad gets a good print, the chances of you catching the burglar are still only seventeen per cent?"

'That's about it."

"But the little bastard shit all over our studio!"

For the first time, the constable looked interested.

"Did he? You'd be surprised how often that happens. He must have been very nervous," he said, nodding in sympathy with the burglar, not with me.

"Look," I said, "I'm a professional artist and I could draw you a portrait of him. Would you be able to compare that to a list of known burglars?"

Even the female cop looked interested, now. She looked at her partner and nodded.

"Sure, that might help a lot," he said, "but if I was you, I'd get a more secure back door, mate."

With a few more homilies on domestic security, they left me to spend all that evening cleaning up the mess. Next morning, I drew a portrait of the skinhead and took it along to the local Newtown police station. The female officer behind the reception desk seemed to know who I was, and received the portrait as if it was a birthday present.

"Oooh, that's very good!" She said. "You're a

very good artist!"

"Do you recognise him?" I asked.

"Oooh no," she said, "but I'll pin it up right here on the wall, and we'll let you know if anyone knows who he is."

And that was the last I heard of it. Once again the cops in the canteen had a good giggle at my expense. I phoned Dawn, and she was upset about losing her jewellery, but quite resigned to it by the time she got back home on Sunday afternoon. I had cleaned everything up and I didn't tell her about the shit in the studio. It was a few weeks later that the weather got colder, and I looked on the hall coat hooks for my treasured Italian leather jacket. That's when I realised the little bastard had been wearing it when he ran out of the house.

But by that time I had more important things to think about. The burglary seemed to have been some sort of last straw for Dawn. She calmly told me that she wanted us to separate into our own places, and that she wanted to handle her own finances, and that we could stay with each other on weekends. I had felt it coming, so was not unduly surprised. In fact, the idea appealed to me as much as it did to Dawn. We had moved to the Enmore house because she had requested it, and I had never liked the poky suburban little place. We had been cohabiting in a succession of places for ten years, so the prospect of separate domiciles assumed an exciting, refreshing aspect. I never had a moment's doubt that it would proceed just as I thought: that Dawn would be happier as an independent in her own place, and so would I in mine, and that we would revert to the status of girlfriend and boyfriend visiting each other on weekends.

And so it was to be. Dawn found a little flat close to her graphic design college in North Sydney, and I moved into a two-bedroom third-floor flat in Surry Hills. We happily maintained these separate domiciles for the next decade.

The Institute

From 1996, when the Neuroscience Institute of Schizophrenia and Allied Disorders (NISAD) became established in offices leased from the Garvan Institute, Darlinghurst, the amount of writing, art direction and print management work I was doing for the new institute steadily increased until I could no longer do it *pro bono*.

As well as acting as the Institute's one-man advertising agency, I was frequently speaking about schizophrenia to audiences ranging from construction workers to Probus groups, and attending fund raising events headed by organisations such as Rosehill Racecourse, and the Law Society. On one occasion, supported by the National Rugby League, I even addressed a half-time rugby crowd from the pitch of the mighty Allianz Stadium in Moore Park. If anyone wants to know how to overcome a stutter, I would say become passionately committed to a worthy cause. It won't eliminate the stutter, but it will eliminate the *fear* of stuttering. I addressed a large Probus group meeting for 15 minutes, once. It was chaired by a retired High Court Judge, and when I sat down next to him afterwards, he leaned confidentially over and whispered, "Very brave." But it wasn't brave, it was just that I didn't care what they thought about me, I cared only about what they learned about schizophrenia and our research program.

As soon as the Foundation Board of Directors established the Institute's head office, we set about replacing ourselves with more influential directors from as wide a variety of professions as possible. It took about a year to attract and appoint an MP, a CEO of an accounting firm, a top rank bank executive, a Senior Counsel, and other heavyweights to the Board. Simultaneously, our scientific director was busy recruiting neuroscientists and other researchers, and negotiating with universities, hospitals and other clinical centres to establish schizophrenia research groups in every appropriate NSW organisation. By the end of the second year of operations, we had such teams and affiliated scientists in Brisbane, Melbourne and Perth, as well as Sydney, Newcastle and Wollongong. Instead of filling the newsletter with reports of what we were going to do, I could write and illustrate articles about what we *were* doing.

It was an intoxicating time. As writer, editor, photographer, art director, finished artist and print manager of the newsletter 'HeadLines', and pretty much every other institute publication, advertisement, and 30-second TV appeal, I ended up having little time for other clients. In 1999, the Board decided that the daily throughput of 'communications and publications' work was so great as to warrant employing a part-time staff member, based at the Central Office. I discussed it with Dawn, and decided to appoint myself to the position – thereby becoming an employee of the organisation I had helped to create. It made sense: I was always hopeless at keeping track of my accounts and tax, so was happy to hand it all over to the Institute's accountant. Likewise, I had managed to put little aside in superannuation, so was even happier to have the accountant manage that for me as well. The prospect of a regular monthly salary was also welcome. As a freelancer, I often had to wait three months for my bills to be paid. It made sense for the Institute, too: whoever we found to act as an in-house publications manager would not be able to handle all the work him/herself on a daily basis as I did, but would have to commission much of the work from outside suppliers – with subsequent deficits in efficiency and costs. Nevertheless there was some talk among Board members about "jobs for the boys", but they eventually were convinced that my appointment was for the best.

So there I was. Just like the other turning points of my life, I found it quite impossible to choose anything other than the road indicated. I quit my North Sydney office and moved my stuff into the Garvan building. The whole event occurred during the time of the great Dawn/Alan split into separate domiciles – which is why I chose my flat in Surry Hills: it was a healthy ten minute walk to the Garvan Institute. I was there for ten years.

Florid Psychosis

What a wonderfully poetic and elastic phrase. What it means is anything from a rabid axe-wielding maniac, to a pathetic person possessed by a ridiculous delusion. Gabriel was the latter case. He used to visit the reception desk in the Garvan Institute regularly, and politely ask for me, his father. The girls on the desk got used to him, even though he turned up in a very strange variety of outfits and personalities. His favourite for a long while was 'Lucinda', a ten year-old girl wearing a tiger stripe mini-skirt and high-heeled sandals – which didn't go at all well with his scruffy full beard, bald head and hairy legs. The reception desk girls would phone me, and I would go down and have a chat. He knew I would never give him money, because he knew that I knew he would only spend it on street drugs. So we would go outside and walk up to the little supermarket in Victoria Street to buy whatever he wanted in groceries and cigarettes. Then we would hug outside, and he would go back with his groceries to Heidi's flat, quite happily. There was nothing I could do, and nothing hospitals or doctors could do. In order to be 'treated' against his will, he had to be 'sectioned', and in order to be sectioned, a doctor had to declare that he was "in danger of harming himself or others", or "in danger of damaging his reputation". And no local doctor or crisis team would do this because there were no psychiatric hospital beds or rooms available.

Well, at least he wasn't as bad as Dawn's brother. Dawn's brother John decided that his mother was to blame for everything, and exhibited such threatening behaviour towards her that she locked him out of the house. The house was in the rural town of Young in central NSW. She was forced to phone the police when he tried to burn down the front door. He was arrested and put in the local gaol, but he escaped from there and was hunted by cops and dogs. After three days a junior constable answered an emergency call from a farmer who had come home to find a stranger eating in his kitchen. The constable arrived outside and shouted to the intruder to come out with his hands up. John came outside but he was eating a sandwich and didn't raise his hands – so the constable shot him. The bullet hit his neck, narrowly missing the jugular. The constable phoned for help and they took John to the local hospital. The cops tried to cover up the constable's mistake by having John declared dangerous and sending him to Long Bay gaol – a top security prison in South Sydney. The family tried to get him transferred back to a psychiatric hospital, and also tried to lodge a complaint about the shooting. No hope. The cops held him in Long Bay for six months before releasing him back to the care of his mother. I wrote an article in my HeadLines newsletter about 40 per cent of the NSW prison inmates having a diagnosed mental illness. That didn't achieve anything, either.

Years passed. The Garvan Institute is just over

the road from St Vincent's Hospital and its nearby psychiatric wing, Caritas, so I became the go-to guy for dealing with wandering psychos and junkies who sometimes wandered into the Garvan's reception area. Outside these encounters, there were crises with Gabriel involving drug overdoses – one of which resulted in stroke and a three-month period with hemiplegia – arrests for various offences, 3-day incarcerations in the revolving-door psyche hospital, and the whole grandson Jack fostering drama. But it's true that we can get used to anything: I remembered my past life as if it was someone else's; some naive chump's who knew nothing about reality. I became adept at cutting off threads of thought that led to feelings of grief, disappointment and betrayal, and expert at nurturing other threads that led to anger and determination. Anger was good, was useful. It was the fuel I burned in my job of drumming up support for more research.

My research institute, NISAD, developed steadily, with occasional hiccups, the worst of which was when a new scientific director employed a completely unsuitable female CEO who wasted $80,000 on crackpot fund raising campaigns which I *knew* would fail. She ignored all that myself and the Research Coordinator said in opposition, and filled the office with meaningless 'corporate speak', like a one-woman motivation seminar. The Board saw sense in the end, and sacked her and the scientific director – all very politely, of course.

Dawn and I became shining exemplars of the successful separate domicile relationship. Truly, it solves all marital frictions if the partners simply live apart and get together on weekends. We phoned each other for a chat most evenings, and looked forward to our Saturday nights together. We both agreed that it was wonderful to come home every night to an empty home, to be sole rulers of our domains. She would do her glass bead work with her blow torch in her kitchen, or talk to her mother and sisters for hours on the phone (a ritual I found annoying), and I would potter about undisturbed in my studio, or use the remote to flick between a number of simultaneous TV shows (a trait which Dawn found *very* annoying). And we had our bathrooms and kitchens entirely to ourselves! We wondered why the world did not know about 'sympatico separation', this perfect way of life.

Everything was as much under control as it could be under the circumstances. And then the circumstances changed. I received a phone call from a psychiatrist at the Cumberland Psychiatric Hospital in Western Sydney advising me that my son Gabriel had been admitted to their locked ward. I was told that he had been arrested in a shopping mall in Sutherland, a suburb about 50 kilometres south of central Sydney. The shop keepers at the mall had dialled the emergency number because Gabriel had been seen talking to toddlers in pushchairs. What had alarmed them was that Gabriel had been dressed in a short pink woman's slip, with very dirty bare feet, a full beard, and using a golf club as a walking stick. The Sutherland police had not taken him to Caritas because *they did not know who he was!* They drove him straight to their own local hospital, the biggest psychiatric hospital in New South Wales, the Cumberland, near Parramatta,

Western Sydney.

I still don't know how or why Gabriel got down to Sutherland, but blessed the day he did. Because he was arrested there, he automatically came under the responsibility of the Cumberland's Western Sydney Health area. If I had tried to get him into the Cumberland he would have been refused because he lived in Paddington, the East Sydney Health area. His arrest and admission into a locked ward was the best news about him I had ever received. The Cumberland, unlike Caritas, was not a revolving door, but a proper psyche hospital with a proper system of treatment. Gabriel remained under the supervision of the Cumberland and its affiliated organisations for seven years. He started in the locked ward, graduated to the open ward, and from there to the rehabilitation system, and from there to outside accommodation, a disability pension, and a job in a protected factory. He is now completely independent, living happily in a rented house with two other 'recovered' schizophrenia patients. His body has suffered some damage from his 15 years of psychosis, but from his gentle manner and friendly speech you would never guess that he had ever been floridly psychotic.

But the moving finger had not got all the way there, yet. In this text it is still writing that the psychiatrist on the phone told me how important family support was in these cases, and that I should visit him at the Cumberland as often as I could.

It was obviously time I bought a new car. Ever since reluctantly parting with my beloved POTATO car, I had been travelling everywhere by taxi or public transport. But this system, though cheaper than running a car, immediately became untenable when I heard that Gabriel was in Cumberland hospital, an hour's drive from Surry Hills. A car would also simplify my weekend rendezvous with Dawn: I could drive across the Sydney Harbour Bridge every Saturday night and pick her up, thus enhancing the boyfriend/girlfriend frisson! Everything was working out. I rushed out and purchased a sensible but nippy Holden Vectra station waggon.

And so the routine of the next five years began. Every Saturday morning I would drive out to visit Gabriel, and return to later pick up Dawn and chauffeur her to my place in Surry Hills. My first visits to Cumberland Hospital were to the locked ward, which was like everyone's assumptions about such places: patients rolling around on the floor, or sitting zombie-like, or banging on the doors of their locked rooms. Fortunately there was a walled patio area available, and the nurses used to open it for me to have a quiet chat with my son. In the beginning he was violently adamant that he really was an eight year-old girl called Lucy. He would stab his index finger hard on the tin table until I feared it would break. But after a few weeks of medication he forgot about that, and was released into the open ward to mix with other relatively stabilised patients. After a few more months, I attended a formal hearing with a Magistrate to review his case and to advocate that Gabriel should be moved into the Cumberland managed rehabilitation system. The doctors agreed, so he became a resident in one of the rehab houses in the hospital grounds. He used to ask

A Noose of Light

his case officers when he would be discharged, and they would tell me, so that I could talk him out of it. I was truly afraid that he would resume his junkie behaviour if he got back to his notorious old Darlinghurst and Kings Cross stamping grounds. At this time, his mother Beverley paid him a visit, and we were allowed to take Gabriel out to a riverside restaurant for lunch. The next stage was when I was allowed to drive him every Sunday to see a movie in the Westfield Hoytes cinema. At last, he was set up in a managed household in a nearby suburb of Auburn with two other 'graduates' from rehab.

Then a new regimen started. Gabriel's household was managed to the minimum extent of one visit every week by a case officer. The household partners were independent, doing their own shopping, cleaning, cooking, and going out every day to whatever work they could handle. Gabriel worked in a protected factory four days a week, assembling shop displays, putting inserts into magazines and scrubbing plastic freight tubs. Reassured by his steady working attendance, I suggested that he could catch a train in to Central Station every Sunday morning. I would pick him up from Central in the car, and bring him home to Surry Hills where Dawn would cook us breakfast before we went across the road to the Moore Park cinema complex to see a movie. It worked beautifully. Dawn liked the new 'sane' Gabriel, and he loved her and the train outing and seeing his old stamping ground through new eyes.

I asked him, "Do you remember being psychotic?"

He said, "Yes, I do."

I said, "What do you prefer, being crazy or being sane?"

He thought about it, and then said, "Being sane."

One such Sunday, we drove past Heidi, who happened to be walking along a street we were driving through.

I said, "Look, there's Heidi."

He said, "I don't want to see her."

Sadly, Heidi did not get a chance to be treated and to rehabilitate. She was always fiercely non-compliant. I was told she had threatened her mother with a knife. Before that, we happened to pass on the street, and she asked after Gabriel. I told her he was in hospital but didn't say where. I dreaded that she might visit him, and that they might resume their crazy druggy relationship.

In 2015, Heidi was found dead in an apartment she shared with an acquaintance. Her family preferred not to reveal the circumstances of her death.

Early Days

My father died when he was ten years younger than I am now. He was a freelance carpenter who never made any money, and of a generation who thought it was unmanly to express affection – even to members of his own family. He somewhat compensated for this by inventing semi-abusive nicknames for all of us. I was 'sludgeguts', my sisters were 'maggots', and my mother was 'delo nith namow', which was south London back-slang for 'old thin woman'. He didn't have a nickname for my elder brother Tony, because Tony had been born with a disability: short hamstrings, which prevented his legs from straightening. Tony spent much of his youth in special residential hospitals, and endured 13 surgical operations on his legs before the age of 12, so he was hardly ever present at home in my formative years.

My earliest memory is from when I was about three years of age, when I was walking up Bellegrove Road beside my father. He was not holding my hand, probably because he considered it unmanly. So far as I remember, it was the only time we had ever been out walking together, so I felt rather self conscious. I don't know what I was wearing, but I remember my father was wearing his Cromby overcoat – an unusually expensive garment in an age when practically all working men wore gaberdine macs and cloth caps. It was a sunny day, but cold, and the pavement was quite crowded with shoppers, so it might have been near Christmas, and that might have been why we were out together. Probably my mother had nagged him into it. There were few cars on the road, because of petrol rationing. Suddenly, the air raid siren sounded, and I watched all the people in front of me scatter like a flock of birds, vanishing into shop doorways all the way up the street. My father, however, carried on walking. The Cromby overcoat was unbuttoned, and he had his hands in its pockets, so all he had to do was extend his right arm to wrap me in a big Cromby wing, and that's how we continued walking up the empty street with the siren howling.

They were howling because someone had spotted a doodlebug, or V1 flying bomb, passing over our town of Welling on its way to London. My father, Alf, was an RAF Aircraftsman working at the Royal Woolwich Arsenal as a carpenter building wood-framed airplanes, so I guess he knew whether the doodlebug was likely to drop on us. The Arsenal was bombed frequently, and he was on duty there in shifts of three months.

My next earliest memory is from the age of six when I was sexually assaulted in the back of my uncle's Wolseley car by my teenage male cousin. My aunt and uncle were sitting in the front seats making jokes about how the hand-hold cords inside the car looked like "willies on the wander". I was siting on my cousin's lap in the back and he was fiddling with my penis. I did not like it, but I did not know what to do. I did not know it was not normal behaviour, so I said nothing to anyone.

A Noose of Light

Before I was born, my family used to live in Plumpstead, even closer to Woolwich, and my mother, Connie, would sneak out at night to rendezvous with Alf when he was on duty in the Arsenal. It was strictly forbidden, of course, but she used to bicycle to a hole in the security fence and crawl through and sit on the grassy bank inside, waiting for him. It was fun because Alf used to raid the officers' mess and bring her a silver tea tray with some biscuits, and sometimes even cake. She used to sit on the high grassy bank in the blackout dark, overlooking the Nissan huts below. If there was moonlight, she would watch him scuttling out of the Officers' Mess with the tray, and across the parade ground and up over the grass to where she was. They used to have a very elegant picnic tea together, with a silver pot and china cups just like a hotel. And when there was an air raid on, they'd watch the bombs come down and the firemen putting out the fires, as if it was a pantomime. The Arsenal was three miles long and a mile wide and employed 100,000 people, so there was plenty of space for the bombs to miss Connie and Alf. I like to think I was conceived on one of those dangerous nights.

It must have been hard for Alf to play the tough guy all the time, to play George Raft or Jimmy Cagney, when his 'soft' side kept breaking through. In his spare time in the Arsenal he made me a wooden battleship and a submarine. He designed and built the whole thing himself. The sub could fire a torpedo at the ship, and if it hit on the right spot, the whole superstructure would explode and fall in pieces into the bath water. Then there was the time when he was home on leave and one of the kids got sick, and he wouldn't go back. They sent some Military Police around to arrest him. Then there were the love letters we kids found a decade later. Connie had tied them all up in red ribbon, and they all began with "Beloved,...". Then there was when I had started to draw. I must have been about ten or eleven, and I was trying to draw a girl. It was pretty lurid, but I was so concentrating on getting it to be less pornographic that I didn't notice when Alf came to look over my shoulder. The next thing I knew, his hand came out of nowhere, picked the pencil from my hand and drew a beautiful female figure beside my own clumsy effort. He could draw like an angel. This had been noticed at his school, but his parents didn't have the money to send him to the art college offered him. No such things as scholarships in those days. At the beginning of the war, most of the women and children in the London area were evacuated to areas deemed safer from the expected 'Blitzkrieg' of German bombers. My mother and sisters were moved to Sevenoaks, but moved back to Plumstead when it became clear that the London-Kent border towns were relatively safe. Four years later, when the V1 doo-dlebugs appeared, the family, now including me, was evacuated to Yorkshire to live in the servants' quarters of a large manor house. My mother wrote to my father complaining that her ration book had been stolen and that we were being mistreated in other ways. He went AWOL, travelled up to see us and to sort things out. The military police arrested him and took him back to the Woolwich Arsenal. The authorities solved the problem by moving us back to Welling, where we remained

A Noose of Light

during the war's closing stages.

My mother had hidden talents, too. When the household duties became less demanding after the war, she became manager of a bakery shop. But her real talent only emerged much later when she got a job in a betting shop. She discovered she had a freakish talent for complex mathematical problems! Everything now done by computers in betting shops, she could do in her head. Yankee doubles, accumulators, she could do all the exotic bets, and pay out on them as well. They could have used her at Bletchley Park on the Enigma machines.

Like everyone else, we had an Anderson air raid shelter at the bottom of the garden. It was never used to shelter from air raids. After the war we kids and a few others from the neighbourhood used it for a club house. We used to gather there around a candle on dark evenings and tell ghost stories. Then the girls made up some black cloaks, and we would glide out from the shelter at night, over fences and under hedges to spy on people through their back windows, or to raid the local strawberry farmer's patch, or to climb the tall pear tree next door and toss down the fruit to our gang below.

I didn't know we were dirt poor until we became teenagers. Then I saw that others were getting smart clothes and motorbikes and holiday trips to the seaside, and I was not. At the age of fourteen, I realised that other boys wore underpants under their shorts, but I had never been given any.

The greatest influence in my childhood, however, was the stutter: it made me terrified to ask for stuff in shops and to speak in class at school. At the age of nine, my mother made an appointment with a speech therapist and my big sister Jeannie took me. The therapist gave me a written IQ test, and told me that I had the IQ of a 20 year-old. It didn't mean much to me, I still had a stutter. I didn't even know that our King George V11 had a stutter. Nobody mentioned the King's stutter or mine. It was like having a physical disfigurement.

Like someone who had a real disfigurement, I tended to avoid company: my favourite place was the local library, and I became addicted to reading because someone reading couldn't be expected to talk, and indeed talking was forbidden in libraries. My favourites were Dennis Wheatley's 'satanist' books, and Edgar Rice Burroughs' Tarzan and John Carter books. I read them all many times, and many others. Wheatley's 'Strange Conflict' was about German occultists using astral projection to spy on British military secrets. I think my later interest in lucid dreaming and other esoteric stuff started with this book, although John Carter's post-mortem trip from the WW1 battlefield to Mars may have influenced that tendency as well. My mother used to call me a 'bookworm'. At the age of nine, I learned what the war was about from Lord Russell of Liverpool's 'Scourge of the Swastika'. No one else I knew talked about why we had fought the Germans.

My sister Wendy tells me that we used to dance around excitedly on our home balcony in Welling whenever a doodlebug flew over on its way to London. Sometimes the engine would cut out and the bomb would fall, and we would cheer. Our home was on the old Roman road called Watling Street, which ran in a

A Noose of Light

straight line from Dover to London, so we were right on the route programmed into Hitler's secret weapons. Neither my sister nor myself thought that dodging bombs was in any way extraordinary; it was just normal life and we had known no other kind. When some distant relatives began to send us food parcels from South Africa, we did not know what to do with the bananas and oranges. We did not know they were food until our mother showed us how to eat them.

My father died at the age of 64 with bladder cancer. The last time I spoke to him was in the mid 1970s. He was sitting alone in the front 'best' room with a plastic bowl on the floor between his bare feet. He was even more taciturn than usual, concentrating on squeezing urine out of his distended abdomen into the bowl. There was not much I could say, but at last he looked at me and said, "I think someone put a curse on me, Al." The last time I saw him was in hospital, but he was unconscious in a bed in a row of beds, all occupied by other dying old men. I vowed I would never allow that to happen to me.

My brother Tony died in 1980 aged 45. He would probably still be alive if today's work safety standards had pertained then. He worked as a glass blower making old fashioned radio valves as replacements for antiquated radio equipment. Something toxic in the hot glass got into his lungs.

In childhood, I saw much more of him when the war finished and he came home from his residential hospital. He was provided with a motorised tricycle 'invalid carriage', which had a waterproof cover over his legs. I was still small enough to hide under this cover, and we would zoom off to see movies at the Bexleyheath Odeon, or to the fun fair at Danson Park. His legs looked as if they were held together with scar tissue, but he never complained. He married a widow who was an enthusiastic member of an evangelical church, and became a popular Deacon.

My mother, Connie, died at the age of 98. She had been in dementia care centres in Kent and Oxfordshire for about 15 years – with my sister Wendy as her visiting relative. I was in my Surry Hills, Sydney flat when Wendy contacted me to say that she had heard from the manager of the care centre that Connie would die soon, and that her surviving children should pay her a farewell visit if they wanted to. I booked a flight immediately, as did my sister Jeannie in Canada. We arranged to stay with Wendy in Wendy's son's house near Oxford. My son Nat was in England at that time, so we all formed a visiting party determined to see Connie every day until she died. Of course, things did not work out so neatly. First there was the shock of seeing Connie's condition. She was a skeleton slumped in a wheelchair, eyes closed, unable to communicate except with occasional utterances of the word, "Toilet" and the phrase, "Nice cuppa tea". We spoon-fed her with lunch in a dining room filled with other old people in various stages of dementia, then we wheeled her out into the spacious gardens, and sat around talking. The manager of the centre, a nice woman, came out to say hello, and to comment on how nice Connie looked in her coral pink cardigan. Somehow we managed to have a good time by resorting to lots of South London black humour. On the second or third visit we had an idea. We wheeled her on to the outside vestibule in front of the grand entrance doors, and started to sing her all the old songs we remembered from the war time: 'Bluebirds over the white cliffs of Dover', 'My old man said follow the band', 'Roses are blooming in Picardy', 'Roll out the barrel', 'Stormy weather', and any others that came to mind. When we forgot the words we just la-la-laad. Some of the other old dears came out to sit on the benches and listen, and pretty soon we had an audience who applauded at the end of every song. This seemed to wake Connie up, and she started to applaud, too, and to call out, "Very good, very good!" We all held her hands and cried.

I don't remember how many visits we made, but three weeks passed somehow. I remember walking with my sister Wendy down a corridor lined with doors to the residents' rooms. Suddenly, the door just ahead of us opened with a bang, and a dishevelled, wild-haired, pop-eyed man staggered out looking like a comic character in a 'Carry On' movie. We suppressed our giggles, but he heard and stared at us as we passed, and shouted after us. "Don't grow old!" He advised.

On another of our visits the nice manager lady told us that this had happened before: Connie had shown all the signs of dying but had come back to life. She had done it four times, and all the nurses called her 'The Immortal Woman'. The nice manager didn't actually apologise for summoning us from the far corners of the Earth on a false alarm, but it was implied. I also think the nice manager had a private word to Connie concerning this issue, because on one of our last visits, and one of our last songs, Connie held out her hands to us and we stopped singing and held her hands and heard Connie say, quite clearly, "If I can die, I will".

Jeannie and I had to go back home, leaving Wendy and Nat to continue the vigil. Connie died a week after Jeannie and I left, and I sent Nat a eulogy to read out at the funeral. It was about Connie and Alf and their night time picnic while the bombs were falling on the Arsenal. Nat organised a new elm bench to be installed on the vestibule. It has a brass plaque inset into the back rest, engraved with the legend:

CONNIE

The Immortal Woman

Most of life ends up lost in the fog of forgotten, so in a certain sense we are all in a state of dementia throughout our lives. Even those who keep diaries can read a page about a distant day, and say, "I don't remember that!" I look back in time and can see this fog stretching back over the years to my birth in 1940, covering up all the billions of events which are deemed not worth remembering. But sticking up here and there through the fog are mountain peaks of memories of particular events. We don't choose them to stick up through the fog, and we can't tell when these events happen to us that they will become one of the peaks. They just happen. People have always known this, and have invented ways to artificially create peaks in the fog by staging ceremonies, festivals, rites of passage, birthday parties, anniversaries, etc. All for the sake of rescuing some events from the fog of forgotten. Sometimes it works, and we really

A Noose of Light

do remember events which were deliberately staged to make us remember them. But mostly, for each of us, the mountain peaks create themselves.

I have read of experiments involving open brain surgery when electrodes have been placed to stimulate certain brain areas, summoning, evoking, conjuring brilliant inner visions of long forgotten experiences. So it might be true that everything is recorded and stored somewhere. After all, the moving finger does not write on thin air, it writes on love and hate and flesh and blood.

Lucid Dreaming

A lucid dream is a dream in which you know you are dreaming. The dream world looks as real as it normally does, with just as many characters and places and weird events, but within this scenario you are perfectly aware that it is not real, and therefore you may decide to leap into the air and fly around, or walk through walls, or have verbal exchanges or sexual encounters with dream people who seem to be completely autonomous.

I have excluded any mention of this activity from this autobiography so far, because it would have made the text too complicated. Nevertheless, my lucid dreams have been a feature of my real life throughout.

The first information I remember receiving about lucid dreaming came to me at the age of 9 or 10 via Dennis Wheatley's book 'Strange Conflict', in which Nazi agents would go to sleep, and travel in their 'astral bodies' to spy on secret British war plans. I don't remember if I was already experiencing lucid dreams at this age, but certainly date my awareness of the phenomenon from this time. Thereafter, whenever I had a lucid or semi-lucid dream, I would associate it with 'astral bodies', and not be too scared. I thought I knew what was happening.

Many people do get scared by the symptoms of lucid dreaming because they have no reference, no knowledge of what is happening. When the body shuts down into sleep mode, the brain activity can lag behind, leaving the awareness still conscious. Therefore normal sleep paralysis is experienced as a frightening inability to move. Quite often this is accompanied by auditory and visual hallucinations as the brain's dream state and conscious state overlap. Consequently, the dreamer may feel paralysed in bed while an imagined burglar is audibly ransacking the next room – or even feel attacked by demons, as pictured in Henri Fuseli's painting 'The Nightmare'. Likewise, someone who is having a normal dream may spontaneously become lucid in the dream, and not know what is happening or where they are. I dare say that many such experiences throughout history account for the reported visions of saints and savants of all races and religions.

Before exploring the esoteric field with Beverley in 1964, I associated my occasional lucid dreams with the astral body theory, and tried a few half-baked experiments trying to prove that, during the experience, I really was in another body, but in the real world – like a ghost. This became very confusing because the dreaming mind is perfectly capable of manufacturing a fair facsimile of my real bedroom. While going to sleep, I could never evoke the initial prelude to such experiences, but when it happened spontaneously, I would, so to speak, float upward out of my body in my astral form, and examine everything around me to verify that it was my real bedroom. I never achieved this confirmation because I always saw something that shouldn't be there – like a hole in the wall, or a strange woman. I should mention how frequent these 'projections' were: they occurred about once a week.

After our nightly Congo Big Stick sessions in Beverley's studio, we both had some memorable lucid dreams. Among others, Beverley had a revelatory vision involving angelic beings who were supervising a spiritual academy, training disembodied people in how to ascend to higher levels. I had a wonderful hallucination in which our Theosophical friend Monika Merlin appeared at my bedside and drew a silver circle on the palm of my hand, causing me to ascend into a state of utter bliss.

When Beverley and I joined the Coombe Springs community, I was pretty sure the astral body theory was nonsense, and began to associate my lucid dreams with my Gurdjieff exercises. It seemed to me that the content of my dreams was linked to whatever I was doing in the Work. This association continued when we became aligned with Idries Shah, and I became convinced that lucid dreaming could be used, was being used as a vehicle of communication in the Work – even though Shah, to my knowledge, never mentioned it nor wrote about it.

When we emigrated to Australia and I became disaffected with Bennett and Shah, my frequency of lucid dreams declined. The already reported appearance of eight year-old Gabriel by my bedside after the diagnosis was the last 'vision' for a long time: the stark reality of Gabriel's illness and the divorce and the ongoing tragedy of the psychosis seemed to overwhelm any tendency toward 'peripheral experiences'. When, however, Gabriel went through the rehab and became established independently, my interest in lucid dreaming revived, and I began to research the subject scientifically – no doubt influenced by my work with the Schizophrenia Research Institute. To my surprise, I discovered that during the 15 year hiatus, lucid dreaming had developed from an occult subject to be found only in esoteric bookshops along with Madame Blavatsky and Aleister Crowley, into a scientifically verified reality. A web site called 'Lucidity' informed me that an American sleep scientist called Dr. Stephen LaBerge had verified the reality of lucid dreaming by devising an experiment allowing a sleeping lucid dreamer to communicate with the 'outside world' while being monitored with brain and body electronic sensors that proved he was asleep.

Becoming a member of the Lucidity web site, I took part in the online forums, delighted to discuss, for the first time, all the wonders and puzzles of the lucid dreaming state. The Lucidity Institute also offered annual eight-day seminars in Hawaii, so I booked myself in for the next one.

In February 2001, I flew to Honolulu and hopped a small plane across to Maui, where the seminar was held in a comfortable meditation retreat in the hills. My testimonial can still be seen on the Lucidity Institute's web site:

> *"Miraculously, everyone shed all inhibitions about revealing personal aspects of their dreams; surreal situations experienced in false awakenings, and bizarre missed NovaDreamer cues. I found myself thinking what a pity it was that all families did not share this degree of frankness and emotional support—and this among a group*

who had never met each other before! In between sessions we cavorted in the pool, sang semi-irreverent chants in the hot tub, endured delightful physical shocks via the sauna and snaky slide into the deep end of the pool, enjoyed deep muscle massage by a choice of dark-eyed gentle-handed houris, strolled around the tropical gardens spotting woo-woo stone circles left behind by earlier guests, searched for the legendary garden goat, ate excellent food, tripped to the beach and mountain tops, shopped in the little towns, and, delight of delights, discussed nothing but lucid dreaming for seven days. One little cameo begs to be told. After the city life, the silence at night in the Hawaiian hills is awesome. On one such night, I got up at 4am after an intense sequence of attempted lucid dreaming, and crept, silent as an astral projection, out of my room to get a glass of water. There outside in the hallways and dining veranda, creeping and whispering together like Dante's shades, were almost all my fellow attendees. I guess you had to be there."

After the revival of my tendency to dream lucidly, I had a number of truly memorable dream experiences. For the record, I divide dreams into four types: 1. ordinary non-lucid, 2. semi-lucid, 3. ordinary lucid, and 4. special lucid. In the first category are those trance states (ordinary dreams) where my perceptions and responses are completely dominated by the scenario. I seem to get a lot of these in which I am trying to travel home, but can't remember which station to look for, or indeed where I live. The second category is when I am lucid enough to not take the scenario seriously: I know I am dreaming, but am not lucid enough to interfere with the scenario – by flying away from it, for instance. The third type is when I am lucid enough to use techniques to prolong and enhance the lucidity; to change the scenario, and to talk and interact with dream characters. The fourth type is when I am wholly lucid and alert, while involved with a very strong scenario. I see this as the mystical side of lucid dreaming: I am wholly aware that I am being shown something. By what or by whom is unknown, but the scenario being presented is strong enough for me to become, though lucid, a respectful passive audience.

I append here some examples of this fourth type. Where each report ends is where lucidity faded and I woke up.

IT IS JUST AFTER SUNSET and the turbulent sky is windswept and lurid. I am standing at the foot of a very tall cliff face, looking up at a small castle-like building on top. Suddenly, high above, a centaur emerges from the castle, stands on the edge of the precipice and shakes his fist at the sky. With his other hand he holds an illuminated small cubic box to his chest. He is roaring with anger. He is so angry that he throws himself off the edge, and falls down to the rocky ledge where I stand. I think he is surely dead, but the shining little box bounces up in the air and falls back into his grasp. He revives, stands up, and staggers away along the rocky ground. I follow, and notice that his hoof prints are embossed into the hard rock of the floor – as if this scene had been repeated thousands of times before, over and over again. I follow these hoof prints along the ledge and around the curve of the cliff face. The light is fading now, and as I turn the corner I see a large obstruction blocking the way forward. I look up at it and see that it's a gigantic shoe, and that above it is a trouser leg, and above that the huge figure of a man who looks like a college professor. I become afraid and try to run away, but he reaches down and picks me up and begins to adjust me, like adjusting a toy.

I AM WALKING ALONG a dirt road through pleasant countryside with several companions. It's a fine day, and we are all dressed in medieval clothes, like pilgrims from Chaucer's 'Canterbury Tales'. I am perfectly aware and thrilled to be having a lucid dream, and hope that the lucidity will last a long time. To ensure it does, I practice some techniques learned from Stephen LaBerge; rubbing my hands together, and stooping to touch the ground. My companions do not find this behaviour extraordinary. I do not know who they are, and am too busy looking around, marvelling at the details of the landscape to ask them any questions. We approach the brow of a hill, and I can already see, towering over the crest ahead, the top of an enormous tree. But I do not realise its true size until we reach the top of the hill and look down into the valley below. The tree is quite gigantic: taller than a New York skyscraper, with branches and foliage that fill the sky. The massive trunk is pale, like an Ash tree, and I try to remember the name of the nordic mythological tree said to be at the centre of the earth, but cannot remember. We all walk down the hill towards the base, and as we approach, we realise again the massive scale of the roots. They extend to the right and left, ancient and gnarled like a mountain range. We walk closer and come to the top of a slope that angles down under the centre of the roots to where an enormous stone Egyptian-scale entrance facade has been built. I walk down the slope, and notice a figure standing in front of the entrance like a guard or a guide. He or she is wearing an elaborate costume that looks vaguely Chinese or Mongolian. He turns and I follow him through the entrance and into a large room, a temple equipped with a variety of musical instruments.

I AM WALKING ALONE across a flat desert. It is twilight and the sky is grey. I notice that here and there are large pits in the ground, and that a different coloured light is issuing from each pit. I think that I must do a painting of this when I wake up. The nearest pit is glowing yellow. I walk up to its edge and look down and see lots of people down there who are all yellow. They are very busy, talking seriously, agreeing and disagreeing about stuff. I can't hear what they are saying. Then I move away to another pit which is glowing blue, and in it I see lots of blue people having a good time, laughing and chatting and singing. I look up and realise that all the coloured pits across the desert are full of people – all busy about their business. I walk up to a red pit and look down. Sure enough it is full of red people. I step down into the pit to find out what they are doing, and suddenly am among the red people and involved with them. At this time I lose my lucidity and start to have a normal dream. We somehow spill out or overflow the red pit, and start to stream out across the desert. I move along with them until I hear someone call my name. I look up and see Shah. He is standing on a little hill, dressed in a sheepskin waistcoat and baggy trousers. He calls out, "Alan, do this!" Then he whirls around on the spot several times. I do the same.

WHILE FALLING ASLEEP, I transit straight into a scenario where I am flying confidently and happily over a beach and out to sea – fully aware that I am in a lucid dream. I am flying with arms outstretched to the sides over a sparkling ocean into a gorgeous sunset. I experiment to see if I can steer myself, and bank like a fighter jet, soaring around in a tight circle to come back on course. This indicates to me that I am being guided to a destination, so I comply. Pretty soon I see down there an island, and on it a town. I swoop down and zoom into a supermarket in the high street of the town, where I am brought to rest, standing upright, but as fixed and immovable as a wooden Indian. There are other people around but I cannot move my head to see them more clearly. One of these others comes closer and chuckles in a knowledgeable but sympathetic way.

I am still working with lucid dreaming, hoping to develop better control and some understanding. I believe we still have a lot to learn about this ability of the mind to create an inner world as real as the outer world, and to move around in this inner world as if

A Noose of Light

we were not ourselves creating it, and for this bizarre experience to affect us as spontaneously and profoundly as do our experiences in the waking world.

The nature of consciousness, these days, is a study that has grown beyond the province of religion and psychology into the cutting-edge territory of physics and quantum theory. I dare say that lucid dreaming will play a definitive role in this study sooner or later.

Metastatic Cancer

In early 2009, my part-time job as Publications Director of the Schizophrenia Research Institute was chugging along nicely at two days a week, and my long-term *de facto* relationship with Dawn (now lasting about 20 years) was chugging along nicely at one night a week and a phone call every night. Gabriel was catching the train from Auburn into Central every Sunday morning to have breakfast with Dawn and I in my flat, after which he and I (Dawn almost never came with us) went to see a movie. She was perfectly happy to catch a bus home to North Sydney to spend her Sunday afternoon practicing her glass bead-making activities in her kitchen. Nat sometimes visited from Melbourne, and got on very well with Dawn. They used to make satirical jokes about me, which I stoically endured.

The new fundraising Director at the Institute had been there only a year when she decided that her department could not afford to pay for an in-house, part-time graphic designer/newsletter writer. She persuaded the Scientific Director and the Board of her case, and my contract was terminated with three months notice. I had planned to retire anyway at the end of 2010, so it was no big deal to do it a year earlier. But I did rather resent being chucked out in this way after my performance record as a founder Director dating back to 1996.

The problem, however, was that I was 68 years old, and unlikely to find another part time job – nor did I have sufficient savings nor superannuation payout nor pension entitlement to maintain myself in the rented Surry Hills flat without the income from the Institute. Reluctantly I was obliged to ask Dawn to move in with me so that we could pool our resources. It made perfect sense because we would each halve our rent and living expenses by cohabiting again, and Dawn would have a firmer financial base from which to plan for her own re-tirement. Dawn, however, had foreseen this vicissitude even less than had I, and found it difficult to comply. In fact, her dithering lasted almost to the end of my notice-of-termination period, when oblivion was staring me in the face.

The situation was so serious that I started to research possibilities of moving to India or Bali or Crete – all offering a much better standard of living for a pensioner pauper like myself. I became a member of a web-site called 'India Mike', and chatted to many ex-pats there about living conditions in Goa, Chennai and Mumbai. I heard I could live like a king on a thousand dollars a month, and pay a full-time cleaner $10 a month. Similarly tempting reports came through regarding inland Bali and off-tourist Crete. I showed these researches to Dawn, and that's what decided her to move in with me. She realised it was serious; that I really would have to leave Australia. She thought there might be a way to avoid the moving finger, but there was no way! She looked a little bit like someone walking to the gallows at first, but after a few weeks, she was standing in the middle of the living room saying, "Alan, I really feel comfortable now. I feel happy to be here." That's the way she spoke about things. Really.

We celebrated by purchasing two Burmese kittens, and we named them Ghengis and Attila. My next door neighbours had a cat called Mister Meeyowgli, who used to spend as much time with me as with them. When the neighbours moved away, we missed Mister Meeyowgli, so the kittens were his replacement, and they made more of a home for Dawn to come home to every night. As for me, all I had to do was give up half the bed, half the studio, all the bathroom and fridge, and most of the wardrobe. I counted myself lucky.

So I retired, and had my retirement party, and my commemorative 'Hero of the Institute' piece in the newsletter, and my acrylic engraved trophy from the Board, and all was well.

In mid-2010, however, the owner of my apartment decided to sell, so we had to move out. I quickly discovered that rents had more or less doubled during the ten years of my Surry Hills stay. I searched far and wide for a place within commuting distance of Dawn's job, and eventually found a third floor flat in Neutral Bay, just over the bridge from The Rocks and her college. The only way I could get it, however, was by not telling the agents about our cats. In October 2010 we moved in. It was not as pleasant as our Surry Hills place, but it was livable and an easy commute for Dawn.

Writing about this period – from the retirement to 2011 – feels like that story about someone who falls

A Noose of Light

off a skyscraper roof, and is asked halfway down how he feels. He says, "So far, so good."

In December 2010 I turned 70, and I had a splendid little party in the courtyard of The Oaks Hotel on Military Road. In February 2011, Dawn complained of a pain in her jaw, and made an appointment at a dental clinic. They gave her a root canal, but the pain persisted. They sent her to a 'facial specialist' who charged her another $300, and to another 'specialist' who also waffled expensively. Eventually I took Dawn to my GP in Darlinghurst, and he sent her for a CAT scan. The results appeared a week later. It was cancer.

So many people wanted to keep up with Dawn's progress – friends, students, family – that I devised a group email list, and a regular 'Dawn Update' email diary to keep them all informed. Here it is:

A History of Dawn's Illness: March – July 2011

29 March

Dawn's health troubles seem to have escalated to the big league, and we now have to log in a bone scan appointment at St Vincents after a CAT scan showed cavities in her pelvic bones. The prospect of bone cancer looms large, and we won't be thinking of anything else until a full diagnoses is obtained. I'm phoning for an appointment first thing tomorrow. She has suddenly developed three conditions: trigeminal facial neuralgia, enlargement of a sub-cutaneous cyst on her neck, and persistent pain in her right thigh. I can't imagine what condition would link all three, but we have been trying to find out what would for two months, now. I'll keep you posted on her progress.

5 April

Sorry to transmit bad news, but we learned today that Dawn has bone cancer, and we are seeing an Oncologist at St Vincent's tomorrow to begin the test procedures to find the primary source of the metastasis which has already spread to her jaw, pelvis and thigh bones. We have reached this step via six weeks of dental and neurological misdiagnosis, and sequential ultrasound, Xray, MRI, and nuclear medicine scans. We hope the oncologist tomorrow will be able to get Dawn started on the appropriate course of treatment. As the old ads used to say, 'Cancer is a word, not a sentence,' and I expect we shall rearrange stuff to comply with whatever treatment regimen arises. I'm already choosing a range of elegantly hued berets for when she loses her hair.

7 April

She's developing new symptoms ever day, but we must wait till next tues for the latest test results. She went for a hairdo this afternoon to cheer herself up, and came back with the hairdresser's comment that she'd got a bald patch on her scalp that wasn't there before. It looks like a melanoma – but there's so many candidates for the 'primary source' that it could be anything. Do melanomas sometimes appear AFTER they have metastasised into the bones? She went to have the CT scan this morning but the sucrose diet she had to swallow before the scan made her throw up – plus the teenager who injected her with the trace serum missed the vein three times, breaking off the feeder. Her later blood test extraction in the Pathology dept. revealed that the operators in the CT scan dept. are infamously incompetent. Would it be better with private health fund support?? I don't know – but I reckon everyone should pay for it JUST IN CASE it's a better service. No one seems to realise that we, as new cancer patients, have been forced to live through three days of not knowing a prognosis after a test – simply because the test happened on a Friday. Right now, at 7.50 PM on Friday, SOMEONE knows what the CT scan has shown – but that knowledge will not be transmitted to us until Tuesday.

A Noose of Light

23 April

She's been very sick since her first 3hr chemo session at St Vincents on Wednesday. I had to pull over twice for her to throw up on the way from there to the radiation at the Mater. Then on Thursday she had another radiation, and she threw up again on the way home. We think they've crammed in as much treatment as they can before the Easter break. I spoke to another patient in the waiting room (a retired GP), and he remembered that his initial chemo session was horrible. What worries me is that she's not eating – and has had hardly anything now for about 10 days. She takes her chemo pills and the anti-nausea ones and the oxycontin pain killers – but it can't be good to keep taking all those heavy drugs on an empty stomach. I keep offering food and she keeps refusing, whatever it is. She's been feeding herself nothing but little bits of muesli, and toast, and morsels of chopped fruit with a spoonful of yoghurt for about a week. This is not a sustaining diet. I've suggested she calls the 24hr adviser appointed by StVincents. She says she will but then doesn't. And she sleeps more or less all the time, and when she's awake she rarely says anything, and she gets annoyed if I suggest bland but substantial stuff like steamed fish or porridge or chicken soup. The only unsolicited thing she's said to me for two days is, "I know what I'm doing". I don't think she does: I think she's silent and sleeping all the time because she's starving herself. I'll try one more time tonight to get her to eat some steamed fish and some baked apple, and if that doesn't work I'm calling the crisis team.

26 April

Dawn sleeps most of the time, but I'm managing to make her eat very small serves of plain food (tablespoonsful), and to come out for little walks – both prescribed as beneficial by the Cancer Council's booklet. The biggest problem is nausea – which is continual despite the twice daily anti-nausea drugs. She's scheduled to have another hospital chemo session (3hrs intravenous) in a few weeks, but meanwhile carries on with the daily drugs. I talked to Domini (who knows about cancer) and she said the first chemo session made her feel so ill she couldn't eat or drink, and she eventually ended up in hospital on a drip feed – so I'm trying to override Dawn's tendency to take the same course. Even so, she's so enervated that she has no energy to answer the phone or check her email or phone messages. We've just found a Saturday voicemail message on her phone from the surgeon who performed the colonoscopy to obtain a biopsy of the putative primary tumor. He said the biopsy was "inconclusive" and that they'd be in touch tomorrow to discuss further action. We don't know what this means – other than that there's probably been another foul up which no one will ever tell us about – so we, as ever, will just have to wait. It might, however, mean that the bowel tumor is not the primary.

30 April
We met with the surgeon yesterday PM and he said that the biopsy of the bowel tumor was "benign", so they'll have to look elsewhere for the primary. He emphasised that finding the primary was important for creating the best chemo treatment recipe. So far they've targeted the bowel and the esophagus without result. Now they tell us that the next target is the liver. It's disturbing that they seem to be just guessing: I'd imagined that cancer treatment was more sophisticated than this – especially after we have paid a grand for a PET scan. I have the CD of the scan and it shows telltale highlights (tumors) just about everywhere. I don't know why they are sure that the bones are not the primary, but they seem convinced that the bone tumors are metastatic. I've made sure they know that Dawn has lost 4 kilos because of nausea since the start of chemo on the 12 April – so they have suspended her chemo, issued her with prescriptions for three new anti-nausea drugs, and referred her to a dietitian. The dietitian gave us a big bagful of 'Sustagen'-style formula foods and told her to try

A Noose of Light

them all to find some she can bear to eat and can keep down. So that's what she's doing now. She's decide not to get any of the newly prescribed anti-nausea drugs, and feels that she needs to be entirely drug free except for the oxycontin pain killer and the anti-constipation drugs which goes with it. It seems to me that the doctor is just chucking every drug available at her on a 'cover your arse' basis – and that it's up to us to find a way through this to restabilise her digestion using the formula foods. So that's what we're doing now: no chemo, no anti-nausea drugs, just formula and pain killers. She's eaten two portions of 'Forticreme', one last night and one for breakfast this am, and so far they've stayed down. We tried a little walk around Woolies yesterday pm, but she had to sit down halfway. She still thinks she can go out alone for walks, but on two occasions she's almost collapsed, so I won't let her until she's visibly stronger. It seems to me that the doctors hit her with too much chemo and radiation in the week before Easter Friday – cramming in as much as possible before the long Easter break – but the sudden impact of heavy drugs and radiation just destroyed her digestive system, resulting in alarming weight loss and fatigue. The next hospital appointment is on Tuesday, when we guess the liver biopsy procedure will be arranged. We'll try to get her to gain some weight.

4 May

Domini says her first chemo was awful but the second was so mild that she did a mile's bushwalking after it. That's what I want for Dawn. She saw Dr E at St Vincent's yesterday at 3.30pm – not his deputy – so I guess he's responding to the severity of Dawn's negative reactions to the chemo. He's decided it's not the right time to do a liver biopsy, and scheduled her in for another meet on Monday 9 for a review and another blood test. Meanwhile, she has to start taking the Xeloda pills again, starting tonight. She's dreading it. She's been so much happier over the past few days just taking the pain killers and eating the formula pap – plus some porridge and stewed fruit I made. It was almost like the illness had gone away. Also, tomorrow she has to see another doctor at St Vincents about the mysterious "vascular cyst" on the back of her neck – which may or may not be related to the cancer. She's pretty fragile atm, but sends love to everyone and thanks for all the good wishes sent. She still insists on going out for little walks down Military Road to the shops, but overestimates how far she can go and comes back very wobbly. Me and the cats have been keeping her cheerful, but nothing much can help if the nausea returns after treatment is resumed. It's just maddening that an exact diagnosis has still not been found after being referred from one specialist to another since 22 February.

5 May

We saw the colorectoral surgeon who did Dawn's bowel biopsy today at 3.30, expecting to talk about the cyst on her neck – but he immediately started describing the procedure for the liver biopsy. Dawn interrupted him to ask if Dr E had told him about the cyst. He said no, he had not. He had assumed that this meeting was preparatory to the liver biopsy. He examined the cyst. It's about 20 cents wide and the bump 5mm high. He said it was a tumor, and was as much a secondary tumor as was the ones detected in her bones and liver and organs. He said he could take a biopsy of this 'cyst', and thereby tell what and where the primary cancer was – because the secondaries reproduce the cellular formations of the primary. Dawn and I have been pointing at this 'cyst' ever since the first CT scan showed bone cancer – because it appeared at the same time as did her jaw and thighbone pains – but the GP and both oncologists had dismissed it to focus on bowel and esophagus. They said they'd "deal with that later" as if it had nothing to do with the cancer. Now, a colorectal surgeon has pronounced it to be a secondary tumor – just like the bowel and esophagus ones that proved to be non-existent after an traumatic operation under general anesthetic. I'm reminded of a story Idries

A Noose of Light

Shah told me about his father. When Shah was a kid, he was taken to hospital with an illness, and the doctor said it was serious but that there was nothing he could do. Shah's father told the doctor that he had a revolver at home, and that if nothing was done about his son's condition he was going to go home for the gun, come back in an hour, and shoot the doctor in the forehead. The doctor suddenly thought of something he could do. After more than two months of "inconclusive results", I sincerely wish I had a gun. As it is, I've excluded myself from attending Dawn's last three consultations at the hospitals because the bland complacence of her medicos was driving me into a degree of anger which I considered to be counter productive to the course of her treatment. No more. I've now decided to attend all consultations with a notepad on my knee, and to make notes like a reporter from 'A Current Affair' – the modern equivalent of a loaded gun. Dawn phoned the surgeon when we returned this afternoon, and requested that he move the procedure up to next Friday, so that the chemo could be adjusted to whatever the results of the 'cyst' biopsy indicated. So now, Dawn is scheduled for another meeting with Dr. E on Monday when, presumably, he will have heard about the surgeon's trespass onto his field, and explain why said surgeon had not been informed that he was to examine the 'cyst', and whether or not he approves of the surgeon's strategy of booking her in for a general anesthetic and biopsy of the neck tumor (not the liver} on the 20th May – two weeks in the future: a period of time in which Dawn is prescribed by Dr E to take 3000 milligrams of Xeloda (the chemo which caused her nausea and 4 kilo weightloss) per day; a prescription based on the now defunct assumption of bowel cancer. Dawn has intervened in this careless and incompetent ruling to take one pill last night, two pills this morning, and three pills tonight – in order to allow her system to adjust to the medications. So far, she is experiencing no nausea, and is eating her formula pap, and has even agreed to have some toasted bread with chicken soup – just to appease my manic demands. She was little before, but now any wind could blow her away. She's also on 40mg oxycontin (the morphine-based prescription pain killer of the stars) twice a day, so I'm monitoring her cognitive reactions on the basis of opiate effects. I've resumed smoking again, so was able to laugh when one of the cats fell into Dawn's relaxing Radox bath this evening.

6 May

I'm happy to report that D's softly-softly approach to resuming her home chemo dosage has worked very well. She's now up to her proper daily dosage of Xeloda without reappearance of nausea, and felt well enough today to pop into her college for a few hours work. The affectionate support of her lecturers and students has given her a big lift, and she's even going to eat a sausage tonight – with a small portion of my chef's speciality mushroom risotto: apart from her pap and chicken soup, it will be the first solid food she's ingested in two weeks. She has to watch her energy expenditure, though: today's excursion has left her pretty exhausted, and she's now tucked up on the couch ready to watch 'Home and Away' and 'MasterChef'. For research purposes I tried one of her oxycontin pills last night, and am now resisting my rock star impulses to have a few more. It certainly reduced my own stress levels, bringing that old Floyd number 'Comfortably Numb' to mind. We are expecting the Monday meeting at St Vincents will finalise arrangements for the neck 'cyst' biopsy – which involves a general anesthetic – on the following Friday. So I hope some good solid eating twixt now and then will build her up for the op. Our friend Jay in the States reports that his cancer biopsy was completed in three days from diagnosis – but also that he'll be paying for it for the rest of his life. As it stands, D has been billed $3,000 for her radiation therapy to date – but Dr E says it was a mistake and he'll sort it. Again on the finance front, I have a four-page formal complaint about her dental misdiagnosis going through the Dental Council of NSW, and am assured by our solicitor that they usually refund these fees as a matter of course. The direct effects of the illness are bad enough, but truly most of the stress in this situation arises from the systemic ineptitude of the medical system. On two key occasions, instructions to the referral doctors from the referring doctors were not been passed on by their staff. Jay says he took an highly visible audio recording machine to all his NY consultations to sharpen their self-preservation instincts. Would it have been different if Dawn had medical insurance? I don't know. It seems to me that these people deal with many cancer sufferers per day: for them it is normal life. But this exposure causes them to forget what the situation is like for their first onset patients – particularly when they prescribe massive doses of toxic drugs and radiation to new patients. Dawn's terrible first week of nausea could have been avoided with a gradual build up of dosage, allowing her system to adjust. But so far so good, the prospect of her settling down to a chemo/radiation regime with minimum disability consequences now seems possible.

13 May

On Wednesday Dawn went in to St Vincent's for an operation to excise her neck lump under general anesthetic. The surgeon says it's a tumor, so the biopsy may identify the all-important primary from which the correct chemotherapy can be formulated. She returned in fine form, but had some pain trouble when the anesthetic wore off, so was prescribed another brand of pain killer which, in combination with her oxycontin and Xloda chemo, has depleted her energy levels a bit. We don't seem to be doing much but watch telly and hang out at hospitals, so we've bought a BlueRay DVD player (recommended by my son Nat) and a wooly bed jacket so that D can recline on the couch with a snuggly blanket to see some old movies she's missed ('King's Speech' tonight). We should get the results from the lump biopsy on Monday, when we go in for another checkup – and then again on Tuesday, when D is scheduled to have a 'Port' implanted into her chest to facilitate intravenous chemo treatment (they have trouble getting a needle into her arms). She's eating better now – but nowhere near her usual diet: more like porridge oats with stewed fruit, chicken soup and toast – and that formula custard pap she can eat. She's just now decided that she wants Bolognaise-style mince on toast, so we'll see how she does with that. She thought she fancied some smoked trout last Tuesday, but couldn't face it. She never gets a full night's sleep, so spends much time dozing with the cats in the day. She's reading 'Water for Elephants', and I might get her to venture out to see the movie on Sunday. She also gets 'restless legs' syndrome (which is common with chemo), for which regular exercise is recommended – so I force her to push me up and down the Military Road in my wheel chair. Thanks for all the cards and flowers. Your good wishes are a real source of uplift for her.

18 May

Dawn is now a bionic woman. Her intravenous 'port' was implanted into her upper chest yesterday under local anesthetic, and today she feels fit as a flea, and is cooking her 'spatchcock a la Dawnie' tonight (recipe available on application). The port will get its first workout on Friday, when she's scheduled for her second chemotherapy session at St Vincent's – where the regular chemo patients sit around in armchairs during the drip-feed process and read books or fiddle with laptops and iPhones as if they're at a hair salon. We look forward to Dawn participating in the routine as complacently as they – but dread a repeat of the first session, which caused her to become severely nauseous and zombie-like. As if we did not have enough to cope with, I have developed an extremely painful condition which feels like someone is poking my right shoulder blade with a cattle prod, causing lightning flashes down my arm to the forth and pinky finger. Dawn immediately diagnosed it as the result of me playing with the cats every night. One of their favourite toys is a much-abused tape measure they call 'tapey', which I whip back and forth while sitting on the sofa

– causing them to pounce back and forth like little Ninjas. I went to our local GP today to get it sorted, and explained to her that I had taken three Panadeine Forte pills but the pain was still cutting through. The GP said that I was not supposed to take three Forte pills; two were the maximum. I asked her what was the use of taking two when three failed. Clearly, she had no idea what the cause could be, and her impertinent questions about how many drinks I drank per week, and her cult-like advocacy of an immediate colonoscopy, and her referral to a neck CT scan quite put me off. So I came home and Googled it: "Nerve pain in right arm". Immediately, I was presented with a photo of a famous US baseball player called Beckett performing the exact motion with his right arm that I nightly performed with 'tapey'. The headline over the Google article read "Ulnar Nerve Entrapment for Beckett?", and underneath was an exact description of my symptoms. So Dawn was right, as usual, and I will tomorrow ask our old Surry Hills GP for a referral to a St Vincent's neurologist – thus short circuiting umpteen likely chain referrals to irrelevant 'specialists'.

24 May

No improvement this morning, so we called the hospital and went there at 2pm for an extra chemo treatment –this time to boost the anti-nausea drugs. We also scored a new 3-dose anti-nausea drug called Emend, the first dose of which D has taken tonight. Fingers crossed that she feels a bit better tomorrow. Some good news is that her CsA levels have come down from 70 to 30 – which means that the chemo is restricting further growth and spread of tumors. She's just developed a new one in her right armpit, though. Still haven't found the primary yet, and we gather that they've suspended further biopsy probes in view of her depleted condition. Steve and Anmarie Ingram sent her some pink ugg boots to keep her little feet warm. Here's a picture:

27 May

A Noose of Light

This is getting like a noire comedy movie. Last night, D was distressed and complaining of breathing difficulties and agitation, so I called the Palliative Care team at 6.30pm and got a please-leave-a-message auto response. So we dressed D up in her big overcoat and pink ugg boots and drove to the Emergency Ward at St Vincents at 9pm and sat around with the OD'd junkies and kitchen casualties for an hour before a doctor moved her to a cubicle and started an ECG, blood test and Xray. Halfway through that, I suddenly remembered that I'd put my leg of lamb on to roast in the oven just before our emergency departure. An instant vision sprang to mind of the crisped joint bursting into flame, filling the apartment with smoke, setting off the alarm, terrifying the cats and summoning the fire brigade. So I left D to the doctors, and zoomed back across the bridge in a panic – to find that I had not turned the oven on at all, merely put the joint in. I called D to say all was well, and she said she was ready to come home, so I arranged to pick her up outside the Emergency entrance. I zoomed back over the bridge and parked in a no-waiting zone outside, but D called to say she'd be about 15 minutes more. So I moved the car to a parking spot at the top of Darlinghurst Green, and sat there in the dark playing the radio to wait for the call. After about 10 minutes, someone rapped on the passenger-side window, and I turned to see a young man smiling in at me. He opened the door and climbed in and stared at me. I said, "Who are you?" He said, "Hi! I'm Paul!" I realised I'd parked alongside the infamous 'Darling-hust Wall' where young catamites lurked for trade. I explained that I was waiting for my wife to get out of hospital, and he apologised nicely and got out. On the way home with D, she reported that the doctors had said she was okay, but having a panic attack, and had given her a couple of Valium. This morning we called the Palliative Care Team, and a nice lady made a house call. She thought that D's trouble was constipation, explaining that the anti-nausea drugs caused ferro-concrete-style blockage which required regular doses of powerful bowel movement agents. No doubt of

A Noose of Light

interest to the objective mind, we are now aware that Xeloda is the cancer-fighting drug, and Oxycontin is the pain killer. But these, as well as causing nausea, deliver severe constipating side effects which must be offset with lorazapam, nexium, maxalon, motilium, coloxyl, movicol and microlax. The care team nurse then delivered to D two enemas and a double dose of movicol, after which D lay in bed like an unexploded bomb, fretting about not being able to attend today's appointment to have her neck stitches removed and to pick up renewal drug prescriptions. I've now picked up the drugs, and D is snoozing, exhausted, on the sofa. She now has approval to suspend Xeloda doses until her system is restabilised. One bright note is that the care team lady examined the in-house pharmacy collected over the course of the illness, and mentioned that Tegretol (prescribed to D when they thought she had trigeminal neuralgia) was a powerful nerve pain suppressor. So I took two immediately, and it's done wonders for my inflamed ulna.

31 May

Writing these reports is a major help for my stability, because it's the only way I have of exercising my artistic daemon while my right arm can't paint. I'm seeing the neurology guy Dr O at StVincents tomorrow, hoping he'll have some better solution than the "sports injury physio" I saw yesterday – who massaged my neck for 10 minutes and charged $80 for it. Meanwhile, it's massive doses of Panadeine that enable me to skivvy the household and drive Dawn around. The most unsettling thing about D's treatment is the absence of a central authority to manage it. Technically, the guy in charge is the oncologist Dr E, but he has assigned his post grad student to do the shop floor work, and just drifts in and out of meetings occasionally to utter platitudes. His student is a nice girl with little experience of hands-on care, who provides schedules of daily drug taking – with footnotes naming six alternative drugs to choose from if the scheduled drugs don't work or cause nausea.

A Noose of Light

This 'system' of leaving the patients to treat themselves from a pile of drugs seems to me cavalier if not downright dangerous. It's now 11 days after D's last chemotherapy session, and she's still disabled by weakness and nausea and inability to eat. The oncology team is evidently too busy to monitor and deal with these quality-of-life effects of their treatment, and it was their reception and coordination officer who referred us to Robyn, the palliative care nurse who visited us on Friday to give practical help for D's nausea and constipation. And it was Robyn who considered D's condition to be serious enough for a booking to see the doctor at the palliative care centre at Greenwich Hospital. We went there at 1.30 today, and it was this doctor who took out the stitches from D's 'port' implant, and who observed that the surgical wound from her neck tumor excision wasn't healing properly: it's an open, dry wound with red edges, and even I can see it's bloody dangerous. The doctor also considered that D's condition was serious enough to warrant a stay in the hospital for a few days, during which her digestive problems, the neck wound and her fatigue could be sorted out. She also introduced us to the Greenwich support team to organise her super access, my 'carer allowance', and other benefits we didn't know about. Just one of the past treatment prescriptions has been Lyrica (pre-scribed to treat the misdiagnosis of trigeminal nerve pain) costing $600 a box, and the other drugs don't come cheap, either – not to mention that I can't take on any freelance jobs while looking after Dawn. So the friendly care, understanding and practical support provided by the Greenwich team made me burst into tears. So D is going to check into the Greenwich hospital tomorrow at 11am to receive some proper attention. The doctor also gave us some welcomed straight talking about the choices to be made when facing a terminal illness such as metastatic cancer – which has a 5-year survival rate of 11%. What is the point of continuing with the 3-weekly chemotherapy sessions if each one totally disables D for 2 weeks afterwards? She has shown that she can tolerate the home doses of Xeloda and oxycontin once she has recovered from the chemo, and the blood tests have indicated that such Xeloda doses inhibit tumor spread and growth. Given the survival rate of her illness, wouldn't it be better for her to stop the chemo sessions and to enjoy relatively normal life activities for the indefinite time she has left? Her next appointment with Dr E is early next week, and we will put these questions to him – but I think he will say what the doctor said: that the decision must perforce be her own. His job is to fight the illness to the end: quality of life is secondary. We are going to ask him if the degree of chemotherapy can be somehow reduced to provide some inhibition of tumor growth and spread with minimum nausea side effects.

1 June

It was touch and go when D checked in to the Greenwich hospital at 11am, because the doctor had said she could probably get a private room, but it turned out that the only spare bed was in a ward with four other patients – some of them in a bad way. She was on the verge of cancelling the stay and coming home with me, but the staff jollied her along and demonstrated that she could draw the curtains around her bed for some privacy – so she was persuaded. I went to my StVincent's neurology appointment at 1.30 (he pronounced my ulna nerve okay, said the trouble was probably at the C7 neck vertebrae, and sent me back to my GP – huh!) and when I got back to D at 3.30 she was chatting happily to the doctor and staff around her bed. When the conference ended, she told me that they'd already got all Dr E's notes, and that they revealed that he thought the primary tumor was pancreatic. Also that she had expressed dissatisfaction with Dr E's team, and that the Greenwich doctor had recommended an oncology specialist friend at the Royal North Shore Hospital. As D found the doctor far more sympatico than Dr E, she has determined to move her case over the bridge, and as this must be via a referral from our GP I will put it to him when I see him about my arm/neck problem at 9am tomorrow. The main thing is that she is now at Greenwich until Friday, by which time her peripheral digestive/ nausea problems will be sorted, and her intro to the new team at RNS arranged. We still have to solve the quality-of-life versus chemo problem, but I'm confident that D will do much better with a team that values the former in balance with the latter – given the general prognosis of her illness. To be fair to Dr E, he had no way of knowing that D was particularly sensitive to the chemo until her reactions to the second chemo session were recorded: she might well have adjusted to it. But still, I would justifiably expect that his team would be more alert to such new cancer patient reactions than they have been, and our experience is that the team treats all patients as an homogenous production line – with no follow-up to check on individual reactions to treatment. This exposure has opened my eyes to the general pernicious 'culture' of speciali- sation in medicine. Dr E clearly believes that it is not his job to assiduously monitor adverse reactions to his therapy, just as my neurologist considered that his job was fulfilled by checking that my ulna was working properly, and by referring me back to the GP for further referral to (possibly) a C7 spinal ulna nerve inflammation specialist. We must remember that Dawn's original exhibiting condition (the jaw tumor) was originally diagnosed in January by her dentist as a tooth abscess, and that they referred her to two consecutive other 'specialists' when the pain persisted after the unnecessary root canal. She ended up with a diagnosis of 'trigeminal nerve pain' and was prescribed 'Lyrica' at $600 per pack. It was our humble GP who ordered a CT scan whereby the metastatic tumors, including the jaw tumor, were revealed. I sent a 4-page complaint of this misdiagnosis to the appropriate NSW body, and they have replied that the practitioners involved acted appropriately and that there is no case to answer. I spoke to a lawyer and he said that it's impossible to prove that such misdiagnosis adversely affected the outcome of Dawn's true illness. So there you have it. I'm too tired to report the whole thing

A Noose of Light

to 'A Current Affair', in pursuit of some transiently embarrassing media exposure. On the bright side, I'm relieved to at last find the humane people at Greenwich, who genuinely take the patient's well being to heart, and we will follow their lead to others of like mind.

3 June

The sensation persists of being maybe Tom Hanks in a Hollywood black comedy. I called on our old Darlinghurst GP at 9am to get a referral to a physiotherapist for my arm, and to brief him on D's progress regarding her transfer to the Royal North Shore oncology team. He said he'd be happy to refer her when we knew the name of the RNS doctor; agreed that my problem was irritation of the ulnar nerve at the C7or C8 vertebrae, and wrote me out a referral to the RNS physiotherapy team. From there I drove to Greenwich to find D walking about chatting happily to the bedridden patients. She was in good spirits, still waiting for the results of tests for her tummy troubles. Then I drove to RNS to deliver the physio referral, and wandered about the appallingly chaotic building site of the vast hospital until I found the physiotherapy department in a grim Dickensian building that could well serve as a scenario for Oliver Twist. I made my appointment for Monday morning, got home at noon, judged it probably safe to swallow two Lyrica capsules (after my early morning dose of Panadeine Forte), and laid down on the bed with the snoozing cats. A few hours later, I woke up to answer the phone and was barely able to speak coherently. The world had become a mildly amusing abstract. I still felt the arm pain, but found I didn't care about it. Neither did I care that the cats had indulged in a new game of pulling papers out of my household accounts file and chewing them to bits. I called D to tell her that I was unable to drive to Greenwich this evening in view of my spaced out condition, and she told me that the test results had found a bug in her digestive tract: a bug that is only generated by ingesting antibiotics. It was decided that the culprit was the antibiotics D had been given after the misdiagnosis of tooth ulcer back in late February/March. The 'good' news is that this bug is contagious enough to warrant D's move to a private room. She has also received permission to spend tomorrow night here at home. I've told the cats, and they said they're looking forward to it. On the basis of Lyrica's outrageous cost I have decided to give it another go this evening, judging that any further spacey side effects will have dissipated before tomorrow morning, when I will visit D again. It's a good job that I've stocked up on microwave dinners as cooking anything is quite beyond me.

11 June

Dawn came home for an overnight stay yesterday afternoon, and she's due back in Greenwich hospital today – and then will come home again over Monday and Tuesday – the latter being her birthday. She's even weaker now than she was when she went into palliative care – although she has not taken any of the chemotherapy drugs since her second disastrous session on Fri 20 May. It is odd to report that she is now in hospital largely because of the cancer treatment, not the cancer – but that's the truth. Of course, we have no way of knowing what her condition would be now had she not complied with the chemotherapy schedule, and there's the added complication of the tummy bug and its antibiotic, and also the different antibiotic for her unhealed neck wound – not to mention the four other drugs she is taking for constipation, anxiety and sleeplessness. To add to the confusion, they keep changing the drugs when Dawn reports any inadequacy of effect, and there seems to be an infinite number of different drugs for each symptom. Perhaps the worst of these symptoms is the inadequately named 'restless legs' syndrome: a truly awful state of being simultaneously exhausted and unable to keep still. It keeps D walking like a little zombie from the bed to the couch to the bathroom to the kitchen and back again. So far as I can work out, the drugs she is currently taking for this specific condition

A Noose of Light

are Temazepam, Lorezepam and Clonazepam, but these seem to make her very woozy and incapable of watching TV or videos or reading a book or making conversation. They also make her want to go to bed at around 7.30, only to get up repeatedly during the night – leaving her exhausted in the morning. She's now still sleeping in bed at 1pm, and will be monosyllabic at best when she gets up – probably just in time for me to drive her back to hospital. All she has had to eat since I picked her up at 5pm yesterday has been a small tub of yoghurt last evening, and two spoonfuls of porridge at 11 this morning. It's no good urging her to eat more, she simply can't – even though she no longer has nausea. The drug regimen seems to be out of control, and I think about trying to stop all drugs but the pain killer oxycontin. But that would disconnect her from the palliative care and the prospect of further treatment with the RNS oncology team. It's difficult; the palliative care doesn't seem to be working but there is no alternative. We just have to hang in there and hope things get better.

16 June

Not much to report. Dawn's back in Greenwich hospital, and they've adjusted her meds a bit, but she's still exhausted and restless. It's better for her to be there, though, with the nurses popping in and out. They're going to give her another CT scan on her legs – because she has increased pain there. I convinced my physio to give me some neck traction on Tuesday – which relieved my arm pain for an hour – so I've ordered a neck traction collar to use at home.

18 June

D is staying in the Greenwich over the weekend. Her CAT scan on her legs revealed enlarged tumors in her right thigh bone, and she has been given a wheeled walking frame to protect from fracture. Her neck pain has been traced to small tumors in her upper spine, and she now has a foam collar to relieve muscle spasm resulting from that. On Tuesday she will be bussed to the oncologist at Royal North Shore for a review regarding possible renewed chemotherapy and radiation treatment. The HR director of CATC college has kindly assured her of continuing support on a sick leave basis – saying that it is but a small return for all she has done over the years for the college. The Cancer Council is assisting her to access her super and prepare her Will – both routine measures in such cases. Several supporters have asked me what the prognosis is. The Greenwich doctor told me that she has handled many similar cases of metastatic cancer, and her policy is to tell patients the prognosis only if they ask for it. D says she would rather not know – so I'm honouring that choice. Many thanks to all for the gifts and messages. D is too weak to respond personally, but is appreciative of the love and respect expressed by friends and family. It's a weird business. D has just called me asking me to bring her a bottle of Bailey's Irish Cream for her after dinner tipple. She's never liked it before.

21 June
Gruelling day today. I was at RNS Physio at 9am for a neck traction. The home pneumatic cushion traction I bought doesn't work for me because every kilo of upward traction also bears down on the shoulder-emerging ulna nerve at C7/8, so I'm trying to get a door-hung hangman's noose setup – but the US bastards don't mail to Australia, so I have to get it sent to my sister in Canada for forwarding on to me. From RNS I parked at Greenwich at 12 to accompany D on the little bus ferrying her to the Mater hospital where she met her new oncologist who has set up a cautious new chemo treatment (4 Xloda pills per day) to see how much chemo she can stand. From there we were bused to the RNS radiation guys where they scanned her neck and thigh to set up the radiation targets. She didn't feel up to the trip. The Greenwich team set her up with an electronic pain relief pump piped into her tummy, but it kept malfunctioning, and she

found the wheelchair very uncomfortable – but we made it back to the Greenwich and her bed at 4.30. She's being very brave about the pain – which is now majoring in her legs and neck – and has some faith that the radiation might prove effective on the evidence of her jaw, which the earlier radiation sessions seem to have relieved. I'm very grateful for all the offers of help, but the truth is that there's nothing to do. I'm handling the domestics pretty well, and D is in the hands of the medicos. It's all a boring nightmare and if I didn't have the cats to look after I'd go batshit. Dogs are slapstick clowns, but cats are stone faced comedians. I'm thinking of smuggling in Dawn's favourite Atti in a bag to see her, but am worried that Ghengi might feel left out. Don't worry, I'm still relatively objective. For instance, I fully recognise that attempting to smuggle TWO Burmese cats into a hospital in a bag, while suffering from a semi-paralyzed right arm, carries a lowish likelihood of success.

27 June

I'm accompanying D on her daily wheelchair-bus trips from the Greenwich hospital to the radiation dept. of the Royal North Shore – where she is having targeted treatments on her neck vertebrae and thigh bone tumors. This will be followed next week by daily low oral doses of Xloda to see how she tolerates the tumor inhibiting drug, now. She remains very frail, but is sleeping better, and is less restless with doses of clonazapam and temazapam. Her mother, sister and niece have travelled in from Young and Townsville to see her. Many thanks for all your good wishes.

11 July

Dawn has got some benefit from her radiation therapy: her neck pain has diminished, but her right femur remains painful. The doctors have increased the constant doses of pain killers, so she is a little more comfortable. She's developed an infection of the esophagus and has difficulty keeping any food down – so she's also on antibiotics. The planned resumption of low-dose chemo-therapy has been postponed due to her continuing frailty. The traction treatment seems to have cured my ulnar nerve problem, so I am better equipped to manage her affairs via my Power of Attorney – and my doctor has put me on an SSRI called Lexapro to boost my spiritual fortitude. The naughty cats keep me smiling, though. Ghengi (the hustler) sits on my chest purring every morning at 7.30 on the dot; pokes me in the eye with his nose and nips my arm to let me know it's time for his munchies. Many thanks for all your good wishes, and please forgive me if I have not responded to particular emails. My son Nat is coming up from Melbourne on Thursday to lend support for a few days.

19 July

Our dearest Dawn was scheduled to go to Royal North Shore from Greenwich for a CAT scan at 1pm today, but when I got there to accompany her she was sitting on the side of the bed with three nurses around her trying to get her to drink the barium meal necessary for the scan. She was trying to do it, but said it was making her feel dizzy and "spaced out". The scan had been scheduled because the doctors thought her inability to eat and constant reflux might be due to an obstruction (maybe another tumor) in her esophagus or stomach – which the scan would detect. It seemed to me that she was far too weak to endure a wheelchair bus trip to the RNS, and an uncomfortable procedure on the scanner bed. The nurses went to fetch the doctor, who explained that the barium was necessary for an accurate detection of any obstruction. I asked the doctor what they would do if an obstruction was detected, and she cited a selection of invasive procedures – including surgery. I said that Dawn was obviously far too frail to undertake any such procedures (her condition is near-skeletal), and suggested that the scan might be postponed until Dawn was feeling stronger. The doctor agreed, and said that she would reschedule the scan. I tucked Dawn up back into bed. Her

A Noose of Light

mind is wandering a bit, and she was worried about clearing her desk at her college office, and when her mother's next visit was scheduled. I assured her that everything would be taken care of by those who loved her. In more lucid moments, Dawn is aware that she is going to die, and is trying to come to terms with that. I talked to her about all the good she has done in nurturing her students, and how her beloved father had already gone to where she is going, and everyone she loves (including our beloved cats) will eventually follow her there.

21 July

There's not long for her to go now. A matter of days. Her mum and sister Jenny and me are seeing her every day, and the doctor has prescribed doses of largactil at night to ease her distress and help her sleep all night. The family and I will assemble at their hotel tomorrow night to discuss funeral arrangements and her Will – of which I am the executor. Thanks for all your messages of love and support. I can't reply personally to all of them, but Dawn knows that everyone's thinking of her.

22 July

At dawn's request, 'Dr. Jo' has arranged for a bed to be installed in her room for me to stay overnight with her indefinitely. The Largactil is helping her sleep through the night, but she has been distressed by what may be its side effects of waking hallucinations. Dr. Jo thinks these may be not due to the medication but to 'pre-death' visions commonly experienced by terminal patients. The one Dawn had this morning involved two old friends of ours coming to tell her that they had arranged for her to move to a better place. She phoned me at 7am to ask me to come and pick her up in the car to drive her there. I drove over and it took a while for her to realise it was not real. She is resting well now, and is content that I will be there beside her at night time. D continues to drift further away. I took the cats in to see her today but she didn't show much interest. The nurses gave her a shower and a shampoo. All she wants to do is sleep. Her mother, sister and niece and nephew are visiting every day, but she's too weak and comatose to say much to them. Here's my favourite photo of her.

31 July
They say Dawnie will probably die today. I've been staying in her room for a week or so – she's now in a semi-coma. They say she's still breathing because she's young and has a strong heart.

31 July
Our dearest Dawn passed away at 12 noon today, with her mother, sister, niece and me by her bedside. The cremation will occur towards the end of this week. I'll let you know the time and place when it's arranged. Love to all – Alan T.

Post Mortem

Looking after Dawn from February to July had drained my bank account, and my efforts as her appointed 'Power of Attorney' to release her superannuation on the grounds of her terminal illness proved lengthy and frustrating. Despite constant badgering for months, Dawn's super fund trustees did not pay her due benefits into her bank account until a day after her death. I received a letter from them saying the money had been transferred, so I dashed along to the bank to switch some cash from her account to my own. Foolishly, I told the bank clerk that Dawn had died, and was horrified when she told me that, in that case, the account was sealed awaiting something I had never heard of called Probate – which is granted by the Supreme Court after receiving proof that the assets of the deceased should be handled by me, the Executor, in accordance with Dawn's will. So I had no money to pay the rent, let alone the funeral company, let alone household bills or an urgently due car service.

With a supremely ironic twist, Gabriel was the only family member able to lend me some money. Over the years of his disability pension and work in his protected factory, he had amassed a tidy sum in his account by the simple technique of never buying anything – or hardly ever. He transferred some funds, enabling me to pay some bills, and to hire a lawyer to speed up the Probate process.

I also went to see the nearest funeral director, who spoke about the necessary arrangements for the cremation, and showed me some coffins. I asked how much the cheapest one cost, and he said $1,700. I was in a rather estranged state, what with all the stress.

"Are they really burnt?" I asked.

"The caskets? Of course," he said, his eyes unwavering.

"It seems like a waste of money," I said.

"I suppose some would think so," he said, coldly.

"What if I want to actually see the coffin go into the furnace?"

"I think that could be arranged, though I've never been asked that before. I'll ask the manager at the crematorium."

I left him to make all the arrangements between the hospital and the cemetery/crematorium, and went home to Nathaniel, who was staying with me to lend support.

Next morning I woke up with a brilliant idea. Five minutes googling located a packing case manufacturers in the suburb of Marrickville. I phoned the manager and arranged to see him at noon, then I called the funeral director to check on the required dimensions of a casket to fit the furnace, and whether the crematorium would comply with my special request. By the time I met the packing case manager at noon, I had the go-ahead from all concerned. The manager was tickled pink at the idea, and called in his foreman to show him the sketch

I had drawn. The manager said he would make Dawn's casket in plain pine for $320. I got him to photocopy the drawing, and then took it to Dawn's college in The Rocks. The graphic design lecturer who had deputised for Dawn throughout her illness agreed to create the artwork and stencils for screen-printing some signs onto Dawn's packing case casket. And that's how my darling Dawn was laid to rest in a packing case with 'THIS WAY UP' and a bold arrow stencilled on the sides, and 'WE LOVE YOU DAWN' stencilled on the lid. She would have loved it. The funeral director also told me that the crematorium would charge $850 for me to witness the casket being fed to the flames. I told him that it was no longer necessary. Probably due to my stress levels, I was convinced that undertakers and crematoriums were in cahoots running an ancient racket involving expensive caskets being recycled. After all, none of the bereaved ever wanted to actually eyeball the deceased being burned up, did they? How easy it would be for the cremation team to tip the body into the fire, and reload the valuable casket into the van waiting at the back door?

When the funeral day came, my two sons and I arrived two hours early to arrange the chapel. I wanted to decorate the casket with Dawn's strings of beads, and check that the CD medley of her favourite music played okay. I walked into the chapel I had not had a chance to visit before, and feared it was too small. Fortunately, the people in the office said that a bigger one was available, so we switched everything over – just in time for the first mourners to arrive. About 150 turned up. I had been offered a 'celebrant', but preferred to handle it myself. It was a simple secular affair. I spoke about Dawn, and then asked anyone else who wanted to say something up to the lectern. Dawn's sisters and some of her fellow lecturers, and some of her students spoke. It went well, but I had entirely forgotten that funerals were to be followed by a reception. Fortunately, some friends and associates from the Institute had suspected this shortfall, and arranged for tables to be booked at The Oaks Hotel, so about fifty of the attendees went there.

I had no idea what was involved preceding and after a death, and no idea how to manage it. My impression after it was over was that everyone, even professionals I had never heard of, all lined up to charge me as much money and to load me with as much stress as possible. Foolish of me, I should have realised that death was big business. Next time I will leave the whole damned thing to accountants, solicitors and undertakers.

After the funeral, I was obliged to immediately search for a less expensive place to live. I had to move out of Sydney to reduce my rent costs down to a sustainable level. In October 2011, I moved to a pleasant little house in Terrigal, on the New South Wales Central Coast, and here I remain at time of writing. Two minutes drive away is one of the prettiest beaches in NSW. I admire it, but do not use it. My son Nat uses it when he comes to visit. He loves being flattened by the big surf he can't get around Melbourne.

Gabriel came up to look after the cat, Atti, last year when I went to attend grandson (Gabriel's son) Jack's

A Noose of Light

21st in Adelaide – staged by his wonderful foster parents Liz and Gregor. During that party Nat got Jack to accept a call from his biological father Gabriel, and they spoke for the first time since Jack was three years old. So I tell you this: stick around, because good stuff sometimes happens.

I've got a level of emphysema from smoking a pack a day since the age of nine, but have stopped now, and use a prescribed inhaler every morning, which keeps me breathing. That's too dramatic: I breathe pretty good without it. I also go to a gym on most week days for about 25 minutes on the machines. It keeps me able to bend down and pick up medium sized parcels.

Last year I also did a 'Farewell Tour' to see my sister in Canada, and my other sister and some friends in the UK – dropping in on New York to see the 9/11 memorial, which design I consider to be the best of type. I do not foresee any further journeys, but you never know, do you?

I am expecting my sons Gabriel and Nathaniel to visit me for a few days over Christmas. Their mother Beverley has Alzheimer's, and is comfortably residing in a Melbourne care centre.

It's December 18 2014, and my son Nathaniel has phoned to say that he has arranged a meeting on Christmas Eve between my grandson Jack (aged 21) and my son Gabriel, his biological father. Due to his illness and its attendant complications, Gabriel has not seen his son for 18 years. I will therefore catch the train down to Sydney on the 24th to attend this momentous lunch, after which Jack will proceed to visit his maternal grandmother, and I will ride back home in Nat's rental car with Gabriel and Nat to spend our usual Christmas together at my place.

A Noose of Light

I thought that the "momentous lunch" would be a good place to end this autobiography, and indeed the first edition did end there. I had a small quantity printed and distributed among my friends, relatives and other interested parties, and received a number of favourable reviews.

I did not try very hard to lure a publisher to market the book for me after the first one to which I sent it advised me that I was not famous enough to publish an autobiography. Self marketing proved arduous: I got fed up with addressing envelopes and standing in post office queues and fretting about 22-day delivery times from Australia to the northern hemisphere. Also several potential buyers complained about the high price imposed by the postage costs. It was these discriminating grumblers who suggested I republish as an e-book through Amazon.com – thus reducing the price and relieving me of the mailing task. But this was not the only reason I welcomed the republishing idea.

While distributing the first edition, it occurred to me (and Mister B's son Ben Bennett implied) that I should have written something about what I had *concluded* from my little adventure through life. So, as the clock is still ticking, I will take the opportunity to add a concluding chapter. After all, as Omar *might* have said:

> Be yourself! The Sufis say
> And let your words fall where they may
> For where they fall, no one can tell
> Nor what they will mean – some day!

Some neuroscientists will forgive me for saying that *they* say that an individual's character and fate is dictated 80% by genetic inheritance and 20% by environmental impacts. What I think this means is that *most* of who you are is written in your genes at your moment of conception, but this 'script' can be somewhat modified by what happens to you when exposed to life. And life, by the way, includes life in the womb – which accounts for why identical twins differ in character: one was on top of the other, or one was on the left hand side when the pregnant mother was rammed by a supermarket trolley, slightly modifying the unfortunate twin. No! Not unfortunate, because that little bang may have been the shock that made the sibling a little more perceptive.

Either way, there's no escape from the fact that you did not design or choose yourself: you did not choose your body; you did not choose your brain; you did not choose your predispositions to certain illnesses, nor your talents or lack of talents, nor your feelings! Nor your thoughts! Do you know what thought you will have before you think it, or what feeling before you feel it? Worse than that, you did not design or choose the environment you were born into – whether it was the society of princes or peasants.

Having got that straight, it's no surprise that

A Noose of Light

most of us fall prey to an 'identity crisis' in which we wonder what, who and where we are; how we got here, and how to get somewhere better. Herein lies the origin of religion and mysticism, not to mention science and psychiatry. Most of us simply cannot bear not knowing who we are or what the universe is all about, so most of us accept the explanation supplied by science and/or by one or another of the popular religions and/or by your local crackpot.

Many are trained from infancy to believe in this or that religious myth, and it never occurs to them to question it. But in every generation there pops up a cohort of people who are unable or unwilling to accept the local faith, or their parents' traditional belief. Some of these are content to simply go along with the scientific ideas of the day; others actively profess atheism, and yet others decide to explore the world's supermarket of different philosophies and esoteric narratives, looking for a way to get an eyeball meeting with the Truth.

As reported in this book, my wife Beverley and I were predisposed to be in the 'yet others' category. We eventually decided that Gurdjieff's teachings and techniques attracted us more than other available alternatives, so we joined the Coombe Springs community.

In doing so, we were not really aware that we were surrendering something very precious: our independence. Theoretically, we could have stayed outside and continued to study the 'spiritual' field and the behaviour of its different inhabitants in a detached academic or scientific manner. But this was never a possibility. What appealed to us about the Gurdjieff Work, as contrasted with the easy-going airy-fairy alternatives, was the prospect of enduring tough austerities: the super effort, the Work face, self-criticism and discipline. We believed that submitting to such a regimen would demonstrate the seriousness and commitment that would fast-track us to becoming transformed into superior versions of ourselves. This impulse, I now accept, was no different in quality to that of the male or female novice wishing to join a monastery or nunnery. We had the enneagram and self remembering, they had the crucifix and guardian angels.

Since those days everyone has become familiar with the term 'radicalisation', and is aware that dominant old people radicalise willing or vulnerable young people. What is less understood is that the radical impulse is driven by the young person's craving for seriousness and certainty in a world where such qualities are hard to find. In times gone by there were fewer choices, but nowadays such young people arise in every generation to explore a whole supermarket of spiritual paths of every description and tradition; markets where the elders stand waiting to snare the seeker in their particular noose of light. Some of these elders are well-intentioned and mild, but others, as we have become aware, like to use young seekers as human bombs.

We did not know we were giving up our independence. Indeed, we felt our independence to be the uncomfortable burden we wanted to get rid of. What Beverley and I could not be aware of was that in joining the Coombe Springs community we were committing ourselves to a lifelong sequence of events and experiences which would *exclude all other* possible events and experiences. It is a simple truth, but one rarely considered. John Bennett and Idries Shah became the most profound influences on our entire lives, so it's appropriate that both should be examined here.

We joined the Coombe Springs community in 1965, when the 'swinging sixties' and hippie culture were blossoming, so our radical impulse was driving us in the opposite direction to the flower power ethos of our general society. It would be three more years before the Beatles went to sit at the Maharishi's feet in India, heralding a cultural redirection away from fun and free love towards spiritual development. It was as if the 60s youth became disenchanted with simply overthrowing the old rules, and looked around for some new rules to follow. During those three years, Beverley and I attuned ourselves to the Gurdjieff discipline, only to have it negated and discarded when Shah took over and we struggled to adapt to the new fun-loving Sufi regime.

"I take the Work very seriously, but Mr. Shah seems to think it's a joke!"

So said Mister B after he had given away to Shah the splendid 7-acre West London estate called Coombe Springs, which he had spent 21 years of his life developing into the Institute for the Comparative Study of History, Philosophy and the Sciences. Anyone who finds this fact remarkable can purchase Mister B's autobiography, 'Witness' and search through its 379 pages for an explanation. It won't take long to discern that the gift of Coombe Springs was just one remarkable event in a truly remarkable life.

John Godolphin Bennett was an Army Corps Intelligence Officer in WW1 who was blown up by German artillery and who woke up in hospital, but found he was outside his own body. When his body was taken to the operating theatre, he went with it. Later he was told he had been in a coma for six days. When the nurse came to take the stitches out of his head, she wondered aloud why they had used coarse thread. Startling her, Mister B awoke to explain that the surgeons had no fine thread left.

"How did you know that?" Exclaimed the nurse.

From there he progressed to becoming a key intelligence officer in Constantinople, where he met Gurdjieff and Ouspensky, who were bringing a group of followers out of Russia during the Bolshevik revolution. He also befriended groups of dervishes, some of whom became his agents. Really! A handsome young British intelligence officer who used Turkish dervishes as secret agents? Ian Fleming might have written it.

This was just the beginning of an astonishing career in which he became, in turn, a diplomat, a legal representative of the usurped Turkish Princes, Managing Director of the British Coal Research Board, and leader of Ouspensky, Gurdjieff and Subud groups. In between these activities he wrote research monographs, a 'Unified Field Theory' accepted by the Royal Society, and a major four-volume work called 'The Dramatic Universe'. Throughout this colossal work output, he was having visions, transcendent experiences and guiding intimations from higher powers. He was forever intuiting or actually being instructed by voices in his chest that he should go somewhere and do something, and always it was to do with the yearned for 'great work' or 'supreme teacher' or 'second coming' or indeed the end of the world. In 1948 he decided that Western culture was going to collapse, so he travelled to South Africa to find land suitable for a Noah's Ark-style community. There, he discussed the matter with Prime Minister and Field Marshall Jan Smutts, changed his mind and came home. He never lost faith when the latest enthusiasm didn't quite work out, and always rushed off after a new and more splendid wild goose.

No doubt it was 'higher powers' that suggested he should give away Coombe Springs. It should be noted, however, that immediately after this transaction, Mister B moved his operations into an even bigger and more splendid establishment at Sherborne House in Dorset, where he initiated a new institute called the International Academy for Continuous Education. Not even content with that, at the age of 77 he travelled to the USA to view 950 acres of woodland in New Hampshire which he had been offered as the base for yet another new institute. He turned that down, but accepted another offer of a grand mansion in the Shenandoah Valley called Claymont Court. Soon after that, he died. Many were surprised that, having contacted and participated in and founded more esoteric mystical schools than most people have even heard of, Mister B had become a Roman Catholic in 1960, and had died in that faith.

I am now three years younger than he was at his death. What can anyone say about a man like that? He might have been a fictional character in a book, but he was real. Everyone loved him and looked up to him.

I happened to be passing when one of the old lady residents at Coombe Springs encountered him as he strode up the drive one sunny afternoon.

"Oh, Mister B!" She cried, "where *do* you get your energy from?"

"From YOU, Rosemary. From YOU!" He said.

On the other hand, I remember working hard on a drawing; a design for the stage backdrop for a play Mister B had written about the building of Chartres cathedral, due to be performed in the Jami. The drawing was in the style of the Bayeux tapestry and told the story of the play in sequential panels. Had it been produced full size, it would have been about ten metres wide by three metres high. I asked Elizabeth Bennett to show it to him at one of the House Meetings. She did, and put in his lap. But he was thinking of something else, and let the drawing fall unseen to the floor. No one, not even Elizabeth, dared to make him look at it. We all thought (yes, even me) that he may have been deliberately offending me – as a Gurdjieff 'shock'. I don't think he was, now. I think he was just not sensitive to visual things, and was also absent minded at the time. How many such mistakes had been mistaken for deliberate actions by his followers over the years?

Some people are still upset that he gave Coombe Springs away, and that Shah sold it all to property developers. But when Mister B was asked what he had

A Noose of Light

got from Shah, he said, "My freedom!"

What that may have meant was that Mister B was trapped by all the old residents that had lived at Coombe Springs since 1944, and Shah's appearance and credentials presented a golden opportunity to let them go and to make a new start – which he did at Sherborne House with a lot of fresh young American students: a new lease of life, indeed.

I have described the effect of the exodus from Coombe Springs on my little family with a new baby, and dare say that many other ejected residents suffered a similar trauma. But Mister B seemed to have washed his hands of us, and organised no links between ex-residents which may have softened the blow. If a town council had suddenly ejected 70 tenants of a large boarding house, and left them to their own resources, it would be viewed as a reprehensible and possibly illegal act. But as Mister B cheerfully said soon after this event, "I may well be a spiritual teacher, but I still make mistakes!"

Despite seeking and finding and promoting so many different types of spiritual development techniques, Mister B was never content. No sooner had he started teaching each new method to his followers than he was off in search of another one; a new holy man in India, or a new Sufi in Turkey. No matter how many followers he collected, he never ceased to search for approval from other group leaders. Many of these actually told him to stop his restless searching and to settle down and teach his own methods. Even his wife, Winifred, said the same thing, and Mister B himself repeatedly berates himself for this characteristic in his autobiography. But it was no good: he could not give up his addiction, his thirst for the final answer, the absolute confirmation that does not exist.

What does this imply about his life's work, his quest and his teaching? If the teacher himself finds the teaching inadequate, incomplete, unsatisfying, ineffective, what use is it to his students? Is it not significant that after spending colossal amounts of spacetime energy on learning and applying the psycho-spiritual transformational methods of Gurdjieff, Ouspensky, Subud, Shah and a number of other 'masters' over the course of 50 years, he finished his quest by returning to the Catholic faith and writing these words in the preface of his autobiography's second 'American' edition?

"In the last volume of the 'Dramatic Universe' published in 1965, I gave my reasons for believing that we are in the early stages of the Parousia, the Second Coming of Christ which heralds the end of the present world.....The facts are plain: the old world is disintegrating and before the end of this century will have disappeared."

1965? That was when Beverley and I joined the Coombe Springs community to study and practice Gurdjieff's 'Harmonious Development of Man'. Little did we know that we were placing ourselves under the guidance of a Prepare-to-Meet-Thy-Doom exponent. Mister B certainly never spoke of the second coming or end of the world at any house meeting or seminar. But even if we *had* read that excerpt from 'Dramatic Universe', which we had not, and even if he *had* spoken about it, we would not have been dissuaded from our commitment. The noose was around our necks. We were on the path. We were radicalised. We even believed that the bungled, brutal eviction from Coombe Springs was a deliberately applied Gurdjieff 'shock' for the benefit of our spiritual development. Whereas, of course, it was simply a bungled, brutal eviction.

Shah was entirely different. I feel a sympathy and fellowship with Mister B, because he exposed himself to the beady eye of everlasting history by writing his autobiography 'Witness'. In all his books, Shah never wrote a word about his own Sufi or other training and experiences. At one of the first meetings I had with him alone, he performed a boastful, swaggering description of how he had persuaded Mister B to hand over Coombe Springs. I say 'performed' because that's what it looked like. I felt quite sure he was doing it to test my attachment to my old teacher, so I was embarrassed. He strode up and down the room in the Big House, waving his arms about and puffing on his cigarette, saying something like, "I said to him, I said, look here *Bennett*, you claim to be connected to higher powers and have the interests of your people at heart? Well, here's your chance to prove it, *Bennett*. If you are sincere, you will give me this property, lock stock and barrel, with no strings attached!"

As with many of the 'set pieces' performed by Shah in my presence over the following years, I did not know how to respond. Maybe that itself was the response? Maybe he was acting out my own suspicions about him; my doubts about his authenticity? What else could have been the motive?

Another time we were in his study at Langton House, and he was wearing a 'fire opal' ring, which he repeatedly twisted so that it flashed, attracting my eyes. I knew he was doing it on purpose but did not know why. Was it to mirror a suspicion he had detected in me: a suspicion that he was trying to manipulate me? Or was it that he was bored with having to talk to me, so was amusing himself by conducting a little experiment with my attention?

Another time, I was sitting in the Elephant hall at Langton with about 50 other dinner guests, listening to Shah hold forth about a particular subject. I forget what it was about, but distinctly remember Shah glancing across the room at me and saying, "You can say something here." He inserted it so smoothly into his speech that I am sure nobody but myself noticed it. I had, in fact, been thinking I knew something about the subject, and so I did say it, and I did see how the fact that I said it and not Shah augmented the value of the event for the listeners.

Another time, a group of about 20 Langton weekend attendees were gathered by the sandpit outside the schoolroom, when Shah, out of the blue, indicated that we should form a sort of conga line and dance around in a circle. Some of us did, and others stood by and clapped in rhythm. I happened to have my guitar nearby, so I picked it up and strummed out a conga-style rhythm. After a while it occurred to me that I could add an appropriate chant to the guitar chords, so I started singing, "Hu! Hu! Hu! But stopped when a very loud and sharp voice in my head said, "NO!"

Many other such occasions over the years convinced me that Shah did indeed possess special powers, but this conviction did not stop me wondering what he was using those special powers to achieve. I did not know at that time that he had been a close companion of Gerald Gardner, a self-confessed wizard and founder of modern Wicca, and that Gardner possessed skills in (and a most extensive library on) hypnotism, magic spells, psychological manipulation, telepathy and other occult arts: a perfect training ground, one might think, for a young man planning to exploit hierarchical weaknesses in long-established Gurdjieff communities such as Coombe Springs?

Sure, but consider this as I considered it for 20 years. If Shah was who he said he was, that is a 'scout' sent by the Guardians of the Tradition to introduce knowledge of Sufi lore and history into Western culture, why should he restrict his activities to those considered permissible by that culture? After all, Shah made it quite clear from the very beginning that we Westerners were all asleep! He even made TV programs about it. Why then should he obey the petty and delusory rules of a bunch of sleepwalkers? So what if he published self-serving books under assumed names? So what if he snared the attention of a Coombe Springs associate with an article about Gurdjieff in 'Blackwoods' Magazine – triggering an introduction to Mister B? So what if he discerned and used Mister B's secret wish for freedom to get control of the valuable estate? Was it not all necessary for him to fulfil his mission and his life's work? History records that it was, because he *did* fulfil his mission. Before Shah, hardly anyone had heard of the Sufis. Now try Googling 'Sufis', and watch a million hits pop up: really, a million! Shah did that.

Another time, I was alone with Shah in his Langton study. He interrupted our discussion about a book jacket or something, to say, "You can't *think* your way out of it, you know?" I knew what he was referring to: it was the giant cooking pot inside my head, and my tendency to keep stirring the soup, hoping for the ingredients to change.

But they didn't change, and I am now still stirring at the end of my autobiography.

I was never a good student. Over the course of my 22 years association with Shah, I developed from being a cringing sycophant to a favoured lieutenant, and then into a resentful and rebellious loose canon. In mundane terms, my services to him were nothing compared to his services to me: he more or less set me up in a good business, and gave me more of his attention than he gave to many others. The issue of what I would have become if I had not met him remains forever moot. No, more than moot, it remains forever the pearly, translucent impenetrable barrier which surrounds and channels all our individual fates. No hard feelings? No, I have no hard feelings about Shah. If we were written as characters into one of his stories, he would be the Prince who bestows favour on a peasant boy, causing his affairs to prosper. But then a terrible calamity falls upon the boy, who blames the Prince for not protecting him.

But the world and posterity will continue to

A Noose of Light

blame Shah for the scandal of the Robert Graves translation of Omar Khayyam, and for the tragic disaffection of Richard Williams, the genius artist who introduced and endeared Nasrudin, the exemplar of Sufism, to Western culture. These were terrible mistakes, and no one has stepped forward to explain them. But I see in both disasters the initiating involvement of that familiar literary figure and icon of resentfulness, the overshadowed elder brother. Whatever Shah thought about these calamities, he was bound to stand by his brother, Omar.

And what was it all about for Shah's followers? What were they looking for in the whimsical stories, and the tortuous texts of the didactic books? It was partly about feeling wiser, steadier and certain in life, instead of stupid, unstable and confused. But these are mental health objectives, not spiritual aspirations. Shah used to say that most of the people around him had been "damaged in the field", and what he needed were well-adjusted, financially stable, level-headed citizens who had "spare capacity" to study his ideas, to receive what he had to give.

Excuse me, Shah, but no such people ever became involved with fringy foreign mystical traditions. We, your followers, were mostly misfits, oddballs, disaffected and restless aliens in our own societies – to one degree or another. Some were professionally well established, true, but most viewed their own mainstream cultures with the eye of the man from Mars; most looked down on the cultural changes of the 1960s and 70s from a distance, rather like tourists, or even anthropologists in a foreign and primitive land. We had rejected the inculcated superstitious beliefs of our parents' societies, and disdained the fossilised feebleness of alternative groups such as Theosophy, Buddhism, Druids and Rosicrucians.

What Mister B offered us through Gurdjieff's teachings was a muscular, physical system for achieving clarity of consciousness, and indeed the daily discipline, the movements and other exercises worked to stabilise us and provide startling moments of insight and elevation. We focussed on these and ignored the Blavatsky-like mythologies of 'Beelzebub's Tales', which I now categorise as a crackpot mish-mash translated and compiled by Jeanne de Salzmann, Alfred Orage and a host of other 'contributors' – all heroically wrestling with the Master's utterly indecipherable Russian/Armenian text. It sounds rather like the way the King James Bible was created, doesn't it? And even *that* was composed after the editors of the (AD325) Council of Nicaea had ruthlessly tossed out as heretical about half of the original texts available.

There they stood as they stand today: the elders, dangling their nooses.

Nevermind! Whatever it was, Coombe Springs worked for us until Shah arrived. Shah offered us no exercises at all: just the never ending flow of books to read. We used to read every one over and over again until the next one came out. We even comprehended that Omar M Burke and Arkon Daraul were Shah's pen names, and felt privileged to conspire with him in keeping that secret. Like many others we loved the Nasrudin books: the all-purpose, wraparound Sufi exemplar, sometimes

A Noose of Light

playing the fool, sometimes the sage, but always playing. But then came many books of translations of Eastern traditional stories, which seemed to us to be like our familiar 'fairy stories', but which we were told were 'teaching stories' relating to our quest for higher consciousness. Thence followed many more translations, but this time of unedited reprints of Hafiz and other traditional Eastern authors, including dense expositions of Sufi lore on such psychological concepts as the 'Naffs', the 'Commanding Self' and other levels of putative mental influence. And then came the didactic books, starting with 'Reflections' and 'Learning how to Learn'.

This was when I started to lose Shah, or he started to lose me. I came to notice that each of the didactic books had a common characteristic. Each point they made constituted an inward circling literary spiral: they led me on through successively tighter turns until I was faced with a blank wall: a *cul de sac,* a dead end. And written on the wall of this dead end was this graffito:

WAIT HERE. DO NOTHING
AND SOMETHING MIGHT HAPPEN.

We waited for 15 years, but then lost patience. I wondered what others thought about this, but did not ask any of my fellow Langton attendees. Like Coombe Springs, no one at Langton talked about the Work.

Once upon a time in the 1980s, we had a garden party at The Old Rectory. Wizz Jones was playing cricket on the lawn with Gabriel, Nathaniel and others, and I was talking to Richard, who helped supervise weekend work at Langton. I forget what we were talking about, but at one point I objected to something he said by exclaiming,

"Oh, come on, Richard, that's elitist and you know it!"

Without a blink, he replied, "So? What's wrong with that?"

There, in his amused ice blue eyes, was the certainty that the elite existed, and that he was either one of the elite already or was on the path to it. What about those who were not? What happens to them? Nothing happens to them, said the elitist blue eyes.

He's safely dead, now, as Shah would say, and Shah is safely dead, too, and Mister B and my darling Dawn, and John Walker, and my mother and father and brother, and lots of my old Beatnik friends who had never heard of Gurdjieff or Sufis are all safely dead. The mother of my grandson, Heidi, is dead after a life blighted and finally destroyed by mental illness. Did some of these manage to coat their Kesdjan bodies, or suppress their Commanding Selves sufficiently to experience different and better after-death conditions than the others? None have come back to report. In the endless silent space, the great lumps of planets have circled around our big brazier many times, and still no one has come back to report. Not even Gurdjieff, not even Mister B, not even Shah.

At bottom, after the teaching has perhaps given you the comfort of a path and a belief, is it all about staying alive after you're dead; staying intact when others disintegrate; standing firm in the lucid dream while others drift away like autumn leaves? Whether Sufi, Gurdjieff, Buddhist, Muslim, Christian or Pagan,

A Noose of Light

is it all about being saved, when others are lost?

Earlier in this book I quoted a joke by the 1930s American radio comedian, Will Rogers:

"If I get to heaven and there are no dogs there, I'm going to ask to go where they went."

I know what he meant, now, and I agree. People I really loved are dead and gone (*"deadibones"*, as Dawnie would say). Wherever they went, I will be content to join them there. Dawn loved her father, who died about 10 years before she did. At the end, she told me she was afraid of dying, and I said she need not be afraid to go where her father had already gone.

Meanwhile, however, I well remember another of Shah's pet sayings. It was "Dog in the manger", and I cannot help wondering if that's how he would categorise the end of this autobiography. That silky noose is still around my neck, and I am unable to discount, deny or reject the possibility of something miraculous and uplifting coming along to change my mind about this whole history.

Terrigal, New South Wales, May 2015.

A Noose of Light

10866396R00184

Printed in Great Britain
by Amazon.co.uk, Ltd.,
Marston Gate.